T0395759

POLICY LOGICS AND INSTITUTIONS OF
EUROPEAN SPACE COLLABORATION

To Noriko and Yukiko

Policy Logics and Institutions of European Space Collaboration

KAZUTO SUZUKI
University of Tsukuba, Japan

Routledge
Taylor & Francis Group

LONDON AND NEW YORK

First published 2003 by Ashgate Publishing

Published 2016 by Routledge
2 Park Square, Milton Park, Abingdon, Oxon OX14 4RN
711 Third Avenue, New York, NY 10017, USA

Routledge is an imprint of the Taylor & Francis Group, an informa business

British Library Cataloguing in Publication Data
Suzuki, Kazuto
   Policy logics and institutions of European space
   collaboration
   1.Astronautics and state - Europe 2.Astronautics and state
   - Europe - International cooperation
   I.Title
   327.1'7'094

Library of Congress Cataloging-in-Publication Data
Suzuki, Kazuto.
   Policy logics and institutions of European space collaboration / Kazuto Suzuki.
      p. cm.
   Includes bibliographical references and index.
   ISBN 0-7546-3014-5
      1. Astronautics--Europe--International cooperation. I. Title.

TL788.4 .S88 2002
387.8'0604--dc21

2002074731

ISBN 13: 978-0-7546-3014-2 (hbk)

Contents

List of Charts, Figures and Tables

Preface

This book is intended as a study of European collaboration in space policy. Though it is fascinating to learn about space exploration, this study strictly focuses on political decisions, negotiations and implementations. It examines the potential and the limit of European collaboration in a security-sensitive, highly politicized policy area.

The study of space policy collaboration is to understand how and why governments voluntarily give up opportunities to develop their own technological competence in strategic industry and open themselves up to a vulnerability of technological interdependence. The major proportion of this book focuses on how and why governments decided to collaborate within a European framework, and how the institutions have developed throughout the history of collaboration. In so doing, this study emphasizes the concept of *policy logics* explaining the changes of decisions, negotiations, and institutional frameworks. Although it is essentially an empirical and historical study, the book also addresses some new theoretical implications.

This book is based on the product of four years of study at the Sussex European Institute in the University of Sussex. Starting with very little knowledge about space technologies and programs and shallow understanding of European affairs, it was not possible to complete this study without warm support and encouragement from many people.

First, let me express my deepest gratitude to Professor Helen Wallace and Dr Peter Holmes, who tirelessly advised, corrected, questioned, and encouraged me at every stage of my research, even when I returned to Japan. I also am indebted to Professor Jim Rollo, Dr Paul Taggart, Professor Mary Caldor, Dr Alasdair Young, Dr Jeremy Kempton, Ms Henrike Müller, Dr Lucia Quaglia, Dr Alasdair Smith, Professor Anthony Fielding, Dr Kevin McCormick, and my friends at the University of Sussex for encouragement and moral support. I am equally grateful to Dr Keith Hayward, who kindly accepted all my ignorant questions and initiated me into the correct path for my research and for educating me on the politics of European aerospace collaboration. I am also heavily indebted to Professor John Peterson and Professor Alan Cawson for thoughtful comments on this study.

My gratitude also goes to Mme Isabelle Sourbès-Verger and Dr Xavier Pasco of the *Fondation pour la Recherche Stratégique* in Paris, who not only guided me through a complex labyrinth of policy-making process of European space collaboration, but also arranged on a number of occasions interviews with people in French and European space communities. Equally I owe sincere gratitude to Mr Takahiro Shinyo, Ms Kanae Aoki and Ms Kazuna Inomata for providing support while I was on research trips in various countries in Europe.

The study of a security sensitive area like space is not an easy subject for a foreign student. Even access to official documents of national and European authorities was not easily obtained. I wish to acknowledge the numerous people who not only facilitated access to official and unofficial documents of the European Space Agency, European Union, and national space agencies and governments, but also provided opportunities for qualitative interviews.

The process of learning about European space collaboration was also keenly encouraged by many politicians and officials whom I interviewed inside and outside of the national governments of Britain, France and Germany, the European Space Agency, the *Centre National d'Études Spatiales*, the *Deutschen Zentrums für Luft und Raumfahrt*, the British National Space Centre, Eurospace, the UK Industrial Space Committee, the European Parliament and the European Commission.

In writing this book I was also encouraged by my colleagues and students at the University of Tsukuba. In particular, friendly but professional discussion with Dr Seifudein Adem motivated me to finalize this book.

Let me conclude these acknowledgements by thanking my parents and close friends, without whom the entire process of being a Ph.D. student would have been much more difficult. Special thanks and dedication to my wife, Noriko Kitakura Suzuki, whose love and attention has given me the strength throughout the years of ups and downs, and our baby Yukiko for giving me a reason to move on.

Last, but not least, I would like to thank those who were helpful but for reasons of space and confidentiality cannot be mentioned here. Whilst this book could not be finished without help and support from those mentioned above, the responsibility for this work is solely mine.

Kazuto Suzuki

List of Abbreviations and Acronyms

ASI	Agenzia Spaziale Italiana (Italian Space Agency)
ATV	Automated Transfer Vehicle
AWST	Aviation Week and Space Technology
BAe	British Aerospace
BARSC	British Association of Remote Sensing Companies
BCRD	Budget Civil de Recherche et de Développement (Civilian Research and Development Budget)
BDLI	Bundesverbandes der Deutschen Luft. und Raumfahrtindustrie (German Aerospace Industrial Association)
BMBF	Bundesministeriums für Bildung, Wissenschaft, Forschung und Technologie (Federal Ministry of Education, Science, Research and Technology)
BMBT	Bundesministerium für Forschung und Technologie (Federal Ministry of Research and Technology)
BMF	Bundesministerium der Finanzen (Ministry of Finance)
BMPT	Bundesministerium für Post und Telekommunikation (Ministry of Post and Telecommunications)
BMV	Bundesministerium für Verkehr (Ministry of Transport)
BMVg	Bundesministerium für Verteidigung (Ministry of Defence)
BMWi	Bundesministerium für Wirtschaft (Ministry of Economy)
BNCSR	British National Committee for Space Research
BNSC	British National Space Centre
CASA	Construcciones Aeronauticas SA
CEDSP	Common European Defense and Security Policy
CEO	Centre for Earth Observation
CEPT	Conference Européenne des Postes et des Télécommuniations (European Conference of Post and Telecommunications)
CERN	Conseil Européen pour la Recherche Nucléaire (European Council for Nuclear Research)

CETS	Conference Européenne des Télécommunications par Satellite (European Conference for Satellite Telecommunications)
CFSP	Common Foreign and Security Policy
CLRC	Central Laboratory of the Research Councils
CNES	Centre National d'Études Spatiales (National Centre of Space Studies)
CNET	Centre National d'Études des Télécommunications (National Centre of Telecommunications Studies)
CNRS	Centre National de la Recherche Scientifique (National Centre of Scientific Research)
COF	Columbus Orbital Facility
COPERS	Commission Préparatoire Européenne de Recherche Spatiale (Preparatory Commission to Study the Possibilities of European Collaboration in the Field of Space Research)
COREPER	Comité de réprésentants permanents (Committee of Permanent Representatives)
COSPAR	Committee on Space Research
CSE	Centre Spatiale d'Evry (Evry Space Centre)
CSG	Centre Spatiale Guyanais (Guiana Space Centre)
CST	Centre Spatiale de Toulouse (Toulouse Space Centre)
CTV	Crew Transport Vehicle
DARA	Deutsche Agentur für Raumfahrtangelegenheiten (German Space Agency)
DASA	Deutsche Aerospace
DBS	Direct Broadcasting Satellite
DEA	Department of Space and Aeronautics
DERA	Defence Evaluation and Research Agency
DFG	Deutsche Forschungsgemeinschaft (German Research Community)
DGA	Délégation Générale pour l'Armement
DGE	Délégue Général de l'Espace
DLR	Deutsche Forschungsanstalt für Luft. und Raumfahrt (German Aerospace Research Institution) renamed as Deutschen Zentrums für Luft. und Raumfahrt from 1997 (German Aerospace Centre)
DTI	Department of Trade and Industry

EADS	European Aeronautic, Defense and Space Company
EBU	European Broadcasting Union
ECJ	European Court of Justice
ECS	European Communications Satellite
EEA	European Environmental Agency
EEC	European Economic Community
ELDO	European Nuclear Energy Agency
ENEA	European Launcher Development Organization
EOPB	Earth Observation Programme Board
EP	European Parliament
EPIC	Établissement public à caractère industriel et commercial (Public Body of an Industrial or Commercial Nature)
ERS	European Remote Sensing Satellite
ESA	European Space Agency
ESC	European Space Conference
ESDI	European Security and Defence Initiative
ESOC	European Space Operations Centre
ESPRIT	European Strategic Programme for Research and Development in Information Technology
ESRO	European Space Research Organisation
ESS	European Strategy for Space
ESTEC	European Space Technology Centre
ETG	European Tripartite Group
EU	European Union
Eutelsat	European Telecommunication Satellite Organisation
FESTIP	Future European Space Transportation Investigations Programme
GATT	General Agreement of Trade and Tariff
GDTA	Groupement pour le Développement de la Détection Aérospatiale
GEERS	Groupe d'Étude Européen pour la Collaboration dans le Domaine des Recherches Spatiales (European Spare Research Study Group)
GEO	Geostationary Orbit
GfW	Gesellschaft für Weltraumforschung (Company for Space Research)

GIFAS	Groupement des Industries Françaises Aéronautiques et Spatiales (French Aeronautics and Space Industrial Association)
GLONASS	Global Navigation Satellite System
GMES	Global Monitoring for Environment and Security
GNP	Gross National Product
GNSS	Global Navigation Satellite System
GPS	Global Positioning System
GTO	geotransfer orbit
ICBMs	Inter Continental Ballistic Missiles
IGY	International Geophysical Year
Inmarsat	International Maritime Satellite Organisation
Intelsat	International Telecommunications Satellite Consortium
IRBM	Intermediate Range Ballistic Missile
ISS	International Space Station
ITU	International Telecommunications Union
JRC	Joint Research Centre
JSSAG	Joint Space Strategy Advisory Group
JTF	Joint Task Force
LEO	Low Earth Orbit
LTP	Long Term Policy
Marecs	Maritime European Communications Satellite
Marots	Maritime Orbital Test Satellites
MERT	Ministry of National Education, Research and Technology
MHT	Matra Haute Technologies
MMS	Matra Marconi Space
MoU	Memorandum of Understanding
NASA	National Advisory Committee for Aeronautics
NATO	North Atlantic Treaty Organization
NERC	National Imagery and Mapping Agency
NIMA	Natural Environment Research Council
OEEC	Organization for European Economic Cooperation
ONERA	Office National d'Études et de Recherches Aérospatiales

OST	Office of Science and Technology
OTS	Orbital Testing Satellite
PPARC	Particle Physics and Astronomy Research Council
PPP	Public-Private Partnership
PSC	Parliamentary Space Committee
PTT	Post, Telegraph, and Telecommunications
RACE	R&D in Advanced Communications Technologies in Europe
RAE	Royal Aircraft Establishment
RTA	Le plan de recherche et technologie amont (Research and Technology Upstream Plan)
SA	Selected Availability
SAG	Space Advisory Group
SAI	Space Application Institute
SBAC	Society of British Aerospace Companies
SCG	Space Coordination Group
SDI	Strategic Defence Initiative
SEA	Single European Act
SERC	Science and Engineering Research Council
SEREB	Société pour l'étude et la réalisation d'éngins balistiques
SETIS	Société pour l'étude et l'intégration de systèmes spatiaux
SNIAS	Société nationale industrielle aérospatiale (Aérospatiale)
SPOT	Satellite Probatoire d'Observation de la Terre
SRG	Space Research Group
SSAC	Space Science Advisory Committee
TCI	Transpace Carrier Inc
UKISC	UK Industrial Space Committee
UNCOPUOS	UN Committee on the Peaceful Uses of Outer Space
US	United States
USAF	US Air Force
VFW	Vereinigte Flugtechnische Werke
WEU	Western European Union
WTO	World Trade Organization

Chapter 1

Introduction

The aim of this book is to propose a new analytical framework for understanding the dynamics of international collaboration and to place European space collaboration in a historical and analytical context. One of the institutional frameworks for European cooperation other than the European Union, the European Space Agency (ESA) brought together the technological competence of national space agencies, companies, and laboratories. Originally two separate international organizations, the European Space Research Organization (ESRO) and the European Launcher Development Organization (ELDO), the ESA currently consists of fifteen Member States — all of the EU Member States except Greece and Luxembourg, plus Switzerland and Norway — and one non-European Associate Member State (Canada). Having developed the technically and commercially successful Ariane rocket and a number of scientific and applications satellites, the ESA and its Member States have acquired highly advanced space capabilities in most activities in space (except, perhaps, in military and manned activities). But, in a very security-sensitive policy area such as space, why did the European governments decide to collaborate, and what were the reasons behind the successful development of technological and commercial capabilities that the European countries enjoy? Moreover, in light of recent dynamic change in the European space industry, namely large corporate mergers and aggressive commercialization, what would happen to European space collaboration and to the process of wider European integration (European defense cooperation in particular)?

At the most fundamental level, I see European space collaboration as a consequence of a dynamic process of interactions between the subjective understanding of (mostly national) policy-makers about space activities and the external environment (or one might call it the international structure), in which the United States has been the dominant actor. The genesis and evolution of European space collaboration were essentially rooted in changes in the international environment, particularly the policies of the American government and the commercialization of the space market, and of policy-makers' preferences. But the dynamics of European space collaboration cannot be explained only as a reaction to the changes in the international environment. It was also a consequence of choices made by European policy-makers to adjust to a new environment, and moreover, to increase the chances for Europe to improve its technological, commercial and political capabilities. This is by no means to say that policy-makers inevitably chose to collaborate. Instead, they developed unique institutions for collaboration that provided a variety of choices between national, multinational, or European solutions. This book develops a new framework of analysis for the study of this dynamic process of European space collaboration, focusing on these two variables: policy choice and institutions.

Implications of this Study for the Study of International Relations and European Integration

The explanation of the evolution of European space collaboration is dominated by the students of international relations who hold the theoretical assumption that monolithic and coherent states are by far the most important actors at the European level. Policy-making at the European level is made through negotiation among the representatives of those states who behave only on account of their respective national interests. The analysis from this 'neorealist'[1] perspective is limited to examine how states bargain at the European level, and why states have desired certain outcomes from the negotiations. From this perspective, the change and transformation in the practice of European space collaboration are viewed as state-oriented and self-interested activities. States collaborate because they seek to reduce transaction costs and to maximize their capabilities through economies of scale. Some argue that European states collaborate in order to challenge large American capacities (Hayward, K. 1994a; Moravcsik 1990). Institutional changes — for example, the creation of the ESA — are regarded as reflections of changes in states' preferences.

Neorealist Assumptions

Much of the analysis of the European space collaboration that had been done by social scientists, historians and journalists was based implicitly or explicitly on the neorealist perspective of international relations (Collins 1990; Hayward, K. 1993; Madders 1997; McLean 1992; Skolnikoff 1993). It is not my intention to review these individual arguments here, but, instead, to reveal three core features of the neorealist perspective in the analysis of European space collaboration.

Assumption of rational 'state'   The core assumption of the neorealist perspective is the rationality of the 'state'.[2] The behavior of governments is rationally calculated and assessed so that the actions of 'states' are in principle predictable and understandable. Neorealists use concepts such as 'power', 'national interest', and 'balance of power' as criteria of rational action (Waltz 1979). The costs and benefits of international interaction are the determinants of the behavior of governments, while the intensity of national preference, the national political situation, and the possibility of a package deal provide a range for possible resolution of differences through international negotiation (Gilpin 1987). Governments actively and purposefully seek to achieve their goals or objectives, and, when they do not possess sufficient means to achieve them, seek alternatives to minimize the costs and to maximize the utility.

The literature on European aerospace collaboration (see, for example Thornton 1995)[3] is not predicated, by definition, on hostile engagement with other states, as the neorealists argue, but it is assumed that cooperative actions are taken to meet the interests of the states. Nevertheless, the analytical focus is on the rational behavior of the 'state'. As Moravcsik (1993b) argues, states "are assumed to act purposively in the international arena, but on the basis of goals that are defined domestically" (p.481). In this framework, the emergence and evolution of European collaboration is explained as a consequence of the convergence of national interests: all governments participating in the collaboration pursue it (1) to gain economies of scale; (2) to avoid or share research and development risks; (3) to increase financial support from partner governments; (4) to increase the market size for the product; and (5) to strengthen European industry to win and survive in the international competition with much larger American counterparts (Golich 1992; Hayward, K. 1988; Jones 1996; Klepper 1991; Thornton 1995).

In general, the analysts share the idea that the rationale of European collaboration is a coalition of 'weaks'. Because the European technological and financial capabilities are limited compared to those of the United States, European governments have to choose between collaborating with the US, while accepting the status of junior partner, or forming a European collaboration to challenge American domination. The neorealist perspective tends to conclude that European governments would choose the latter because governments prefer to preserve national control to security-related activities such as space. As Nau (1974) put it, "the global solutions they might favor would tend to go far beyond what stronger participants would be willing to accept. Weaker states may insist that global resources be redistributed rather than simply regulated to permit exploitation by those who are already in the best position to undertake such exploitation" (p.31). Given the big difference in technological capabilities compared to American industry, what one might call the 'technological gap', analysts argue that the preferences of European governments have converged to meet *le défi américain* (Servan-Schreiber 1967) and therefore promoted collaboration.

Protection of autonomy   Protection of national control over the aerospace industry is another central issue in the debate about European aerospace collaboration. Because space technology is a dual-use (civil and military) technology, the neorealists argue that governments have preferred national R&D and production in order to retain the capacity to produce security-sensitive technology on their own and to reduce the vulnerability that results from depending on other countries for crucial technology. This echoes Keohane and Nye's (1977) observation: "[g]overnments continually sacrifice economic efficiency to security, autonomy and other values in policy decisions" (p.41), even in an interdependent world. By the same token, Skolnikoff concluded, "technological change has had important but limited effects on governmental autonomy and authority" (Skolnikoff 1993, p.226). These analysts suggest that governments would not give up their autonomy in controlling important security-related technologies at any expense.

For other analysts, however, security concerns do not play as decisive a role as economic concerns for governments in the preservation of autonomy. On the one hand, governments seek to secure job opportunities, technological spin-offs, and export potential from highly competitive technological programs. On the other hand, it is no longer possible for European governments to fund capital-intensive programs for aerospace technology single-handedly (Hayward, K. 1986). Therefore, governments choose to collaborate as a "second-best solution" to fulfill their desire "to maintain domestic military-industrial capacity on the one hand, while incorporating capital and technology from abroad on the other" (Kapstein 1992, p.657).

Neorealists often argue that a greater degree of interdependence will increase the vulnerability of a country's security; thus governments try to limit collaborative programs to relatively marginal areas such as sub-systems or basic R&D (cf. Edmonds *et al*. 1990). Shaffer and Shaffer (1980) also argue that states act to protect both military and economic autonomy, since space covers both areas and these are vitally important for a state's capacity in the international arena. Among analysts of European collaboration, Nau's (1974) argument, which emphasizes that "technology enhances rather than undermines national autonomy" (p.13), is well accepted.

Centrality of intergovernmental bargains   Since neorealists assume the state as a unitary and monolithic entity, the dynamics of European space collaboration are explained by intergovernmental bargaining. The governments play games to maximize their national interests under a certain set of rules. Analysts of European aerospace collaboration are especially focused on intergovernmental bargains because they assume that the aerospace industry is a government-led industry and is dependent on government for defining collaboration strategy. Therefore, they argue that many collaborative projects in Europe are conducted under the principle of *juste retour*, or fair distribution of industrial return, through which governments negotiate industrial work share and benefits. This assumption clearly tells us that the neorealists see the aerospace sector as a typical case of 'military-industrial complex', which implies that government and industry are mutually dependent and collude to achieve or defend their interests at the expense of the taxpayer.

These three core assumptions of the neorealist approach are, from my point of view, insufficient for the analysis of European space collaboration. First of all, the neorealists assume that the rational behavior of 'states' is based on the concept of 'national interest', which is vaguely defined as what is best for the nation in its relations with other states. As an analytical term, the concept of 'national interest' has a critical weakness, in that there is no agreed method to identify "what is best for the nation" (Clinton 1995). In other words, there are many 'national interests' – economic, political, military, technological, social, and financial – and they may often conflict with each other. Furthermore, these 'national interests' may not serve the nation as a whole, but each national interest would serve for some particular groups within the nation, and hence, governments may need to take into account those groups in its decision-making process.

In addition, the notion of the rationality of 'state' raises the question whether the state is free to behave as it wishes. Although the fundamental neorealist assumption that the world is in a condition of anarchy is already challenged by many scholars (see, for example, Ashley 1986; Bull 1977; Grieco 1990; Keohane 1984; Milner 1997; Oye 1993), the neorealists who study European collaboration maintain their view that the states have created mechanisms of cooperation that preserve national freedom to ensure national interests. However, it is often wrong to assume that governments are able to shape their interests and strategies independent of international and domestic contexts. On the contrary, international and domestic structures, institutions, and contexts shape and influence the objectives and strategies of policy-makers.

Furthermore, the concept of the protection of autonomy does not suit the analysis of European space collaboration. Ironically, the European governments sometimes claim to maintain the *European* autonomy in which each national government is required to give up some of its autonomy. Thus, it is necessary for the analysis of European space collaboration to include the concepts of both national and European autonomy.

Finally, the notion of the centrality of intergovernmental bargains also seems questionable. The history of European space collaboration tells us that the governments, though they were the most important actors, were not the only driving force of collaboration. The scientists, engineers, and other experts were involved in the creation and change of the institutions of European space collaboration. They participated in the decision-making process at both national and European levels, and persuaded governments in negotiation to realize their objectives and interests in space programs.

Challenges to the Neorealist Perspective

The neorealist approach and its three assumptions are, therefore, not sufficient for the analysis of the study of European space collaboration. Although there is virtually no theoretical challenge to the neorealist perspective in the existing literature on European space collaboration, some critical frameworks for analysis can be found in international relations and European studies. We shall discuss two useful frameworks from political science, which have different sets of assumptions, to challenge the neorealist account of European collaboration.

New institutionalism The first framework comes from the scholars of 'new institutionalism'. New institutionalism was introduced as a criticism for behavioral science, which was fashionable during the 1960s and 1970s among the social sciences, particularly in the United States. The core assumption of new institutionalism is that "institutions matter" (Bulmer 1998, p.368) for understanding political and social outcomes. There are a wide variety of versions of new institutionalism, which try to shed light on how the political process is mediated by institutions. The challenge from new institutionalism may well suit the purpose of this study. Unlike the neorealist perspective, the institutionalists seek to make the importance of institutions an independent variable, influencing the process of preference formation. Their assumption starts, not from the rationality of the 'state', but from the subjective understanding of (human) actors who tend to follow rules and procedures without a completely rational understanding of those rules and procedures. The institutionalists also seek to explain how the institutions comprising European space collaboration influence the behavior of policy-makers.

Two-level games There are some emerging arguments in the studies of European integration which deny the neorealist assumption of a 'unitary state' and introduce an analytical framework that emphasizes the role of individual ministries as well as sub-national and non-national actors in the decision-making process of the European Union (cf. Fuchs 1994; Grande 1996; Hix 1994; Peters 1994; Scharpf 1994). Conventional analysis of European space collaboration assumes that the actors within government, such as ministries, space agencies and companies, are acting uniformly, and few have done a detailed analysis of the process within governments.

A useful synthesis is proposed by a group of scholars who support the idea of the 'two-level games' (Evans *et al.* 1993; Putnam 1988). In short, it separates the decision-making process into international negotiation and domestic ratification phases, and focuses on the Chief of Government (COG) as a pivotal actor between the two levels. This framework emphasizes the importance of the constraints imposed by domestic actors in international negotiation. States are no longer regarded as uniform and monolithic, although they speak in one voice at the international level. Even if it may not be immediately applicable to European space collaboration, this framework seems to have an explanatory power in analyzing the decision-making behavior of governments.

Beyond the neorealist approach   Although the neorealist approach may have some explanatory power for the study of European space collaboration, it seems clear that this approach is inadequate. Thus, this study seeks to develop a new framework, which focuses on two important aspects. The one, which is inspired by new institutionalism, is to take institutions into account with regard to the process of decision-making. From the beginning, the institutions of European space collaboration have influenced the objectives and strategies of national governments. The neorealists argue that international institutions are not as binding as national ones, and therefore, the institutions of collaboration are so weak that the governments can manipulate them. Although transnational institutions are relatively weak, they represent important constraints for national governments to make certain decisions, policies and strategies, which might not be taken otherwise. Once the institutions have been established, they become an independent variable in influencing the national decision-making process. Institutions at the national level also shape the decisions of governments. National governments have their own rules, procedures and codes of conduct for decision-making with regard to space programs, and the actors (ministries, space agencies, engineers, scientists etc.) behave within those institutions.

The other aspect which this study emphasizes is the plurality both of actors within and objectives of national governments. As the two-level games framework suggests, the domestic actors are widely divided into different policy groups, with their own objectives and interests, and policy-makers (COGs) are strongly influenced by those groups. Furthermore, in a highly technological policy area such as space, policy-makers depend on policy input from experts, hence these play an important role in the policy-shaping process. In other words, instead of a concrete 'national interest' or single objective, the objectives and strategies are defined by a more complex process of policy-shaping in which experts from different policy groups exert strong influence. These points (which will be developed more fully in chapter 2) are made to place in proper context our discussion of the emergence and development of European space collaboration.

Methodology and Structure

The dynamics of the interaction between actors and institutions are difficult to grasp, at least partly because the methodology of conventional social sciences — implicitly and explicitly — relies on a causal relationship in one way or another. For example, neorealist arguments see the actors (states) as an independent variable, while new institutionalists tend to regard the institutions as an independent variable. In other words, social scientists adopt one of two views between "(1) human beings and their organizations are purposeful actors whose actions help reproduce or transform the society in which they live; and (2) society is made up of social relationships, which structure the interactions between these purposeful actors" (Wendt 1987, pp.337–338). This so-called 'agent-structure problem' has attracted the interest from many social scientists (Bhaskar 1979; Bourdieu 1977; Giddens 1979 and 1984; Layder 1981), and from scholars of international relations (Onuf 1991; Ruggie 1993; Wendt 1987; 1992 and 1995; Wendt and Duvall 1989) and of European integration (Carlsnaes 1992; Christiansen and Jørgensen 1999). Although their arguments are sophisticated and theoretically interesting, they have not developed a practical and empirically useful analytical framework.

Thus, chapter 2 seeks to develop an analytical framework for understanding the changing historical dynamics of European space collaboration. As will be discussed in detail, two central analytical axes, policy logic analysis and institutional analysis, are introduced. Policy logic analysis, on the one hand, focuses on the logics that actors may follow for defining their long-term interests and goals, their policy conduct and behavior, and a set of values which would provide criteria for judging policy performance. On the other hand, institutional analysis focuses on the role of institutions at different levels of action and the implications for the behavior of the actors. At the end of the chapter, a proposal will be advanced to the effect that these two brands of analysis are not mutually exclusive and may fruitfully be combined into one framework.

Chapters 3 to 5 examine three different periods in the history of European space collaboration under rather different sets of institutions. The chronological approach is followed here, since the aim of this study is to see historical changes over a certain period. The chapters are separated according to institutional differences, to facilitate illustrating the changes in policy logics of the actors under specific institutional frameworks, but, at the same time, close attention is paid to the process of institutional change during these periods. That is to say, even under a stable set of institutions the changes in policy logics would influence the mode of policy conduct by the actors, and when the institutional framework becomes unable or unsuitable to coordinate the policy logic of the actors, the institutions may change to adjust to circumstances. Through the examination of different periods of institutional settings, it should become clear that the changes in policy logics and institutions are closely linked.

Chapters 6 and 7 focus on the dynamics of institutional change at national level and the relationship between ESA and the EU respectively. These chapters will provide a picture of how the changes of policy logics influenced the changes of national and European institutions.

The concluding chapter will review the analytical framework set out in chapter 2 and applied in chapters 3 to 7, and reorganize the findings into a framework for the analysis of the historical dynamics of European space collaboration. It should be noted, however, that the primary aim of this study is not to create a new theory for the study of international relations or European integration. Rather, the aim here is to understand why and how European space collaboration emerged and evolved in the course of history, and to identify the driving forces behind the changes. To this end, this book develops an analytical framework which constructs an argument as to the nature of European collaboration.

Primary and Secondary Sources

The study of a security-sensitive area like space is not an easy subject for a foreign student. Even access to official documents of national and European authorities is not easily obtained. Nevertheless, there have been a lot of support from numerous people who not only facilitated access to official and unofficial documents of the European Space Agency, European Union, and national space agencies and governments, but also provided opportunities for qualitative interviews. These amount to some 60 in total, some of whom were taped. The interviewees included three current and former Director-Generals of ESA, two current and former Director-Generals of national space agencies, and one former national minister for space. Given the limited time and financial resources, interviews were mainly conducted with officials in three countries — France, Germany and Britain — and in the ESA and the EU. Speeches and proceedings of conferences in which government representatives participated were also useful written material as primary resources.

Given the scarcity of social scientific research on European space collaboration, an extensive survey was done of the daily and weekly publications on space, among them *Space News* and *Aviation Week & Space Technology* being the most valuable resources, as well as business journals and monographs of the ESA, European aerospace companies, and national space agencies. In addition, resources available on the Internet provided extensive background information. However, it should be noted that these materials contain information on relatively recent issues. Secondary resources, thus, constitute a major source of information for chapters 3 and 4, supplemented by several interviews with current and retired officials.

Notes

1   Though the term 'neorealism', in the narrowest sense, describes Waltzian theory which focuses on anarchic nature of international structure, it is used in this book in a slightly broader sense in order to extend its scope to economic issues (overlapping with neomercantilist perspectives) as well as security issues in this book.
2   In the literature of neorealist argument, the concepts of 'state' and 'government' are often used interchangably. This study attempts to avoid this confusion.
3   It should be noted that even though this literature covers the 'space' components of the 'aerospace' industry and its industrial policy, the main focus is on 'aircraft' components. Therefore, this literature may not be relevant to European 'space' collaboration.

Chapter 2

Theoretical Framework for Analyzing European Space Collaboration

The study of European collaboration in space has not been fully exploited by the political science literature. Most of the work has been done by officials who are involved in both national and European decision-making processes, by lawyers whose perspective is understandably focused on the legal aspect of collaboration, or by the technical specialists in science and technology. A wider area of study, such as European armaments collaboration, has attracted some attention among scholars of political economy, but their studies are largely focused on individual programs or historical description. Because of the nature of international collaboration, the dominant paradigm of these studies regards collaboration as the practice of rational state actors who create institutional frameworks to minimize the transaction costs and to maximize national strategic and technological capacities.

This chapter aims to create a research framework, which would range more broadly beyond what appears in the neorealist approach. Its main aim is to seek an analytical framework which can overcome international/domestic division, and which can explain the dynamics of the evolution of European space collaboration, even though the main emphasis of the study is analytical rather than theoretical.

Do Institutions Matter? The 'Institutionalist' Approach

As mentioned in the previous chapter, the focus here is on both rational choice and historical institutionalism. Although there are important differences between these two institutionalisms, both approaches have advantages and disadvantages for the study of European space collaboration. This section seeks to find out how important institutions are in the process of decision-making, and how institutions will make a difference in the outcome of that process.

Two Institutionalisms

Rational choice institutionalism Rational choice institutionalists regard institutions as a solution to the collective action problems[1] which reduce transaction costs (North 1990;[2] Williamson 1985). They presume that politics is a series of collective action dilemmas and of conflicts of self-interested actors. In their view, institutions impose constraints on such self-interested behavior by providing a set of the rules of the game. Institutions are created to realize gains from cooperation (such as minimizing the transaction costs), and if institutions cannot provide benefits, institutions may become subject to change, or another form of institution will take

9

over. Presumably, the process of creation of institutions revolves around "voluntary agreement by the relevant actors" (Hall and Taylor 1996, p.946), and this agreement emerges as the "lowest-common-denominator" (Moravcsik 1991a). Such an approach is also attracting attention from other scholars — mainly the neorealists who are preoccupied with 'prisoner's dilemma' — of international relations (Grieco 1990; Krasner 1983; Oye 1993, Young 1989) as well as of European integration (Breckinridge 1997; Tsebelis 1994). They argue that under the anarchy of the international system, rent-seeking actors (states) seek to reduce the transaction costs of collective activities and to avoid a 'tragedy of commons'.

This perspective certainly has an explanatory power for the study of European space collaboration. Many would argue that European countries collaborate because they want to reduce the risks and costs of R&D, to strengthen national industry, to increase financial support, and so forth. Governments clearly seek gain from collaboration and reduction of transaction costs by associating with other Member States. There were no coercive actions to force governments to collaborate; therefore governments agreed on their association voluntarily, and the rules of collaboration were set to satisfy all the participating actors.

Historical institutionalism   Among a wide variety of scholars who claim to be institutionalists, there is a general consensus of what historical institutionalism is. It is historical because it emphasizes path-dependency[3] and unintended development of institutions. It is institutionalism because it stresses the role of institutions for constraining and shaping strategies, preferences and behavior of actors, and for structuring power relations. Historical institutionalists assume that actors do not stop and calculate each time they make decisions, but turn to established routines or familiar patterns of behavior, since actors "are not so much as all-knowing, rational maximisers, but more as rule-following 'satisfiers'" (Thelen and Steinmo 1992, p.8). They tend to use the concept of institution more broadly than an instrument of interaction. Some emphasize that particular institutions such as norms, beliefs and ideas influence actors' world view (cf. March and Olsen 1989). There are various scholars of international relations who think that the international system is also structured by historically developed institutions (for example, state sovereignty)[4] in which beliefs, ideas and norms have an important role (cf. Goldstein and Keohane 1993; Keohane 1989; Kratochwil 1989; Milner 1997; Wendt and Duvall 1989). Likewise, those who see the importance of the acquis communautaire in the process of European integration employ this perspective to stress the role of institutions (Bulmer 1998; Garrett and Weingast 1993; Pierson 1996).

Differences of two institutionalisms   Historical institutionalism distinguishes itself from rational choice institutionalism in three respects: the role of institutions; preference formation; and actors' rationality. First, for rational institutionalists, institutions are important as constraints on self-interested behavior. The rules and procedures are determinants of the strategies of actors in, for example, international trade agreements (GATT, WTO etc.), and when these rules are changed, actors' strategies may also need to be changed (see the classic example of prisoner's dilemma). For historical institutionalists, institutions influence more than actors' strategies. Institutions shape actors' worldviews and define their identities, self-images and preferences. Historical institutionalists tend to see that institutions distribute power asymmetrically among actors, that is, institutions are created for powerful actors to support their dominance in the international system (Cox 1986; Gill 1990), and the way in which institutions are maintained is dependent on 'intersubjective understanding' among actors (Ruggie 1993; Wendt and Duvall 1989).

Secondly, there is a sharp distinction on the issue of preference formation process. Rational choice institutionalists take the preferences of actors as given, whereas historical institutionalists try to reveal how and why such preferences were made. Because rational choice institutionalists do not deal with them, they tend to take a deductive approach to the process of preference formation. Allison (1971) revealed some of these theoretical shortcomings in the rational choice-neorealist approach to preference formation in his famous work on the Cuban crisis: his three typologies of explanations on preference formation were all deduced from the outcome of decisions.[5] On the other hand, historical institutionalists problematize the process of preference formation, and ask how actors' preferences are historically, socially and politically constructed. In other words, the rules, procedures and norms play a great role to prescribe not only actors appropriate behavior, but also their strategies, preferences, and ends and means. However, it should be remembered that historical institutionalists carefully avoid taking institutions as the only determinant of actors' preferences and strategies. Their emphasis is rather on how institutions influence and shape preferences and strategies of actors, as well as distribution of power and outcomes. They reserve room for other factors to influence those processes.

Thirdly, both institutionalisms deal with the rationality of actors differently. Rational choice institutionalists deal with rationality of actors as a prerequisite of their theoretical construction. Rationality is observable and calculable from the outside, and therefore it is clear and objective. The outcomes of interactions are rationally justified by actors' preferences, and vice versa. Historical institutionalists, on the other hand, would not deny the role of rationality of actors. They also tend to see that actors may strategically pursue their goals and ends as well as rational choice institutionalists.[6] However, the important point is that historical institutionalists go beyond simple instrumental rationality, and try to unveil why actors choose certain preferences and goals. March and Olsen (1989) stress that the criteria of what is rational is not based on the expectation of the consequence of action (logic of consequentiality), but actors' insight into how appropriately they are behaving within the rules, norms and values of society (logic of appropriateness). Works by institutional economists[7] extend the stress on the role of values: "a society is a collection of institutions, while an institution is a collection of socially prescribed behaviors correlated or held in relation to one another by a value" which are said to rationalize behaviors (Edgren 1996, p.1017).

What is an 'Institution'?

For any framework using the concept of institution, it is necessary for it to clarify what is meant by 'institution'. The definition of institution varies among institutionalists, such as "the formal rules, compliance procedures, and standard operating practices that structure the relationship between individuals in various units of the polity and economy" (Hall 1986, p.19); "the formal or informal procedures, routines, norms and conventions embedded in the organizational structure of the polity or political economy" (Hall and Taylor 1996, p.938); "both formal organizations and informal rules and procedures that structure conduct" (Thelen and Steinmo 1992, p.2); "social practices consisting of easily recognized roles coupled with clusters of rules or conventions governing relations among the occupants of these roles" (Young 1989, p.32); or "the routines, procedures, conventions, roles, strategies, organizational forms, and technologies around which political activities are constructed" and "the beliefs, paradigms, codes, cultures, and knowledge that surround, support, elaborate, and contradict those roles and routines" (March and Olsen 1989, p.22). In addition to this diversity of definitions, Bulmer argues that an initial policy choice subsequently restricts the policy choice of today, thereby creating a kind of path-dependency which has its own internal logic (Bulmer 1998, p.372). This is rather confusing, and therefore we ought to have our own operational definition of institution.

In order to do so, three distinctive aspects are of particular concern: organizations, norms, and existing policies. First, following the distinction made by Young (1989), formal organizations should be treated separately from institutions.[8] Formal organizations are "material entities possessing physical locations (or seats), offices, personnel, equipment, and budget" (p.32). North (1990) emphasizes the purposive intent and objectives of members which form organizations, and therefore organizations are not a part of institutions per se. Indeed, he argues that organizations are influenced by institutional structure, and in turn, organizations may act as actors of institutional change. Such distinctions will be useful in this study which will pay a great deal of attention to organizations such as the European Space Agency which is certainly influenced by an institutional framework, but may also be a source of influence of institutional change.

Second, the normative aspects of institutions will be stressed by including norms in the definition. Institutions are neither instrumental nor apolitical. Rules and procedures are created and reproduced on the basis of the shared norm and paradigm on which participants generally agree. The ideas and concepts of 'what these institutions are' and 'what these institutions are good for' should be shared by participants; otherwise, participants would find the institutions inappropriate and irrelevant, and thus, the institutions may need to be changed. However, it should be emphasized that norms, ideas and paradigms should be distinguished from what we define as 'policy logics' later in this chapter. Policy logic is a concept which explains the logics that are employed by actors to persuade and convince decision-makers and negotiation counterparts: actors develop policy logics that consist of a set of policy rationale and objectives deriving from their long-term interests and goals, policy guidelines, and a set of values and criteria for policy performance (see below). A norm is more abstract and an epistemological understanding and interpretation of the reality. Although it is hard to draw a line between these two concepts, it should be distinguished for our research purposes. Norms are important to sustain and reproduce institutions. Without what March and Olsen term 'logic of appropriateness' which underpins actors to behave appropriately according to rules, procedures and conventions, institutions may not be able to exist.

Third, although existing policy commitments may be counted as a part of the relevant institutions, they should also be treated as constraints. Because of the lengthy lead-time to develop certain technology, initial policy decisions influence and constrain subsequent decision-makers' choices. Once a government is committed to participate in one program, it becomes difficult to withdraw. But this can also be explained by the sunk costs and international obligation (which is another institution, not a policy), rather than the institution. Thus, institutions are defined in this study as *the rules, procedures and conventions which structure the relationships between actors, and the shared norms and paradigms which underpin and support those rules, procedures and conventions.*

Perhaps the most problematic term in this definition is 'rules'. We use 'rules' in various ways: rules of sport, traffic rules, rules of etiquette, and of course legal rules. Sometimes we conceptualize a 'rule' as a regularly repeated action such as 'waking up at seven as a rule'. What is common in these expressions may be, as Thompson (1989) points out, "how to go on": to know the rules of a game is to know how to play; to know the rules of etiquette is to know how to behave properly in certain situations. Rules are not neutral instruments but resources which facilitate the exercise of power. In the context of European space collaboration, rules are not only defined 'formally' as in the ESA Conventions, but also 'informal' rules of 'working together' such as information sharing or rule of equality (Zabusky 1995) which facilitate not only interactions among participants, but also generate the base of the exercise of power.

Different Analytical Levels and Institutionalism

As discussed above, both rational choice and historical institutionalisms have relevance for the analysis of European space collaboration, despite the conceptual differences between the two. Some scholars have tried to articulate or, at least, to accept some elements from the two approaches. North (1990), based on rational choice analysis, agreed that institutional evolution does not happen *tabula rasa*, but is constrained by a historical path. Some historical institutionalists, such as Pierson (1996) and Bulmer (1998) in the study of European integration, also employ methods of rational choice analysis as a tool to explain actors' behavior. These 'softer' approaches may be applicable to the analysis of certain policy issues, but this study takes a different view. It regards both types of institutionalism as useful frameworks when they are applied to different levels of political interaction.

Having been inspired by Peterson's model of three analytical levels (Peterson 1995), this study makes an analytical distinction between three levels of analysis; European, national government, and expert levels. As we will argue in the next section, values, norms and policy paradigms are different among actors, and such rules of behavior differ according to the level at which actors play.

First, institutions at the European level may only be instrumental, and decision-makers' behavior may be driven by interest or calculable rationality. Because of the low degree of socialization, the norms and paradigms may not be developed, as some historical institutionalists would expect. Actors may have choices upon which they can impose their policy logics. At this level, the rational choice institutionalism seems a suitable framework, but even so, it is important to remember that institutions also shape and influence the actors' interests and strategies to a large extent. Actors are relatively free from normative institutions, but rules and procedures influence actors' preferences and strategies and constrain the actors' behavior.

Table 2.1 Level of Analysis and Analytical Frameworks

Levels	Characteristics of institutions	Suitable framework
Europe	Less developed common paradigms, relatively free from path-dependency	Rational choice / Historical institutionalism
National Government	Established rules, shared norms	Historical / Rational choice institutionalism
Experts	Established norms, high degree of socialization	Historical institutionalism

Secondly, institutions at the national government (cabinet) level are firmer and well established. Norms and rules of behavior which are developed through frequently repeated interaction throughout the course of history are shared among members of government. Their criteria of action are not only bound by the existing rules and procedures, but also by norms and conventions which are historically developed. These norms and conventions include national policy doctrine or policy paradigm. The rules and procedures are well established and institutionalized, and actors often share common norms and values. However, interests and strategic and political concerns play a big role in the decision-making process at this level. Sometimes norms or values are overridden by political concerns and institutions only provide instrumental constraints, particularly in times of unstable political circumstances. Thus at this level, it is assumed that rational choice institutionalism will have an explanatory power during a time of turbulence, whereas historical institutionalism is a suitable framework to analyze interaction during a relatively stable period.

Finally, institutions at the level of experts are robust and enduring. Experts who are involved in space policy-making are by and large civil servants in administration, and 'logic of appropriateness' prevails at this level. Experts tend to have life-long values and norms accompanying their professions, which is unlikely to change unless there is a serious paradigm change in their methodology or research objectives. However, it does not mean that these experts are politically neutral and non-strategic. They behave in certain ways in order to strategically influence policy outcome to realize their long-term policy interests.

Experts in the Policy-making Process

This section reviews analytical frameworks which mainly focus on the role of actors and actions other than those of the 'state'. In so doing, we will examine two aspects of the policy-making process. First, we will see how the international domain is inter-related to domestic political circumstances. Individuals representing their country at the table of international negotiation are not free to decide the outcome of negotiation without considering the domestic consequence of the outcome. The two-level games approach seems to be appropriate to analyze this aspect. Second, as neorealists argue, policy-makers may decide the course of space activities beyond technological and financial constraints (one good example is the American Apollo program), and they would define space policy for strategic purposes. But, on the assumption that space is a technologically complex policy area of which the lay policy-makers will not be able to understand completely technological constraints and opportunities, they should seek help from experts. Thus, the interaction between the strategies of policy-makers and the interests of experts should be given consideration. The role of experts has been analyzed in conventional pluralist approaches (interest group model or bureaucracy model) (see Fischer 1990; Lambright 1976; Peters and Barker 1992), but in the light of recent theoretical development, this study will take a closer look at two frameworks: epistemic community and advocacy coalition.

Two-level Games

The argument of the two-level games questions a simple neorealist model of international negotiation where the domestic decision-making process is considered as a 'black box', and where the relative strength of the state decides the outcome. The two-level games framework sheds light on the interactive relationship between international negotiation and domestic political resonance. The essence of the argument is as follows:

> [a]t the national level, domestic groups pursues their interests by pressuring the government to adopt favorable policies, and politicians seek power by constructing coalitions among those groups. At the international level, national governments seek to maximize their own ability to satisfy domestic pressures, while minimizing the adverse consequences of foreign developments. Neither of the two games can be ignored by central decision-makers, so long as their countries remain interdependent, yet sovereign (Putnam 1988, p.434).

In other words, central decision-makers should strategically and tactically seek an outcome of which other states as well as their domestic constituencies will accept. Central decision-makers are not only facing their counterparts, but also their domestic groups at the negotiation table.

Two-level games approach sees that the most important part of this process is the requirement that any agreement at the international level must be ratified — formally or informally — at the national level. The concept of 'win-set', which is a set of all possible international agreements that would gain the necessary majority of constituents, is the decisive factor in international negotiation. Negotiators can only agree upon sets agreement which they can win in the ratification process and then integrate into the agreement.

According to Putnam, the size of a win-set is determined by three sets of factors: distribution of power, preference and possible coalition at the domestic level; domestic institutions; and negotiator's strategy at the international level. First, the win-set depends on the balance between the size of the 'isolationist' who may not benefit from agreement, and 'internationalists' who support international agreement. In the case of space collaboration, some actors in larger countries may take the 'isolationist' position because they have the capacity to 'go it alone', whereas actors in smaller countries tend to take the 'internationalist' position. But usually, the concern for most of governments is not if they participate in a certain program, but *how much* of a share of a program they will get.

Secondly, the size of a win-set depends on domestic institutions. As we will see in chapter 5, each country has a different domestic institutional setting and degree to which the negotiator (head of ministry or space agency) has their autonomy over decisions. For example, the British negotiator (minister for space) may have a strong position *vis-à-vis* the space agency, but under the severe constraints of the Treasury whereas a French negotiator (head of *tutelle* ministry) may have a weaker position *vis-à-vis* a strong space agency (see chapter 5).

Thirdly, the size of a win-set depends on the tactics of the negotiator. There are several ways that a negotiator/statesman can induce domestic actors to ratify the agreement. First, the negotiator can use side-payment in order to expand win-set. A typical example is the case in the 1976 crisis in France when the CNES Toulouse Center went on strike and the French government had to offer side-payment (see chapter 4). The other tactic is to use international agreement as a legitimization to expand the win-set. This tactic was used to persuade public to accept the agreement for participation in the International Space Station, particularly in Germany (interview with DLR official, 4/6/98).

The two-level games approach has adequate explanatory power in many cases of European space collaboration. However, in the process of European space collaboration, two points should be added to the framework of the two-level games. First, for most of the cases, major actors in the ratification process are narrowly limited within space community and to governmental actors. The distribution of power among these actors will be a factor in deciding the size of a win-set. Second, it is not only the ratification process but also the agenda-setting process which is important. Particularly, on the assumption that space activities involve a vast amount of expertise which many politicians do not understand, we should take a closer look at how experts and scientists are involved in the policy-making process.

Role of Experts in Policy-making

Governing modern society may not be easy without highly skilled, competent, and well-trained experts. Space, in particular, is an area where the government needs help from such experts. Decisions for space policy should be based on technological capabilities (or the prospect of technological evolution) within limited financial constraints. Central decision-makers have to be informed about what is possible, and what is desirable. The decision has to be made as to which issues to consider and which should be left alone. The role of experts, scientists, engineers, and space companies becomes relevant in this respect. Their knowledge and advice influences their path of policy. In other words, experts can transform their knowledge into power to pursue their own personal and organizational goals. Although the focus here is on the role and power of experts, the argument departs from the literatures of 'technocracy' which concern itself with the role of experts in *governance* rather than decision-making (Bell 1973; Firscher 1990; Galbraith 1967; Kraft and Vig 1988). Instead, this study finds the approach of Aberbach and others (1981) which distinguishes the relationships between bureaucrats and politicians in four images useful (Table 2.2). They argue that modern democracy is moving from Image I, the classical administrator-decision-maker relationship, to Image IV, a "pure hybrid" of bureaucratized politicians and politicized bureaucrats. In between, Image II is described as a "facts-interests" relationship where bureaucrats bring knowledge and politician bring "interests and values" into the decision-making process, and Image III as an "energy-equilibrium" relationship in which politicians articulate broad interests, whereas bureaucrats do so for narrow interests.

The relationships between politicians and bureaucrats in the space policy-making process in Europe, despite significant national differences, fall into a category between Image II and III. On the one hand, in a technologically complex policy area such as space, as Baumgartner and Jones (1991) argue, issues "are portrayed as technical problems rather than as social questions, experts can dominate the decision-making process" (p.1047). But on the other, in a strategic policy area such as space, decision-makers commit themselves in the policy-making process to link space policy with other strategic goals. The degree of strategic importance of space policy may make differences in the 'images' of policy-making process among European countries.

Epistemic community   Many studies about the role of experts in recent years refer to the work of Peter Haas (1992) on 'epistemic community'. While the definition of epistemic community is commonly known as "a network of professionals with recognized expertise and competence in a particular domain and an authoritative claim to policy-relevant knowledge within that domain or issue-area" (*ibid.*, p.3), Haas repeatedly implies that the epistemic community, which consists of professionals who share not only expertise and competence but also a set of normative beliefs, causal beliefs, and common policy enterprise, should be distinguished from functional units such as interest groups or bureaucracy. Members of an epistemic community distinctively act on a value-based rationale, shared methods and criteria of analyzing, validating and linking problems and desired outcome, and have common practices in their exercise of competence. The epistemic community perspective provides insights into how the networks of experts play in articulating cause-and-effect relationships of complex problems, helping states to identify their interests, and proposing specific policies.

The concept of epistemic community limits its scope of application to the process of policy transformation. According to Haas, epistemic communities significantly influence the process of transformation in the following three stages.[9] First, the policy area should be under a condition of uncertainty. It is assumed that decision-makers do not always seek help from epistemic communities until they recognize that their understanding of issue and exercise of power is limited. "It is difficult", writes Haas, "for leaders to identify their potential political allies and to be sure of what strategies are most likely to help them retain power" (*ibid.*, p.14) under a condition of uncertainty. Under such conditions, existing institutions become unworkable and unstable,[10] thus room for epistemic communities to play a large role is created. Second, once an epistemic community establishes its foothold in the policy-making process, control over knowledge and information becomes a new dimension of power and the diffusion of new ideas and information will be able to set a new pattern of behavior. Diffusion of new ideas and information lead to the third stage of transformation: institutionalization. New ideas and information are accepted by wider policy communities and form mainstream policy beliefs. Once the ideas are institutionalized, the entrepreneurial role of an epistemic community should be concluded, and wider policy communities (bureaucracy) will take over. In this sense, the concept of epistemic community is not suited for the analysis of the day-to-day bureaucratic exercise of power but the role of experts in dynamic policy transformation.

Table 2.2   Four Images of Politician-bureaucrat Relationships

	Type of relationship	Characteristics
Image I	Classical	Bureaucrats implement decisions made by politicians
Image II	Facts-interests	Bureaucrats bring knowledge and politicians bring "interests and values" into the decision-making process
Image III	Energy-equilibrium	Politicians articulate broad interests, whereas bureaucrats do so for narrow interests
Image IV	Pure hybrid	Bureaucratized politicians and politicized bureaucrats jointly make decisions

Source: Adapted from Aberbach *et al.* (1981).

Haas and other contributors emphasize the process of learning as a linchpin of the transformation process. They regard learning as "changes in the epistemological assumptions and interpretations that help frame and structure collective understanding and action" (Adler and Haas 1992, p.385). Learning implies that policy-makers can absorb not only new ideas and information but also new ways of drawing linkages between causes and effects, and therefore can change their interests and objectives of actions. Moreover, learning also means that their alteration of behavior can become not momentary but enduring and institutionalized (Heclo 1974, p.306). Hence, the power of experts is characterized not only by the manipulation of information and expertise but also by their power to change and maintain policy-makers' epistemological interpretation.

Members of epistemic communities, therefore, influence state interests "either by directly identifying them for decision-makers or by illuminating the salient dimensions of an issue from which the decision-makers may then deduce their interests" (Haas 1992, p.4). These changes of interests in one state may diffuse to other states, and therefore increase the likelihood of convergence in state behavior at the international level, influenced by transnational alliances of epistemic communities. It is clear in his argument that state interest and behavior is a 'dependent' variable which is framed by the ideas and beliefs of an epistemic community.

However, two important reservations should be made. First, as Adler and Haas (1992) assert, "[e]pistemic communities create reality, but not as they wish" (p.381). If decision-makers are familiar with the issues concerned, they tend to use experts whose idea may resemble the pre-existing preferences of decision-makers. Political factors and the priority of the subject concerned decide how influential members of epistemic communities can be. In short, power and influence of epistemic communities is dependent on access to the decision-maker (Barker and Peters 1993). Second, it is misleading to suggest that the process of policy transformation is automatic. The new ideas informed by the epistemic community have to compete with the ideas of other epistemic communities. The outcome of the competition is not presupposed or fixed.

Advocacy coalition   Even though it is less popular than epistemic community, the concept of "advocacy coalition" proposed by Sabatier and Jenkins-Smith (1993) provides a more elaborated research program on groups of actors similar to that of an epistemic community. They define advocacy coalition as "actors from a variety of public and private institutions ... who share a set of basic beliefs (policy goals plus causal and other perceptions) and who seek to manipulate the rules, budgets, and personnel of governmental institutions in order to achieve these goals over time" (Jenkins-Smith and Sabatier 1993a, p.5). Although as Radaelli (1995) points out, their emphasis tends to be on the role of beliefs rather than knowledge or expertise, it is implicitly assumed that experts play an important role as agents who provide technical knowledge in support of the advocacy coalition as well as agents who share beliefs with other members in the coalition.

The emphasis on shared beliefs implies that actors in the policy process do not make 'coalitions of convenience' which are primarily motivated by their short-term interest, but coalition which is bounded by shared beliefs (Sabatier 1993, p.27).

More precisely, as they argue, the coalition is organized around common beliefs in the 'core' elements which are fundamental normative axioms and policy positions, but less so in 'secondary' elements which are instrumental and technical beliefs. Therefore, it is assumed that the composition of an advocacy coalition is relatively stable over a long period of time, and once one coalition dominates a policy area, the policy may be stable as well.

Perhaps one of the problems for the advocacy coalition framework is the distinction between 'beliefs' and 'interests'. Students of conventional policy analysis would think that policy coalition is usually formed around a common interest, instead of a shared belief. While Sabatier (1993) accepts that "belief systems are normally highly correlated with self-interest and the causation is reciprocal", he uses 'belief systems' rather than 'interest' because "beliefs are more inclusive and more verifiable than interests" (p.28). 'Belief systems' consist of (1) a set of means and performance indicators to attain goals; (2) a set of interests and goals; (3) perceived causal relationships; and (4) a perceived parameter (guideline of actions), and therefore it is assumed to provide an analytical tool which enables us to see various ways of how actors establish their goals. This definition is rather confusing because on the one hand, Sabatier and Jenkins-Smith distinguish 'core' and 'secondary' elements of beliefs which are normative and instrumental beliefs. This means that 'core' and 'secondary' elements of beliefs are non-material, ideological or judgmental beliefs. Such beliefs shape and constrain actions and behaviors. But on the other hand, they include interests and policy goals in the belief system. It almost seems that 'interest' is assumed as the 'secondary' element of beliefs.

Although the advocacy coalition framework is not a particular framework to analyze the role of experts, it may provide a relatively robust framework for the analysis of policy process. However, there is some opaqueness in this. First, it is assumed that advocacy coalition is formed at the 'policy subsystem' level. That means that decision-makers who may share beliefs with members of an advocacy coalition are excluded from the coalition and considered as a politically neutral and instrumental actor. The advocacy coalitions are assumed to compete with each other to get better access to politically neutral decision-makers in order to influence the outcome of the decision. Assuming that space is a strategic policy area, at least for some states, it is difficult to imagine that decision-makers play only an instrumental role in the policy-making process.

Second, because the advocacy coalition framework uses a broader concept of beliefs, which include interest as well as normative beliefs, and assumes that the coalition would be made around the 'core' belief, it tends to neglect the possibility that policy coalition may be made around interests as well as 'secondary' beliefs. This can be the case of space policy where members of the policy community largely share 'core' elements of normative beliefs such as technological evolution and exploration of the unknown: there is a wide variety of policy coalitions that are formed around the 'secondary' beliefs or long-term interests of the members. It would be misleading to ignore the possibility that the members of the policy community may form a coalition around the 'secondary' beliefs or long-term interests.

Policy Logic Analysis

In this chapter, we have seen three sets of analytical framework — two-level games, epistemic community, and advocacy coalition — to evaluate the interaction of domestic actors in agenda-setting and ratification of international agreements. These frameworks suggest that state policies are neither fixed nor enduring, but they are strongly influenced by the limits of win-sets and the beliefs of expert communities. While these frameworks enlighten areas which neorealist perspective neglects, none of them seems to be fully applicable for our research area.

The problems are two-fold: first, the conceptual confusion about the distinction between 'ideas' and 'interests' seems to be very problematic when it comes to operationalizing these concepts. As Hood (1994) notes "the further we move from 'harder' to 'softer' versions of the 'primacy of ideas' approach, the harder it will be to distinguish 'ideas' from 'interests'" (p.7). It is true that at the 'secondary' level of belief, as Sabatier argues, it is difficult to distinguish 'ideas' from 'interests'. These ideas and beliefs frame interests, but at the same time, those interests frame these ideas. For example, the controversy over European participation in the International Space Station was not only a conflict of beliefs (whether manned space is a good science program; *grand projet vs. value for money* argument), but also a conflict of interests (industrial, technological, and scientific returns). Thus, this study proposes a concept of 'policy logic' to fill the middle ground between normative beliefs and material interests.

Second, none of the approaches mentioned above have given a satisfactory framework of the interactive process between central decision-makers and experts. Because the two-level games approach is preoccupied with the ratification process and win-set analysis, it neglects the process of policy formulation. Although Moravcsik (1993c) relies on the two-level games approach as regards domestic preference formation, his argument is rather circumstantial and vague. The advocacy coalition concentrates its focus on the policy subsystem, and politicians are taken as instrumental actors. Perhaps, the epistemic community approach is more concerned about how experts exercise their power on decision-makers, but this framework lacks explanations of the process of competition between epistemic communities and of how decision-makers choose which communities they rely on. Our research framework, which is called the 'policy logic analysis', would bridge the gap of these frameworks and provide a fresh look at interactions between decision-makers and experts.

Policy logic analysis regards policy as an outcome of competition of 'logics'. On the one hand, decision-makers have their own policy 'logic' based upon their strategy for space or use of space for other policy objectives. On the other, experts have their own specific 'logics' to compete with each other to have closer access to decision-makers or to convince them if they have priority for particular logic.

Definition of 'Policy Logic'

As discussed above, in order to analyze the very complex process of policy-making in international collaboration, neither 'interests' nor 'beliefs' seem satisfactory analytical tools in our framework. Actors in space policy — decision-makers and experts — do not consciously differentiate interests from beliefs. Some may believe that space should be associated with national pride and autonomy, others may believe that space should serve for commercial and industrial benefit. Such beliefs and values for space policy are directly reflected on the preferences and interests on the selection of programs or allocation of budget. Experts have their interests to promote certain programs in order to reify their belief or values — such as challenging new technology, sending a probe to an unknown planetary body, and so forth. In other words, as Scharpf (1997) argues, "people act not only on the basis of objective needs but also on the basis of preferences reflecting their *subjectively defined interests and valuations* and their *normative convictions* of how it is right or good or appropriate to act under the circumstances" (p.19, emphasis original).

The concept of 'interest' in particular may change at different levels of analysis — Europe, national government, and experts' levels — and from domestic process to European process. For example, the interests of Member States presented at the ESA meeting are not merely an aggregate of domestic interests. Decision-makers or the Chief of Government (COG) may use different discourses of interest in domestic and international domains. As many critics of 'national interest' argue, the notion of interest cannot be isolated from its subjectivity and ambiguity (cf. Clinton 1994, chapter 2), and therefore, it would be misleading to believe that national interests are objective and "fundamental goals, which change little" (Milner 1997, p.15n).

Thus, in order to avoid confusion of concepts, we will employ a term 'policy logic' in this study. The concept of 'policy logic' shall be defined as reasoning conducted according to a system of policy principles in which experts, group of experts and decision-makers are committed to realize their respective objectives. As discussed above, this study assumes that experts and decision-makers have their own objectives in policy programs to realize their individual values and interests. Particularly in space policy-making, those values and interests are strategically projected in the long-term because of a lengthy lead-time and scarcity of resources. Therefore, the process of policy-making in space appears to be an interest-driven competition for budget distribution. However, the 'policy logic analysis' focuses on the logic (or reasoning) of actors for rationalizing their policy objectives and principles. On the one hand, experts use their own logic to motivate decision-makers to support their objectives and principles if decision-makers are not in favor for experts' logic. On the other hand, decision-makers have to have their policy logics for rationalizing their decisions and convincing certain groups of experts for not adopting the proposed policy objectives, and also decision-makers have to convince their counterparts in international negotiation. The concept of 'policy logic', in short, allows us to analyze rationales of experts, groups of experts and decision-makers/ negotiators behind the outcome of both domestic and European policy process by separating the concepts of 'value' and 'interest'.

The system of policy principles on which actors conduct their policy logic consists of (1) a set of long-term interests and goals, (2) perceived guidelines of policy conduct and behavior, and (3) a set of values which would provide criteria for the judgment of policy performance.[11] This definition may enable us to distinguish the 'core' aspect of normative beliefs, which is historically and socially constructed (and is therefore difficult to change), and short-term self-interests of actors, which may not be suitable for the analysis of space policy which requires long-term commitment in technology development. The concept of 'policy logic' implies that the 'state' is not a monolithic entity because the members of different policy communities within it share different policy values and beliefs. Although this study is ready to accept that there are certain shared 'core' norms and paradigms among all members of communities to support and underpin rules and procedures, it does not assume that governments and experts share the 'secondary' beliefs, values or ideas for detailed political decisions.

By definition, the concept of policy logic explains that interests, values and policy objectives are possessed by individual actors. At this level, policy logic explains the individual motivation and ambition toward space policy. In this study, we will take a pluralist view of policy-making, that is to say, the political decision is made through interactions among individual members in a policy community. The decisions taken at the national or European level are consequences of domestic and international interaction. But unlike simple pluralist model, it does not take a position that a policy is a simple amalgamation of domestic or international interactions. Rather it regards national decision-makers as pivotal actors to reconcile 'domestic policy logics' and formulate national space policy which will be presented as 'national policy logic' at the level of European negotiation. As perceived in the two-level games approach, the decision-makers became negotiators in European negotiation to promote their 'national policy logics' to be realized in policies at the European level. The policy logic analysis focuses on the interaction of policy logics between the decision-makers and experts, and the consequence of which is going to be regarded as 'national policy logics' at the table of European negotiation.

The emphasis on plurality of the concept of 'policy logic' should be explained. We go from single *policy logic* to plural *policy logics* to indicate that there is more than one logic within national and European policy. In fact, space policy itself does not constitute a policy of its own, but it serves for other political purposes. Since the investment in an individual space program is so large, it is often the case that a decision for one program serves to satisfy different policy logics. It is, indeed, more reasonable to analyze political decision as the production of several policy logics. Thus, a policy taken at national and European level is rarely based on single policy logic, but it often contains a complex set of different policy logics, and each policy has its own set of policy logics to drive the policy forward.

The concept of policy logic also explains the importance of the vision of decision-makers for space. Since all policies are ultimately decided by decision-makers, the policy outcome is largely influenced by the policy logic preferred by the decision-makers. It is also important to consider who is the 'principal decision-maker'. The concept of principal decision-maker is almost equivalent to the 'Chief of Government' in the two-level games approach, but the principal decision-maker includes not only ministers of government but also the heads of administrative bodies, particularly the chief staffs of space agencies, who have the authority to make decisions in the ESA Council (see chapter 4). Since the policy competences for space activities are usually held by several ministerial bodies, such as ministries of technology, industry, post and telecommunications, and military, there may be cases that two or more decision-makers are involved as the principal decision-makers. For instance, the position of the British minister in charge of space rotates quite frequently (almost every year) among ministers who have the portfolio of trade and industry or science and technology. In the case of France, the space portfolio is divided among the ministry of industry, post and telecommunications, and research and education, according to different governments. In these cases, the preference, priority, and policy logic of principal decision-maker for space varies according to the political contexts which surround them. Such institutional allocation of the space portfolio in the government, together with personal policy logic of principal decision-makers would have significant implications of the outcome of the competition of policy logics.

It is important to note that the concept of 'policy logic' does not imply that all policies are objectively calculable and rationally measurable. As March and Olsen (1989) argue, there are two senses of 'logics' in collective action; "logic of consequence" which is a logic of action to anticipate the consequence of particular action, and "logic of appropriateness" which is a logic of action to behave appropriately to the rules and institutions. Their argument explains that the logic of actions may not be explained by calculable methods. The concept of policy logic, as we discussed above, is separated from that of calculable interest. Instead, this study regards policy logic as "strategic social construction" (Finnemore and Sikkink 1998) in which actors behave rationally and strategically to reconfigure preferences, identities, or social context. This is to say that strategies and interests of decision-makers and experts are shaped by institutions, but institutions — norms and rules — are significantly influenced by the strategies and interests of actors. The argument in this study, based on a pluralist view of policy formulation, is that actors who have different sets of 'policy logics' compete strategically to influence policy outcomes, and the consequence of this competition of policy logics influences the shape of normative context, but the actors in this competition are strongly influenced by the institutional setting to behave appropriately.

Types of Policy Logics

First, we shall identify which kind of policy logics can be appropriate for the analysis of space policy. There is no question that there is a wide variety of interests, beliefs and policy objectives for space activities, but in order to have a manageable number of variables, we should shortlist the candidates of possible policy logics for space policy. In this section, we are going to bundle up policy logics for space development into six logics; logics of science, technology, commerce, military, autonomy, and finance.

The first one is the *logic of science*. As we will see in chapter 3, the institutional framework for European space collaboration was strongly influenced by scientists who demanded European collaboration at the beginning of space collaboration. Scientists, such as astrophysicists, astronomers, geologists and meteorologists, naturally have strong interests and beliefs in scientific programs. As Polanyi (1968) argues, this community of scientists, or 'republic of science', is relatively autonomous to influence scientific development through authoritative decisions. Although it differs from country to country, decision-makers understand the necessity of government funding for scientific exploration. Some decision-makers who have a scientific background or strong relationship with scientific communities may apply the logic of science as his/her policy conduct. The logic of science emphasizes the responsibility of government to support exploration to open the frontier of scientific knowledge for mankind. Actors in this logic regard space as an object of study, and are often influenced by history-making achievements of space science such as the American lunar landing or the Hubble Space Telescope. One of the particular characteristics of the logic of science is that its normative base is not bound by national activities. Since scientific knowledge is shared by international academic circles, there is no reason that scientific programs should be national. In fact, even in the height of Cold War tension, there were international scientific programs for exploration of comets and other planetary bodies between the US and the USSR.

The *logic of technology* is another policy logic which is strongly supported by experts. Engineers who work in the field of aerodynamics, electronics, and propulsion, particularly those who work at the nuts and bolts level, naturally have interests in building state-of-the-art satellites and launchers. Their personal goal of being in space agencies or companies is to develop spacecrafts which are technologically advanced or on cutting the edge of the technological frontier. New inventions or the development of new technologies would bring personal or organizational reward and honor in the space community. The logic of technology is also a policy logic for decision-makers who are concerned with overall national technological development and capability in the high technology sector. However, on the assumption that the decision-makers' priority is to achieve other political goals by exploiting space technology, it is then that decision-makers use the logic of technology with other policy logics which they put priority on. It is then observed that decision-makers show their concerns for technological development as a step toward strengthening the international competitiveness of their industry. In such cases, the logic of technology of decision-makers often forms a coalition with the logics of commerce. In terms of its transnational characteristics, the logic of technology serves in different ways for decision-makers and experts. The former would have their policy logic to maintain and accumulate national technological competence, and to control under national authority whereas the latter would not care much about the nationality of technology. The experts will be willing to cooperate with other countries as long as they can get funding for programs to develop a particular technology.

The *logic of commerce* is becoming more important these days since the commercial space market for launching service (Suzuki 2000) and telecommunications is dramatically expanding. Strong advocates of this logic are space companies, as well as the user industry, space insurance companies, financiers, and trading companies. For the groups of business and financial experts, space is an industrial area where they can make profit, just like other industries. Their behavior is based on the values of commercial business such as increasing competitiveness, and their interests are simply to make profit from contracts and to win the competition in the market. In the past, space was a typical case of 'market failure' where a commercial market did not exist, and therefore these actors had to rely on government contracts (which implies that the logic of commerce was not given priority in government policies). Even so, the logic of commerce was attractive to some decision-makers, largely because there were government ministries which use and regulate space operation such as PTT and transportation.

However, as discussed above, developing technological capabilities was the imperative for those ministries as well as the companies in order to catch up with the market leader and to make profit. In terms of transnational characteristics, this logic has experienced a dynamic paradigm shift. The aerospace industry was a typical example of the 'national champion' until the 1980s when the government reinforced industrial consolidation into one or two firms of international dimensions capable of sustaining foreign competition. But in recent years, governments are beginning to prefer 'European champion' policy which allows 'national champions' to consolidate into one or two companies at the European level (see Cohen 1992; Hayward 1995). Such a paradigm shift was brought about by a broad consensus that sustaining foreign competition can only be done at the European level, and therefore the logic of commerce should be open to the transnational dimension. However, it is still possible to see, particularly among decision-makers, that they protect or maximize a narrow sense of 'national logic' in the process of European consolidation.

Because the aerospace industry, which includes the space segment, has been a champion of the defense industry in Europe, and space technology in the United States and Soviet Union was developed by the drive for the military use of space, it is therefore easily assumed that the European space sector is developed by the *logic of military*. Although the logic of military played a small role in the development of European space technology as we explain in subsequent chapters, we have to take into account how much this logic drove space policy forward. Obviously, ministries of defense (particularly the Air Force) and chiefs of staff are strong advocates of this logic, but it should be remembered that they are *users* of space technology, and that they are very aware that space is not the only means for communication or surveillance. It is rather the decision-makers, particularly in big countries, who hold strong the logic of military to be important in space policy. For them, it is important to have their own national (or European) sources to gather their own satellite communication system and intelligence information to make strategic choices. Especially in a time of crisis, decision-makers often find that Europe lacks satellite communications and intelligence capability compared to that of the US. However, the logic of military in space policy is not necessarily entirely nationalistic. Since the investment is so enormous, decision-makers have to make a strategic choice between the autarky and efficiency problem (Moravcsik 1991b). In fact, smaller countries cannot afford to have their own national assets for military use, and even a big European country like Britain depends on American capability for intelligence from space.

The fifth policy logic, the *logic of autonomy*, overlaps with other policy logics in many cases, but it has certain distinctive features. Its value and long-term goal is to secure national autonomy in scientific knowledge, state-of-the-art technology, commercial competitiveness, military control over space assets, and so forth. The distinctive characteristics of this logic are that it has a political goal, but it needs to be used with other logics. There is no particular advocate of this logic among experts, but many decision-makers often pursue this logic in their space policy. When we deal with policy at the European level, we should be careful about whether the logic of autonomy applied to national or European levels. In the early days of European collaboration, the concept of 'autonomy' meant *national* autonomy. France, under De Gaulle's presidency in particular, used space as a policy sector to express its national *grandeur* or prestige. Success in European policy directly translated into national glory. However, along with the progress of European integration and intensification of European collaboration, the concept gradually changed its characteristics from *national* autonomy to *European* autonomy.

Last but not least, the *logic of finance* occupies a unique and important position in the constellation of policy logics. Because of its sheer costs and the unpredictability of technological investment, space has always been subject to financial pressure led by the Ministry of Finance or the Treasury. Unlike other logics, its function is to set a limit of spending for national and European activities and to put the brakes on the growth of space expenditure. Its value and interest is to sustain the balance sheet of the national budget and to reinforce financial discipline in space policy. The logic of finance has been in existence all the time, but its influence is heavily dependent on the preference of decision-makers. If decision-makers put priority on space development, the logic of finance is overridden by political force, so that space programs are carried on no matter how much governments are in debt. However, a paradigm shift in fiscal policy, often summarized as a shift from 'big government' to 'small government' or 'welfare state' to 'competition state' (Moreau Defarges 1992), together with the introduction of a single currency and the so-called 'Washington Consensus' (Krugman 1995), has shaken up the importance of the logic of finance in space policy as well as other policy areas. Decision-makers not only became unable to override the legitimacy of the logic of finance, but began to support and prioritize this logic. Although the logic of finance is dictated by national concerns, since there are no common resources for space activities, advocators of this logic are increasingly closing national differences because of the single currency.

These six types may sufficiently cover the range of major policy logics in European space collaboration. We are going to use this set of policy logics to analyze national and European processes of space policy-making. One important reminder of it is that each country has a different set of policy logics for a particular policy — national as well as European — and the weight of policy logics changes throughout the course of history. Domestic institutional settings as well as the external political environment shape the balance and importance of policy logics, and participating countries in European space collaboration seek to reconcile or compromise such differences in negotiations at the European level, in order to reflect their policy logics in the European space policy. In this way, we can use the concept of policy logic to apply to cross-national policy analysis and the historical dynamism of policy change.

Logic Coalition

Individual experts seek to achieve their own interest and values to be included in space programs. But if they pursue policy logics individually, they may not have the political power to influence decision-makers to give priority for their policy logics, and, by all means, experts are not professional politicians and "lack the knowledge which is needed to solve a policy problem or to manage a policy field according to some chosen course" (Barker and Peters 1993, p.1). Thus they tend to create 'policy logic coalitions' around common policy logic to seek to expand their influence on programs. It is assumed that members of policy logic coalitions share the logic of their policy ideas and interests, and these policy logic coalitions compete against each other to get better access to principal decision-makers, to implement their policy objectives, and to gain favorable budget line. It is also assumed that experts form coalitions not only among themselves, but also with politicians who may share their beliefs, values and interests because it is often the case that politicians also have long-term commitment, values and interests on certain issues. Table 2.3 shows the hypothesis of policy logics and logic coalitions in space policy. Among these policy logics, experts tend to have a firm and well-established coalition in the logics of science, technology, commerce, and military, since they have corresponding ministry or industrial organizations. On the other hand, the logics of autonomy and finance are more political and ideological logics, so that they do not have an identifiable logic coalition as such. These logics are however shared among most experts, and are used to reinforce the power of logic coalition when the concerned logic coalition is in an unfavorable position.

The power resources of the logic coalition have two dimensions. First, the power of a logic coalition is influenced by the domestic and European institutional setting. As discussed, our definition of institution is not solely limited to organizational aspects of government, but includes beliefs and paradigms. Each European country has its unique institutional setting which allows certain logic coalition to be powerful. For example, the military logic coalition in larger countries such as Britain and France may be stronger than those of smaller countries which do not have a stake in a military space operation. Some of these smaller countries, for example Switzerland which hosts CERN and other international scientific activities, have a powerful science logic coalition.

Table 2.3   Types of Logic Coalitions in Space Policy

Logics	Dominant Actors	Major Values	Perceived Goals
Science	Scientists	Knowledge	Frontier programs
Technology	Engineers	Evolution	Technologically advanced programs
Commerce	Space Companies	Profit	Increase competitiveness
Military	Military Personnel	Security	Autonomous control
Autonomy	(Decision-makers)	Autonomy	Strategic non-dependence to others
Finance	Financial authority	Value for money	Budgetary discipline

Secondly, the degree of influence can be assessed by the access to, and the preference of, the principal decision-makers. The ultimate goal of the members of a logic coalition — to promote the policy they support — can be achieved only through principal decision-makers who have the authority in political decisions. The principal decision-makers for space policy in European countries are usually ministers for space, but sometimes higher authorities, for example the French President, may play a decisive role. This access to the principal decision-makers is not instrumentally granted to all logic coalitions, but instead it is highly selective according to the preference of the decision-makers. The principal decision-makers may have a set of priorities, so s/he tends to grant better access for preferred logic coalitions rather than others. However, other decision-makers in the policy-making process — other ministers who are directly involved in space decision-making such as PTT, the defense or transport minister, the head of space agencies, and so forth — may also have some voice in the process. For logic coalitions, it is important to find these decision-makers to support their logics, if they are not granted favorable access to principal decision-makers.

The logic coalitions do not always compete against each other, but often they cooperate to promote policies which serve for more than one logic. The commerce logic coalition may cooperate with the military logic coalition when there is strong pressure from the logic of finance when they cooperate to promote a program which would be used for both military and civilian purposes. The autonomy logic coalition may sometimes have a link with the science logic coalition to promote programs such as manned space flight or the exploration of Mars. Such cooperation of coalitions would extend their political resources, and therefore increase their potential to appeal to the principal decision-makers. Perhaps the most isolated logic coalition is the logic of finance which by its own right has rich political resources, not only access to principal decision-makers and supports, but also to the budgets. For example, the logic of finance and the logic of military (or the logic of autonomy) confront sharply in the case of the autarky-efficiency problem (Moravcsik 1991b). However, the finance logic coalition is not always the most powerful logic coalition. In a few cases, principal decision-makers are able to override policy proposals (budget line) and implement their own preference or international agreements.

International Negotiation and Domestic Logic Coalitions

The interactions among domestic logic coalitions determine not only the national policy logic at international negotiation, but the outcome of the negotiation as well. As discussed in the two-level games approach, negotiators face not only their counterparts, but also domestic actors, and the outcome of the negotiation is determined by the size of the win-set. The size of the win-set is determined, in addition to Putnam's three sets of factors, by the distribution of policy logics. If the negotiators face difficulty to achieve an agreement, and if it is necessary for negotiators to alter their negotiating position or priority of agenda, they tend to prioritize the agenda of powerful policy logic. In other words, they prefer to reach an agreement at the expense of the weaker policy logic. Negotiators may find it easier to convince the members of the weaker logic coalition than the stronger one. It is often the case when negotiators use 'cutting slack' tactics which is to use a broader win-set than expected to accommodate an agreement. For example, the ESA Ministerial Council at Toulouse in 1995 decided to freeze the science budget for five years in order to allocate funding for other programs. The ministers found that it was easier to convince the members of the science logic coalition than other logic coalitions, especially the commerce and finance logic coalitions.[12] By contrast, the stronger logic coalitions will 'tie the hands' of negotiators in international negotiations by threatening that they would not ratify the agreement if it was not in their favor.

Sometimes, negotiators do not wish unilaterally to use 'cutting slack' tactics which would undermine their negotiating position or credibility *vis-à-vis* their domestic logic coalitions. Rather, negotiators would prefer to use a 'package deal' approach. The 'package deal' approach allows all participating countries to bring their priority forward to satisfy strong domestic policy logics and, at the same time, to convince weaker domestic logic coalitions to accept the agreement. Options for weaker coalitions are limited because they do not have enough power to overturn the agreement, and the objection to the international (or European) agreement is regarded as undermining the spirit of European collaboration.[13] In the period of early European space collaboration, the least benefited policy logic from 'package deal' approach was, most likely, the logic of finance, because the package deal agreement tended to expand the overall spending level. However, since most European governments came under severe budgetary constraints, particularly in the 1990s, the situation of the logic of finance has changed, and it has become the top priority for many European countries.

It would be misleading if we stop here without mentioning the role of the ESA Director-General (DG) and the Executive as the 'policy broker' in negotiations. Unlike bilateral negotiations, it would be difficult for the participants of negotiation to find a set of 'packages' which would be acceptable for all participants. The ESA Executive, therefore, plays an important role. As seen in Table 2.1 concerning three analytical levels, the ESA Executive is involved at every decision-making level and has close contacts with logic coalitions through Program Boards and numerous working groups. The ESA DG and its Executive are in a position to know the situation of policy logic distribution in each country, and therefore it will be able to intervene in the negotiation as an impartial 'policy broker'. Furthermore, as we will discuss in Chapter 4, the status of the ESA DG defined by the ESA Convention[14] provides an institutional base for the role of policy broker.

Dynamics of Institutional and Policy Logic Changes

Institutionalism and policy logic analysis are useful analytical tools for comparative cross-national policy-making process by focusing on differences of institutions and policy logic distribution, but they tend to limit their analytical explanatory power in the static framework of time. On the one hand, institutionalism, by its definition, assumes that institutions are stable variables that endure throughout the course of history. On the other hand, the concept of policy logic which consists of 'long-term interest' and 'policy values and beliefs' also does not anticipate changes in its framework. The change of policy and institutions is often explained in a causal relationship with externality of events — external shock or impacts — which forced institutions to become redundant. However, the institutionalism and policy logic analysis would bring more elaborated framework to explain historical dynamics of the changes.

As argued above, institutions and policy logics are interactively related, and it is difficult to have a one way causal relationship. Changes of institutions significantly influence the contexts and distribution of the power of policy logics, whereas the outcome of competition of policy logics shapes and defines the historical path of institutions. Thus, framing dynamics of policy change shall focus not only on aspects of institutional change, but also on interaction between institutions and actors during the period of change.

Institutional Change — How Do We Explain?

Presumably, institutionalists see institutions as the framework which shapes the interests and strategies of participants, and therefore those institutions are assumed to be stable and robust. The institutionalist perspective always has a danger to fall into 'static' analytical tendency. Krasner (1984) argues "once institutions are in place they can assume a life of their own, extracting societal resources, socializing individuals, and even altering the basic nature of civil society itself. ... Furthermore, once a critical choice has been made it cannot be taken back" (p.240). But institutions do change and evolve during the course of their history.

Institutionalists in general have struggled with the process of conceptualization of institutional change. Because their research objectives are focused on illuminating cross-national difference and the persistence of patterns or policies over time, they tended toward institutional determinism. Rational choice institutionalists in particular face such a problem since their research scope is rather limited to a short period of time, and they assume static institutional settings. Their 'snapshot' approach invites taking institutions as independent and stable variable. They use an analogy from sports: institutions are the rules of game; no matter how actors behave (play), the rules remain as they are. Even rational choice institutionalists who are concerned with institutional change explain the change according to preference shift and increase of transactional costs (Williamson 1985). Historical institutionalists, by their nature, are interested in the institutional dynamics of the past — how institutions emerged, maintained and took their particular historical path — but did not explicitly theorize institutional change. Their arguments are too often centered around *how* institutions emerged and reproduced, but not on *why*. One of the reasons is, again, their tendency to focus on continuous constraints rather than change.

However, there have been some attempts to theorize institutional change. Krasner (1984) made the first by introducing the concept of 'punctuated equilibrium'. His concept, in brief, implies that once institutions are established, they will have their own life and persist for a long period of time in stability, but this stability will be disrupted by periodical turbulence or crisis such as war, revolution, and depression. When society faces such crises, old institutions become no longer functional or desirable, and new institutions will be created and settled in the society. It is "an imagery that expects short bursts of rapid institutional change followed by long period of stasis" (Krasner 1984, p.242). In his view, institutions can be functional only during periods of stability, and therefore actors are constrained by institutions, but when the institutions are thrown into crisis, actors become the ones to shape institutions. The same tune was played by Thelen and Steinmo (1992), as they argued institutions "are independent variable and explain political outcomes in periods of stability, but when they break down, they become the dependent variable, whose shape is determined by the political conflicts that such institutional breakdown unleashes" (p.15). Historical sociologists, such as Skocpol (1979) and Tilly (1975), tend to concur with this view. They see exogenous forces such as wars and revolutions — although revolutions are often regarded as the consequence of endogenous contradiction — suddenly changing the socio-economic institutional structures.

By contrast, institutional economists and some historical institutionalists who emphasize the importance of norms, ideas and values tend to see rather incremental institutional change. We classify them as belonging to the 'cognitive change' school. For them, institutional change is a change in values and norms (Bush 1987). Driven by technological, social and material circumstantial change, values change progressively to integrate such changed circumstance into society. Actors' perceptions may be changed through a learning process. Actors learn not only how to behave within institutional constraints, but also how to associate their values and norms to changing structural circumstances. But the process of perception change takes a long time. Even though formal rules and procedures change overnight due to wars or revolutions, "informal constraints embodied in customs, traditions, and codes of conduct are much more impervious to deliberate policies" (North 1990, p.6). To break through the persistence of perceptions, they also stress the importance of leading individuals in the process of change. According to North (1990), the change comes from "the perceptions of the entrepreneurs in political and economic organizations that they could do better by altering the existing institutional framework at some margin" (p.8). In sum, they view that institutional change occurs when norms and values of actors, particularly the leading actors, are changed to associate technological, socio-economic and material change.

Table 2.4   Explanations of Institutional Change

	Punctuated equilibrium	Cognitive change
Pace of change	Rapid	Incremental
Force of change	Exogenous	Endogenous

The model of 'institutional dynamics' proposed by Thelen and Steinmo (1992) provides good empirical descriptions on the situations of institutional change. This approach focuses the interaction between institutions and political processes: how institutions structure politics as well as how the impact of institutions itself is mediated by the broader political context. They set four patterns of institutional change with two distinct sources — exogenous and endogenous — of dynamics.

Broad changes in socio-economic and political context can influence existing institutions and produce three different outcomes of institutional change: latent institutions become salient; institutions are put in the service of different ends; and a shift in the goals and strategies of actors. First, changes in socio-economic and political context provide for latent institutions to play the role which was expected but not practically exercised. The revitalization of the WEU after the collapse of the Eastern bloc and dramatic change in international security structure is a good example of this. Second, broad change in political and socio-economic context brings about a situation that old institutions serve a new purpose. Third, exogenous changes can produce a shift in the goals or strategies being pursued within existing institutions. Changes of the roles and goals of international telecommunications institutions such as Intelsat and Inmarsat are good examples in the field of space activities. The fourth pattern of dynamism can occur when political actors adjust their strategies to accommodate changes in the institutions themselves. This seems to be similar to what we have discussed as the learning process of changes in logic coalitions.

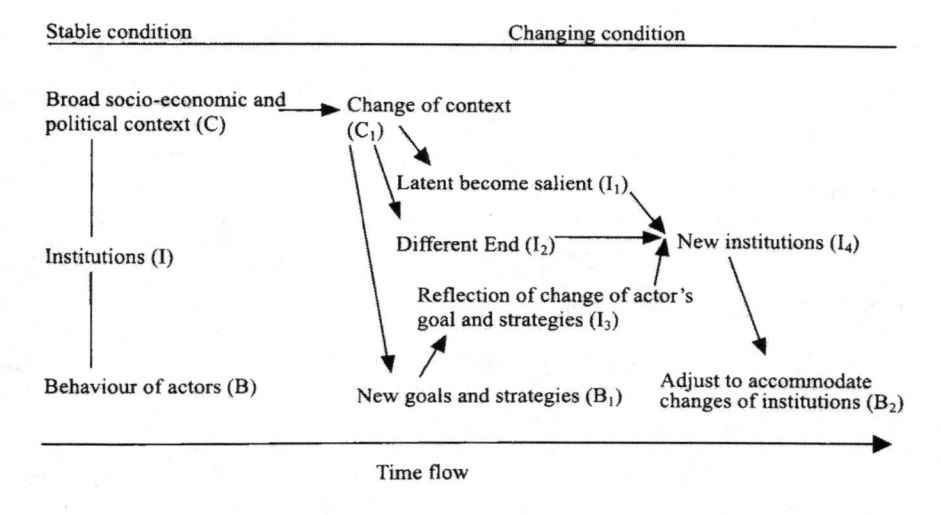

Source: Adapted from Thelen and Steinmo (1992).

Figure 2.1   Institutional Dynamics

Figure 2.1 shows a relational picture of their arguments. As we can see, their arguments are still under a very strong influence of exogenous forces. Their arguments, in order to serve their research purposes, leave aside – or bracket — the process of 'contextual change'. In other words, their arguments lack the dimension of a 'path-shaping' (Nielsen *et al.* 1995) process where actors purposively act within the institution to 'shape' the path and generate new circumstances. The path-shaping approach implies that actors can intervene in the process of history-making and actively re-articulate historical trajectories. The rules, procedures and norms are consciously and unconsciously reproduced throughout history, but there is always a moment when actors subjectively and actively intervene in the historical process and re-shape the historical path which opens up a new future. As Nielsen and others argue, "the path-shaping approach implies that, within specific, historically given, and potentially malleable limits, social forces can redesign the 'board' on which they are moving and reformulate the rules of the game" (p.7). Dynamics of historical change of institutions should, therefore, be explained as an interaction of actors and institutions shaping and reshaping each other.

Norm Life Cycle

Having discussed the shortcomings of institutional change arguments from institutionalists, the argument of 'norm life cycle' proposed by Finnemore and Sikkink (1998) seems to complement the lack of explanation of the 'path-shaping' process. This argument is particularly helpful for constructing our research framework not only because it focuses on interactions of institutions and actors during the period of change, but it also provides a theoretical connection between changes driven by exogenous forces and cognitive changes.

Based on their understanding that norms are "'strategic social construction' in which actors strategize rationally to reconfigure preferences, identities, or social context" (*ibid.*, p.888), their argument focuses on the role norms in the interaction of political change in the ways in which norms change themselves, and in the ways in which they change the political landscape. They set up three stages of norm changes — norm emergence, norm cascade, and internalization of norms — and first two stages are divided by 'tipping point' at which a critical mass of actors adopts the norm. Each stage is characterized by different actors, motivations and pattern of influences.

The first stage, norm emergence, is characterized by the effort of 'norm entrepreneurs'. Norm entrepreneurs are those who have strong notions and visions about appropriate or desirable behavior in their community. They create names, interpretations of concepts, and discourses of anticipated consequences of new norms. In the process of persuading new norms, norm entrepreneurs have to face contestable existing or other emerging alternative normative context. New norms are, most of the time, considered as 'inappropriate' from the 'logic of appropriateness' of existing norms. To face this challenge and conflict with established norms, norm entrepreneurs shall have characteristics of "empathy, altruism, and ideational commitment" (*ibid.*, p.898). In terms of political resources, it is not always that norm entrepreneurs have resources to motivate other members of the community, because powerful actors tend to defend existing norms which make them powerful. Thus, the resources that norm entrepreneurs have are their enthusiasm, commitment and vision. It is also important that norm entrepreneurs shall exercise their leadership in their community. As Burns argues, "leaders address themselves to followers' wants, needs, and other motivations, as well as to their own, and thus they serve as an independent force in changing the makeup of the followers' motive base through gratifying their motives" (Burns 1978, p.20). The emergence of norm entrepreneurs depends very much on changes of external environment. Changes outside of their community such as changes in material resources, international geopolitical context, or global technological standard create a situation in which existing norms became irrelevant or unjustified. Norm entrepreneurs who tend to be inspired by such changes come up with new notion of norms to substitute existing norms. Thus, it is more likely that norm entrepreneurs emerge in the time of crisis where the legitimacy and relevance of existing norms are weak.

New norms persuaded by norm entrepreneurs will reach a threshold or 'tipping' point, the point where new norm is accepted by the 'critical mass' of the community. Since their argument concerns only 'international' norms, Finnemore and Sikkink set up two standards of 'critical mass'; one-third of total states, including states without which the achievement of the substantive norm goal is compromised in the international system. In the case of European space collaboration — one particular kind of international system — the 'critical mass' also can be specified by the contribution to ESA. Since more than two-thirds of the contribution to the ESA comes from a combination of France, Germany and Italy, the 'critical mass' can be achieved with the agreement among these three countries. In other words, if these countries accept new norms, then the norms can step into the next stage of the norm life cycle.

After new norm passed the 'tipping point', it will be put in a different dynamics of 'norm cascade'. Because new norm is recognized by a 'critical mass' of the community, "[m]ore countries begin to adopt new norms more rapidly even without domestic pressure for such change" (Finnemore and Sikkink 1998, p.902). The new norms, they argue, are spread and accepted through an active process of socialization. Since critical members of the community endorse the new norm to "redefine appropriate behavior for the identity" (*ibid.*, p.902), 'peer pressure' — legitimization, conformity and esteem — is placed on other members to accept the new norm. For those who do not accept the new norm, their actions will be illegitimatized, they will be unrecognizable as members of the community and they will be embarrassed. Such negative sanctions through the socialization process advance the spread of the new norm throughout the community.

At the end of 'norm cascade' process, the new norm reaches a point that it becomes internalized and taken for granted. Once the new norm is internalized, it will be reproduced and learned through the process of training, education and policy exercises. Learning is a strong mechanism in this process. In fact, many literatures of institutional change made the learning process a centerpiece of the mechanism of change. For them, learning is a "relatively enduring alteration in behavior that results from experience; usually this alteration is conceptualized as a change in response made in reaction to some perceived stimulus" (Heclo 1974, p.306). This definition implies that members of a community can absorb new meanings and interpretations of a reality, as generated through historical process of policy development and structural change, and therefore, can change the policy logic to adjust to new circumstances. Actors learn not only that they need to adjust to the circumstances, but also it "becomes a creative process by which alternatives and preferences, or 'interests' are generated" (Adler and Haas 1992, p.385). In other words, "those who do not learn are at a competitive disadvantage in realizing their goals" (Jenkins-Smith and Sabatier 1993b, p.44). Thus internalized the new norm becomes a part of institutions which shape and define strategies and behavior of actors.

Summary: The Framework for European Space Collaboration

The aim of this chapter is to demonstrate, albeit briefly, theoretical shortcomings of existing studies and to propose an alternative framework which can be substituted for them. In doing so, we proposed two criticisms of neorealist approaches, institutionalism and policy logic analysis. These two aspects will enable us to analyze not only political interaction at the European level, but also cross-national comparative aspects. To support these approaches, this chapter introduced a discussion of historical dynamics of policy change to analyze changes of institutions and policy logic distributions.

Although this analytical framework was tailored for our study of European space collaboration, it is expected to apply to other policy areas particularly when technology and strategy cuts across areas such as nuclear energy, the defense industry, and aerospace industrial policies. These areas not only share the characteristics of the policy logics and logic coalitions, but also experience similar normative changes. It is my hope that the following chapters will prove the applicability of this framework in empirical studies on European space collaboration.

Notes

1   Olson has described the collective action problems as a situation where actor rationality leads to failure in organizing interest groups because of the potential members' tendency to free-ride (Olson 1965).
2   To the extent that North emphasises the importance of path dependency and historical process of institutional development in the section of institutional change, he may also be considered as an historical institutionalist.
3   Path-dependency suggests that the institutional legacies of past accidents or decisions limit the range of possibilities or options of institutional evolution. Perhaps the best example is the QWERTY keyboard. David (1985) argued that once a certain kind of path was chosen — either rationally or contingently — institutions developed along a particular path, and alternative paths may be shunted aside or ignored even if they are more efficient and rational. He explained that the QWERTY keyboard became standardised and persisted, even in the face of more efficient alternatives.
4   See, for instance, Bull (1979), Bartelson (1995) and Onuf (1991).
5   To be fair to Allison, two of his explanations are not based on the 'calculus approach' but rather the 'rule following approach'. His work was to criticise neorealist approaches which take preference formation for granted, and therefore it is hard to classify him as a typical case of rational choice theorist.
6   Hall and Taylor (1996) divided historical institutionalists into the 'calculus approach' and 'cultural approach', and each gives a slightly different view on actors' rationality (pp.939–942). As an example of the 'calculus approach', Pierson (1996) sees the advantage of employing historical institutionalism as it "cuts across the usual sharp dichotomy

between rational choice and non-rational choice work, drawing instead on research within both traditions that emphasizes the significance of historical process" (p.131). According to him, historical institutionalism also includes rational choice analysis which considers historical evolution and path dependency of institutions.

7 Institutional economists (cf. Adams 1994; Bush 1994) are a group of economists who are influenced by the works of Clarence Ayres (1944–1961) on the historical dialectical process of progressive technology and ideas with the restraints of past-binding customs, ceremonies, and beliefs. In other words, they seek alternative methodological approaches to rational individualism.

8 As an international relations theorist, his image of 'organisations' and 'institutions' should be interpreted as 'international organisations' and 'international institutions'.

9 By definition, there should be more than one 'epistemic community' in a particular policy area, although Haas does not explicitly mention it. For example, there may be 'doves' and 'hawks' in a security policy area, and these groups may have completely different sets of 'shared beliefs' and membership. As Masters and Kantrowitz (1988) describe clearly, even scientists who claim themselves 'unbiased and neutral' become advocates of certain values in the public debate on SDI policy process.

10 See Krasner (1984) for the similarity of argument.

11 In order to be distinguished from 'core' normative beliefs, this set of values may be called 'policy beliefs' or 'occupational beliefs'.

12 The detail of agreement is more complicated than this. See chapter 5.

13 This is where policy norms, beliefs, and paradigms matter most. See the argument in Section 2.3 of this chapter.

14 According to Article XII of the ESA Convention, the Director-General of ESA "may also submit proposals concerning activities and programs as well as measures designed to ensure the fulfilment of the Agency's purpose".

Chapter 3

Formation of Institutions and Policy Logics: ESRO and ELDO Years, 1960–1973

The history of space development in the world has been led by the so-called 'space race' between the United States and the Soviet Union. As numerous studies suggest, this space race was basically driven by the national strategy to demonstrate technological capability and to promote national prestige as if the competition to be the first country to send a human into space or the Moon was a substitute for fighting the Cold War (see, for example, McDougall 1986; Launius 1994; Heppenheimer 1997). As for Europe, space was originally dealt with by individual countries, but as early as 1959, there was a recognition that big science such as space could be dealt with better as a collective action of European countries. While space was largely regarded as a part of military activities by European governments, particularly in France and Britain, there was a slow but steady movement by scientists and engineers to Europeanize space activities in order to follow the speed of technological development of the superpowers.

The creation of the European Space Research Organization (ESRO) and the European Launcher Development Organization (ELDO) was intended to catch up on the technologies of the superpowers, but these institutions had to face many difficulties developed by fast-changing external environment and differences of national policy logics. This chapter seeks to analyze the genesis of the institutions of European space collaboration and early development of national and European policy logics from the 1960s to early-1970s. It seeks to explain why a particular set of institutions were emerged and established instead of other models of European cooperation in high technology, with particular attention to the development of national and European policy logics. Then it focuses on how these institutions were changed and transformed in response to the changes in external environment and national policy logics. The intention of this chapter is therefore to detail the possible alternative paths at each moment in the history of European space collaboration, and explain why certain institutions were chosen.

Our analysis in this chapter relies on secondary documents as the main source of information. Because of the limited extent of research on space policy, much of the data is obtained from the ESA Historical Study Report series. However, the analysis in this chapter does not necessarily reflect the opinion of the agency, as it is also based on other sources and has been reoriented with my own interpretation.

Two Origins of European Space Collaboration

Space has long been a dream of mankind, but it only became possible to observe it from the Earth after the means to do so was attained. This dream has driven many scientists and engineers — including Wernher von Braun — to develop rocket technology before and during World War II. V2 rocket technology, despite the horror it brought to Western European countries, was a groundbreaking success to carry heavy objects into orbit. Allied powers, the United States, Soviet Union, Britain, and France, 'invited' the developers of the V2 rocket from Germany, and those exiled Germans provided the basis for developing satellite launching rockets as well as long-range warhead-carrying missiles. After the deepening of Cold War, the rocket technology evolved primarily through the research for Inter Continental Ballistic Missiles (ICBMs). But many in civilian space science and engineering also saw this technology as opening a new opportunity for further research for satellite-carrying rockets.

The International Geophysical Year (IGY) in 1957 marked the beginning of 'space age' as well as 'Cold War in space'. The idea of IGY was proposed by the US government to establish global cooperation in this new area of science, space research. It was the American intention to foster a world-wide space research community through IGY events by using the non-military launcher (Vanguard), but at the same time, the IGY project was closely related to the Eisenhower's 'Open Sky' initiative – mutual exchange of aerial photography under joint supervision to ease the fears and dangers of a surprise attack. The Eisenhower initiative was rejected by the then Soviet leader, Khrushchev. A more important motivation of the US government was to establish the principle in international law of 'freedom of space' for science or any other activities, which meant that no country could have jurisdiction in outer space, and therefore every country has the right to fly over hostile territory and observe from space (Day 1998, Peebles 1997). Although space reconnaissance was not technologically proven at this time, it represented the American strategic intention behind the IGY proposal.

Despite American motivation, the Soviet Union nonetheless used the ICBM-modified launcher, and successfully launched the first artificial satellite, Sputnik[1], into orbit in 1957. The 'Sputnik shock' overwhelmingly filled Americans with a losing sense of pride and a fear of ballistic missile attack. The irony was, the Soviet Union took the advantage of 'freedom of space' as a means to deploy nuclear warheads to hostile territory. After 1957, the US space development accelerated not only launcher development, but also their capabilities in space communication and reconnaissance (McDougall 1997).

From the perspective of Policy Logic Analysis, the American strategy can be seen as largely based on the logic of the military in coalition with the logic of science. However, the shock of the Sputnik launch was so grave that the logic of autonomy overwhelmed other policy logics. Nevertheless, the logic of military and science remained as operational logics, so that scientists and military could enjoy the enormous political support through the logic of autonomy. The early years of space development (at least within the Western Bloc) began in this way, and set a certain policy environment for Western European countries.

The Impact of the International Geophysical Year in Western Europe

Although IGY is mostly remembered as ushering in the space race in the history of space development, it did bear some fruit in Europe. The Italian physicist and politician, Edoardo Amaldi, who was inspired by the projects of IGY began to speak out on his idea to establish a European organization for space research. Although the first reaction from other European scientists to his idea was generally cautious, he found strong support from Pierre Auger, also a physicist and founding member of *Conseil Européen pour la Recherche Nucléaire* (CERN). Amaldi and Auger were engaged and encouraged by the success of European nuclear research collaboration in the 1950s. Particularly in 1959, CERN had successfully commissioned the proton synchrotron accelerator which gave confidence to European scientists and engineers so that they could coordinate national governments to commit to a European major scientific project (Krige and Russo 1994). The success of the CERN project provided a foundation for a new policy paradigm of scientific collaboration.

Then, the first meeting of the Committee on Space Research (COSPAR) which spun-off from IGY to coordinate international space research allowed Amaldi and Auger to organize European space scientists. Most scientists, according to Carlier and Gilli (1994), shared a sense in which "European countries seemed reduced to the role of mere spectators" (p.78) of IGY, compared with the progress made by Russians and Americans, and expressed their interests in the Amaldi-Auger proposal. A very important factor in the informal meetings of COSPAR was the enthusiastic support from Harrie Massey, who was the president of the British National Committee for Space Research (BNCSR). His involvement in the movement of European space collaboration brought new light to the problem of launcher. For Amaldi and Auger, whose governments had not developed satellite-launching capability, getting access to a launcher was the critical problem inhibiting European space science activities. Massey, as a leading advocate of using the British Intermediate Range Ballistic Missile (IRBM) — codenamed 'Blue Streak' — for satellite launch, produced the idea of using the Blue Streak as a European launcher.

In February 1960, the second meeting of leading European space scientists from France, Italy, West Germany, Belgium, The Netherlands, Sweden, Switzerland, and UK, with apologies from Norway, was held in Auger's flat in Paris to discuss future European collaboration "with great secrecy" (Massey and Robins 1986, p.110). At this meeting, Massey took the initiative in raising the idea of a formal negotiation with governments. In April 1960, two weeks after the British government decided to abandon the Blue Streak as a military weapon and to use it as civilian satellite launcher, European space scientists from ten countries (the above eight plus Norway and Denmark) gathered in London to discuss the possibility of European collaboration. Given that there were possibilities of using the Blue Streak for civilian research in sight, there was a big debate about whether their national governments would be willing to participate in launcher development. Italian and Dutch delegates made it clear that their governments would not be willing to contribute if the Blue Streak could not be properly integrated into European programs (Krige and Russo 1994).

In contrast to what happened between the United States and the Soviet Union, IGY provided a clear opportunity for European space scientists both to recognize the technological weakness of Europeans, and to discuss the possibility of long-term collaboration. Moreover, through the experience of CERN, they knew the advantages of collaboration and shared a belief that Europe should collaborate to catch up with the superpowers. The news of cancellation of the Blue Streak accelerated the discussion further. The beginning of European space collaboration was blessed with these precedents and fortunate coincidence. But the most important factor was the leadership of Amaldi and Auger, in conjunction with that of Massey. Without their enthusiasm, it would have been tremendously difficult to consider European collaboration in the area of science where the logics of military and autonomy were overwhelming at that period.

British Decision for the European Option

Britain, the most advanced country in terms of satellite launching capability at the time, played a crucial role in the formation of European space collaboration. Most observers of British space policy tend to find that the British decision to use the Blue Streak for satellite launchers began after the cancellation of its military use. But according to Whyte and Gummett (1997), the British government — the Ministry of Supply under the authority of Ministry of Defense and the Royal Aircraft Establishment (RAE) — began to study the possibility of launching reconnaissance satellites with the Blue Streak, even though its conclusion was not favorable for using the Blue Streak for space reconnaissance in relation to development cost. Nevertheless, the experience in the US to convert ICBMs to satellite launchers made the RAE consider the option of using the Blue Streak not only for a military satellite launch but also a civilian one with the expectation of recovering the cost by selling launch services. When the estimated cost for developing the complete system of the Blue Streak became £500–600 million, the British government finally took an official decision, which Marsh (1991) described as "a wonderful example of political opportunism" (p.196), to convert civilian launchers on 13 April 1960.

At the time, the British government had four choices. The first option to 'go it alone' was soon dismissed because of the cost. British scientists and Conservative MP Philip Goodhart teamed up to promote British satellite and launching capability in order to secure the autonomy of the British science community. Although there was some understanding about the necessity of developing a British scientific satellite, the government did not believe it was a satisfactory reason to invest in a British launcher. Although Goodhart and scientists led by Massey strongly lobbied both military (Ministry of Supply) and potential civil application users (meteorology or communications), the British government did not show any interest in developing a British owned launcher. After all, space science alone could not justify "a seven-to eight-figure sum" (Whyte and Gummett 1997, p.151). The option was narrowed down either to abandon whole program or to collaborate with other countries to share development costs.

The second option, collaboration with Commonwealth countries, for launcher development was also considered, since all British space scientific activities were based in Woomera, Australia, and space science experiments with Skylark sounding rockets in cooperation with Canada and Australia were carried on during the Blue Streak debate. Canada, Australia, New Zealand and India expressed an interest in space research collaboration with Britain in 1959, but the collaboration was limited to scientific projects and satellite tracking (Massey and Robins 1986, chapter 7). None of these countries was interested in sharing the financial burden of launcher development.

It was considered a more immediate and potential option to collaborate with the United States. BNCSR had already conducted Ariel satellite programs (launching a British satellite with the American launcher SCOUT) with NASA, and it was expected to use the American launcher continuously for scientific experiments. However, through the experience of the Ariel program, British scientists found it was not satisfactory for conducting full-scale research with American counterparts because of the constraints of American launcher availability and capability. SCOUT did not have the capacity to carry the payload which British scientists wanted to launch, and was not always available during particular launch windows.[1] Moreover, there was strong concern about losing Britain's position as a leading industrial power, as well as technological prestige, along with emigration of young engineers if Britain depended on American launchers and did not use Blue Streak (Whyte and Gummett 1997).

Finally, the choice that the British government made was to take the lead in European collaboration. Obviously, the movement of European scientists and Massey's support for a European option injected the idea of utilizing the Blue Streak for European endeavors, but there was a strong force from industry to transform Blue Streak into European civil satellite launcher. Engineers and managers from major British industry such as Hawker-Siddeley, Rolls Royce, and de Havilland announced their preference for Europeanization because they considered that a European launcher would avoid excessive dependence on the Superpowers and would pay dividends in the future (De Maria and Krige 1992). Along with lobbying from scientists and industrialists, British decision-makers seemed to have other thoughts on their mind. Following the decision of Britain to stay out of the European Economic Community (EEC), "the question of how Britain might reach an accommodation with 'the Six' was being considered in the context of a major review of strategic foreign policy options" (Whyte and Gummett 1997, p.169). In fact, Britain had relative technological advantages *vis-à-vis* European countries to be able to place itself in the commanding position in Europe.

The major policy logic in Britain was to convert the Blue Streak to a civilian launcher was because of finance alone, but in the process of choosing this particular logic, other policy logics also came into play. The logic of (British) autonomy and the logic of science were not convincing enough in the face of the logic of finance in the first place, but when the option was narrowed down to an American or European option, the relative autonomy and strategic concern for leadership in collaboration became the deciding factor for a European option. In terms of the political justification of conversion, the logic of commerce emerged as a potential policy logic, but in reality, the only justification came from the logic of science. The British decision was, therefore, based on a strong logic of finance with logic of relative autonomy and a weak logic of science.

Models of Collaboration: CERN, Euratom or Concorde

When both scientists and British decision-makers gathered the momentum to go for the 'European option' in space science and launcher development, the institutional framework of European collaboration was under discussion. This was the critical moment to set the historical path of the development of European space collaboration which eventually created a 'two-Europe' situation for the next thirty years. The CERN model (intergovernmental model) seemed to be the natural choice for European space collaboration since Amaldi, Auger and Massey were all involved in the creation of CERN, but there were other options proposed in the early stages which included the possibility to conduct space research under the European Communities (Euratom model). If the Euratom model had been chosen, the history of European space collaboration might look completely different today. Thus, it is worth reviewing the options in this period and discusses why the Euratom model was not chosen.

For the 'founding fathers'[2] of European space collaboration, it was natural to pursue the CERN model for the institutional framework of space science collaboration. First of all, most of them were involved, to a certain extent, in establishing CERN in 1952. As explained above, it was relatively successful at assembling good European scientists in atomic and nuclear physics, and at maintaining world-class research activities in pure science which meant excluding application research for military purposes in particular. In brief, CERN was a typical intergovernmental research organization: each Member State had one vote in the governing body, the Council, to approve research projects, budget and to appoint the Director. Decisions were generally taken by simple majority vote. For the 'founding fathers', the CERN model was the most suitable for European collaboration for big science. They could not be bothered to find other models to replace it.

However, there were some doubts about adopting the CERN model for European space science collaboration. First, space, more than nuclear research, was believed to be a more military-driven area, particularly the question of launchers. Space research could not be done without access to space, and the access cannot be guaranteed unless Europe had its own launcher. Unlike nuclear physics which would benefit military technology, space science was beneficiary to missile/ launcher development, and vulnerable to foreign policy concerns (in the case of using the American launcher). In short, space depends more on government than atomic energy research. The second question was the location: in the case of CERN, all that was needed was to set up one laboratory (outside Geneva) to concentrate research facilities to carry out experiments, but in the case of space research, the experiments should be carried out in outer space. Scientists could build instruments and sub-systems in their own laboratory and central institutions would hold the responsibility for assembly and operation. British scientists were not willing to give up their autonomy to control operations from their home laboratories, and also argued that heterogeneity of scientific and technological levels in Europe might degrade the quality of research (Massey and Robins 1986, p.111). Third, there were concerns that space science is, unlike any single discipline such as nuclear physics, a complex of many disciplines including atmospheric physics, astrophysics, and solar physics, and therefore it seemed to be irrelevant to create a single organization to encompass such diverse disciplines. Finally, there was a question of industrial and commercial application. The French in particular were very keen to use space research for profitable applications in telecommunications, whereas the British were more science-oriented. CERN had not experienced such problems and difficulties of reconciling differences in interests and policy logics in the setting up of large-scale collaboration.

Alternatively, some people argued that space research should be conducted by a framework similar to the European Nuclear Energy Agency (ENEA) or the European Atomic Energy Community (Euratom). ENEA was created in 1957 as a specialized agency under the Organization for European Economic Cooperation (OEEC), which was later associated with Euratom in 1959. Amaldi and Auger — the 'founding fathers' of CERN — were also involved in establishing Euratom, and Auger recalled that they "considered ... affiliation [of space research] to the EEC" (Auger 1984, p.12). Although their involvement was not as enthusiastic as was the case with CERN, it can be assumed that they must have considered the Euratom model as well as the CERN model since they knew the strengths and weaknesses of both organizations.

While the scientists were arguing the form of space collaboration, politicians also became interested in the debate. David Price, Conservative MP and British representative to the Council of Europe, made a report to Consultative Assembly of the Council of Europe on European space research. In the report, he recommended that the ENEA/Euratom model would be preferable because "it could be largely independent in its day-to-day working but under the ultimate control of a body of responsible Ministers" (Council of Europe 1960, p.79). At the same time, a program called 'Euroluna'[3] was proposed within Euratom countries — Amaldi was again the central figure of this proposal — to catch up with American and Soviet space technology (De Maria 1993a). It was originally designed to be an integral part of the Communities' activities, which meant the exclusion of the United Kingdom (Madders and Thiebaut 1992).

It is not difficult to assume that the reason why these proposals for the 'Community model' were not adopted was because British space technology — the most advanced in Europe — was crucial to European collaboration. As we saw above, the enthusiastic support from Massey was very important in the early stage, and it was impossible to establish any kind of institution without British participation. Furthermore, the 'Community model' was, as Auger himself explained, "not an example to follow, since it was too subject to political contingencies" (quoted in Krige 1992a, pp.7–8). At the end of the discussion, the CERN model which would be acceptable for British politicians and scientists and more independent from political intervention, was preferred to the Community model.

Finally, apart from the European context, NATO set up a Science Committee as a tool for transatlantic science and technological development in reaction to the launch of Sputnik. The Committee prioritized space cooperation as a priority agenda and proposed to establish a 'European NASA' as a counterpart of the American NASA (Massey and Robbins 1986; Sebesta 1994a). Such a proposal was not acceptable to European space scientists and some politicians since it would induce deep commitment to military space activities and dependency on the United States.

Unlike what is suggested by the literature (for example Collins 1990, Krige and Russo 1994), the choice of the CERN model was made not only because the founding fathers were committed to CERN activities. For Amaldi and Auger, however, it was difficult to make a final decision because they were involved in all models. The decisive moment came in February 1960 when Massey "in sudden contrast to Amaldi's earlier 'Euroluna' scenario, swung the initiative towards Britain" (Madders 1997, p.31). There might have been a sense of urgency for Massey for if he had let Amaldi and Auger take initiatives, Britain might have lost the opportunity to join in European collaboration. At the end of the discussion, Massey's initiative was accepted by all participating scientists, including Amaldi and Auger.

Protecting the Logic of Science: Road to Meyrin

While these space scientists were in discussion with their European colleagues in the first half of 1960, they took the leading role in organizing scientists in national institutes and universities to put pressure on their governments. Because of the diversity of disciplines involved in space research, national space scientists were not well-organized to speak in one voice and put pressure on their governments to promote European collaboration. But thanks to the initiatives taken by leading scientists gathered at the European level, national organizations were quickly emerging in Belgium, Denmark, France, West Germany, Italy, The Netherlands, Norway, Spain, Sweden, Switzerland, and the UK. The leading scientists from these countries met again in London under the chairmanship of Massey in April 1960 to establish the CERN model as the organizational framework of European space collaboration, and agreed to lobby on national governments. Following the meeting, national organizations acted as the so-called 'CERN lobby' to put pressure on governments to accept their proposal for the CERN model of institutional framework.

Two months after the meeting in London, leading scientists met in Paris to coordinate their action to persuade national governments by setting up GEERS (*Groupe d'Étude Européen pour la Collaboration dans le Domaine des Recherches Spatiales*). Again, the question of launcher development dominated the agenda of this meeting. British representatives led by Massey started arguing that they could not guarantee British participation unless other European governments are committed to contributing to the development of the Blue Streak. The representatives from smaller countries argued that using the American launcher would cost half as much as developing the Blue Streak, but the British and French representatives insisted that the American launcher (SCOUT) would be too small and unsatisfactory (Collett 1995, p.90). At the same time, those from smaller countries were apprehensive that the big countries — Britain and France — would dominate space science and swallow up a large part of the space budget, thereby threatening their national autonomy of science. From the beginning, GEERS had to deal with a difficult question: pertaining to launcher development and autonomy of smaller countries. The problem was that the representatives in the GEERS meeting were mainly scientists which deprived them from having direct access to national decision-making (though they were mandated from their governments). The atmosphere of the meeting was quite friendly and the vision of participants was optimistic, since the scientists had already socialized on many occasions and were passionate about European collaboration. But this was not of much help in resolving 'diplomatic' problems (Hultqvist 1992).

The question of launcher development was finally taken up by national governments under British initiative (see below). Scientists in GEERS were relieved from the 'diplomatic' issues, and were able to concentrate on the parameters of scientific collaboration. From 28 November to 2 December 1960, scientists and national civil servants from the eleven European countries plus Austria, gathered at CERN Headquarters in Meyrin, outside of Geneva. The representatives from Britain and France withdrew the launcher question since it was dealt with at intergovernmental level and said the meeting should only deal with scientific research. This was a clear suggestion that not only launcher but also commercial applications would not be discussed in the meeting. The French delegate — the most interested party for commercial application — was convinced by other delegates that a new organization should be "as free as possible from detailed governmental interference in its scientific work" (Massey and Robins 1986, pp.118–119). However, in terms of finance, governmental officials in some national delegations — particularly in the British delegation — demanded tight control over the budget in the light of their experiences in CERN, which tended to run over budget. Scientists in many delegations were not happy with the proposal, but at the end of the meeting, all delegations agreed to set up a ceiling on the annual budget and a three-year period review on mid-term spending plans.

At the end of the conference, the 'Meyrin Agreement' was signed to set up an 'official' intergovernmental Commission (*Commission Préparatoire Européenne de Recherche Spatiale*: COPERS) for the preparation of the European Space Research Organization (ESRO). The Meyrin conference was a turning point in the early process of institutional emergence. Not only the question of launcher development was separated from the new organization, but also the development of commercial applications was excluded, which meant that the logic of science prevailed over the logics of military and commerce. It also meant that space science and satellite technology programs would be supervised and funded by national ministries responsible for science and technology, instead of ministries of defense whose budgets — particularly those of Britain and France — might be squeezed by launcher development. The science logic coalitions from smaller countries whose interests and long-term policy objectives were to enjoy relative autonomy from government intervention to develop militarily or commercially potential technologies were the greatest beneficiaries from the Meyrin Agreement.

Building on Compromise: Establishment of the ELDO

Many of those who were involved in the process of establishing the ESRO were scientists and engineers who shared experiences in CERN and policy logics in favor of European collaboration. But this was not true in the case of establishing a launcher development organization. As Massey recalls,

There seems to have been rather little direct contact initially between the groups discussing scientific co-operation in space and those discussing co-operation in launcher development, at least in Britain. One reason may have been the heavy political and military overtones associated with rocket developments compared with the traditional free exchange of scientific views (Massey and Robins 1986, p.226).

Unlike in the case of the ESRO which inherited policy logic from CERN, there was little spin-off from the ESRO experience to the negotiation of European launcher development. A lack of common policy logic among countries made the negotiations quite difficult.

As discussed above, the decision on 13 April 1960 to cancel the Blue Streak development as a military IRBM lead the British government to the 'Europeanization' of Blue Streak-Black Knight[4] as a civilian satellite launcher. Nevertheless, the British government had to face a serious dilemma in this campaign. On the one hand, the United States government, which had provided key technology for the Blue Streak development, set up a policy to avoid assisting "either [France or Germany] develop an independent IRBM capability" (Krige 1993c, p.11). After the COPERS meeting in 1960, the American government space agency (NASA) abandoned the idea of cooperating with European countries through the NATO framework, and approached individual European governments to cooperate with civilian scientific programs such as *Ariel* with Britain, *San Marco* with Italy, and *Helios*[5] with Germany (Sebesta 1994a). On the other hand, the French government, on the basis that they had already developed the *Diamant* satellite launcher as a spin-off from military application, argued that participating in the Blue Streak project would be too expensive unless *Diamant* was used as the second stage instead of Black Knight, and therefore Britain should provide access to launcher technology — developed with American assistance. In reality, French engineers wanted access to military technologies such as warhead re-entry and the inertial guidance system which would be used for ICBM.[6]

For the British Minister of Aviation, Peter Thorneycroft, the first task was to negotiate with the French. He tried to persuade the French through numerous bilateral meetings to accept the Blue Streak-Black Knight option and argued that the Blue Streak-Diamant option was more costly. The French delegates were not convinced, however, and in order to keep France in the framework, Thorneycroft finally made concessions to let France develop the second stage before the end of 1960. The question of military technology transfer was a more difficult issue, particularly since Britain was bound by the agreement with the US government. The French government was increasingly unwilling to commit to European launcher development towards the end of 1960 if Britain could not provide relevant military knowledge.

The breakthrough came dramatically when Prime Minister Harold Macmillan met President Charles de Gaulle on 27–29 January,[7] a few days before the European conference on launcher development was held. According to Carlier and Gilli (1994), de Gaulle was attracted by the idea of Europe becoming the third space power alongside the Soviet Union and the United States and imposed no conditions in the military field (p.80). De Gaulle chose the long-term strategic advantage of having a European presence in the 'space race' over the short-term advantage in military technology.

Having the French on board, the British project to Europeanize the Blue Streak seemed to be going well. The Anglo-French joint conference was organized in the Council of Europe premises in Strasbourg (in response to the Price Report) in January 1961. However, the road to achieve the goal was yet long and winding. The British delegation wanted to share financial costs according to GDP so that no single participant should pay more than 25%, as it had decided in the Meyrin Agreement for the ESRO. But the French and other delegations from smaller countries rejected the proposal because Blue Streak was a British project and therefore Britain should take financial as well as technological responsibility. Again, Britain had to withdraw its primary proposal and agreed to pay one-third of the total cost of launcher development in order to ensure other countries participated. Britain wanted to include maintenance costs of the existing Blue Streak project until the real launcher program began, but again this was rejected by all other countries. Furthermore, the British government formally abandoned its plan to use Black Knight, and agreed that the second stage would be built by France, and the third stage by 'continental countries'. It also had to agree on free exchange of all existing and new technological information.

It seemed that Britain took a negotiating position to bring in other European countries at any cost. Since the discussion of converting the Blue Streak was so complicated, the delegates, particularly Thorneycroft, stuck with the principle of 'Europeanization' and could not find other options. At the end of the conference, all the British government was able to do was to maintain Woomera as a launch site and to make sure that a new launcher development organization should be operated 'exclusively for peaceful purposes', without using the Blue Streak technology for military purposes in the light of the agreement with the US.

Although the conference concluded that a European launcher would be developed, there was no concrete commitment from participating countries for financial and technological contribution except Britain and France. Germany,[8] before the Strasbourg conference, was categorically against the British proposal for launcher development based on the Blue Streak for three reasons: First, politically and psychologically as well as financially, Germany was not prepared to take part in rocket development which would revive the image of V2. Next, the Blue Streak was technologically primitive and uneconomical. The well-known rocket scientist, Eugen Sänger, was a special advisor to the Ministry of Transport with his idea of reusable shuttle, and was the prominent advocate of this position. At last, in order to tighten up the relationship with the US military forces, it was considered to be wise to develop a European launcher under license from the US (Fischer 1994).

Nevertheless, in response to the Strasbourg conference, the German government set up an expert group (Bock Commission) to consult on the issue of the launcher. To the surprise of many German ministers, on 22 May 1961, space scientists, engineers, the directors of big research institutes, industrialists, and even financial experts in the Bock Commission unanimously took a decision to recommend that the government approve the resolution of the Strasbourg conference (*ibid.*). The Commission concluded that participation in European launcher development would contribute to the establishment of a capable industrial and technological base for the aerospace sector, and more importantly, collaboration in space would contribute to the integration of Europe and Germany (Keck 1976). Moreover, the German government recognized that collaboration with the US would not bring technological expertise to Germany, but a European project would, particularly since Britain and France offered to develop the third stage in Germany. Also the idea of 'European collaboration' was preferred in the context of foreign policy and was given strong support by Chancellor Adenauer. In June 1961, the German government decided to join the European launcher development.

What was more difficult was to convince Italy. Since Britain and France agreed to let Germany build the third stage, there was little room left for Italian participation. The Italian government and scientists were almost unanimously against the arrangement made between Britain, France and Germany. The Anglo-French team offered that Italy could develop test satellites for the European launcher. According to Krige and Russo (1994, see also De Maria 1993a), Edoardo Amaldi, the 'founding father' of European space collaboration, was furious about the deal because: (1) developing the test satellite was not in the interest of the Italian industry, (2) separating work by four countries would be wrong with regard to international collaboration as well as for the efficiency of the organization, (3) given that the bilateral arrangement with the US would bring opportunities for using the US launcher for the Italian national program, there was no immediate need for the European launcher, and (4) the Blue Streak technology would be obsolete when the launcher became available in five years. The Italian dissatisfaction carried on until the establishment of the ELDO.

Participation of smaller countries was another headache for the Anglo-French team. Although it was obvious that the contribution of smaller countries could not be significant to improve the financial burden on Britain, Thorneycroft actively flew around European capitals before and after the Strasbourg conference to persuade them to participate with the hope of spreading the cost and adding more 'European' color on the Anglo-French project. One observer in Norway commented that "Thorneycroft's presentation to a meeting of members of government, scientists and civil servants in Oslo on 14 January 1961 was a forceful demonstration of salesmanship" (Collett 1995, p.95). The salespoint of Britain was that Europe needed to develop telecommunication satellites, that it was necessary to have a European launcher development organization since the American launcher was not likely to be available for application satellite launch and that ESRO excluded the possibility for application satellite development. The problem for smaller countries was a lack of resources and low priority for space, particularly in the case of Sweden (Stiernstedt 1984). As for the neutral countries – Austria, Switzerland, and Sweden – they did not at all appreciate the military origin of the Blue Streak. Their policy logics were a mixture of the logics of science and finance, and an evasion of the logic of military. According to Collett, there was some discussion among Scandinavian countries to participate in launcher development if there were some possible industrial returns (development of a test satellite for instance). After Italian negotiations, Thorneycroft was left with no option but to offer to transfer British NATO contract of missiles to Norway (*ibid.*, p.104). However, it was not enough to convince smaller countries to justify such huge costs.

Such desperate attempts by Thorneycroft did not pay off in the meeting at Lancaster House from 30 October to 3 November 1961 which was called to draft a convention for the ELDO. Norway, Sweden and Switzerland, out of the eleven European countries, sent only observers to demonstrate that they had no intention of participating in launcher development. Italy had not changed its position of being against the Anglo-French deal, and to make matters worse, France suggested that it would call off the whole project if Italy would not join, since the French government did not want to replace the Italian share of the financial burden. The Italian problem was still blocking any significant progress.

Eventually, the Italian government began to shift its position under pressure from intensive diplomatic efforts by Britain, France and Germany (Krige 1993c). And some Italian scientists and engineers felt that development of a test satellite would be beneficial for their national program for scientific satellites and new propulsion development (De Maria 1993b). When the ELDO convention was signed on 30 April 1962, there were only seven countries: Belgium, France, Germany, Italy, The Netherlands, the UK, and Australia (Woomera launching site). Belgium would be responsible for the down range guidance station, and The Netherlands would take charge of long-range telemetry links and ground equipment. In response to the lack of participation by smaller countries, the final share of costs were agreed as follows: Britain 39%, France 24%, Germany 19%, Italy 10% and 17% for the rest.

It is often described as the ESRO/ELDO twins, but the processes of establishment of two organizations were completely dissimilar in terms of institutions and policy logics. Unlike in the case of space science, the major players in the negotiations did not share policy logics. The British initiative was dictated by the logic of finance to save the cost of the Blue Streak conversion project with the ambition to be a leader in Europe, whereas French policy logics were the logic of (European) autonomy and the logic of technology in conjunction with the logics of military and commerce. The German and Italian behavior, on the other hand, reflected the logic of technology without a clear strategy on the implication of space technology. The British initiatives in numerous occasions lacked the mechanism to reconcile the differences of policy logics among countries, but only the means to make concessions to them just so as to keep enough players in the 'Europeanization' scheme. As a result, the British share of costs became 39% from the expected 25% (in retrospect, it might have been more efficient and cheaper if Britain had chosen to go it alone).[9] In contrast to the ESRO, there was neither enthusiasm nor vision on the future of European collaboration in launcher development. Such diversity of national policy logics reflected the institutional arrangement of launcher development. There was no prime contractor or technical center for the overall program, and "a tenuous management chain in a project of such complexity could not but aggravate the problems of overall system design" (Massey 1986, p.227). Although British industry had accumulated certain technical and managerial expertise on launcher development, it was wasted on such inefficient institutions. In short, the launcher development project was an odd political compromise on different policy logics of major countries and was only able to produce a bizarre launcher without a properly integrated system.

Policy Logics and Institutions at the Beginning of European Space Collaboration

From the perspective of policy logic analysis, European space collaboration in science and launchers was very different. First of all, there was a simple but strong sense of sharing policy logic. Scientists were well-organized both on the national and the European level to form a logic coalition for science, and put strong pressure on their governments. Although those scientists were coming from different disciplines, they shared the idea of collaboration through their CERN experience. When government officials and diplomats came in to negotiate, they used the logic of finance to push back the logic of science, but there was no serious alteration of the process of establishment. Second, there was a group of core actors to lead and inspire the other members of the coalition. Amaldi, Auger and Massey were key figures in this process. They acted as 'norm entrepreneurs' who created names, interpretations of concepts, and discourses of anticipated consequences of new norms (Finnemore and Sikkink 1998). Their proposal of introducing the CERN model for space collaboration shaped the idea and perceived institutions of the ESRO. Finally, there was general understanding among European governments that the US and the Soviet Union were competing head-to-head in the 'space race', and Europe would be left out if it did not act immediately. In this sense, the logics of (European) autonomy and technology played mutually supporting roles in pushing national governments toward the ESRO.

On the other hand, the process of establishing a collaboration framework for a launcher was more difficult. There was a clear gap in the capabilities and expertise among European countries. Britain and France had already developed certain missile and sounding rocket capabilities whereas other countries had almost no technical expertise. Because European countries were in different stages of technological development, the policy logics of each country were quite different and difficult to reconcile. Britain was dominated by the logic of finance, whereas France (and Belgium to some extent)[10] was acting on the logic of autonomy, but Germany and Italy were acting according to the logic of technology. There was no single, coherent policy logic to articulate the difference among European countries. The role of the United States was not explicit in this process, but it influenced, to a certain degree, decisions of European governments on launcher development. Italy and Germany had individual arrangements to collaborate with the US to use SCOUT, which made the negotiations more complicated. For these countries, European autonomy in launching capability was not important as long as they believed that they could rely on using the American launcher. Thus, the logic of autonomy did not exist in Germany and Italy, so that Britain and France had to offer other logics (logic of technology) to convince them. Finally, in the case of launcher organization, there was no 'norm entrepreneurship' to motivate, visualize, and create discourses of anticipated consequences of new norms. Thorneycroft was the central figure in the process, but he did not provide practical concepts to attract other national governments. European collaboration in launcher development thus begun with a fragile balance of different policy logics.

New Institutions and New Situations

As new organizations, the ESRO and the ELDO had to face a number of difficulties as well as rapid changes in technological development. The initial enthusiasm and idealism for European space collaboration was gradually fading away, and the scientists, engineers and policy-makers had to deal with the cold harsh reality. During the 1960s, space technology evolved quite dramatically, due to the 'space race' and the success of Intelsat (International Telecommunications Satellite Consortium). At the same time, continuous failure of launchers and economic recession in the mid-1960s generated severe criticism against space activities in Europe.

The ELDO/ESRO Conventions

The ELDO and ESRO conventions entered into force on 19 February and 20 March 1963 respectively. The ELDO consisted of six European countries and Australia as the owner of Woomera site (see Table 3.1). Three distinctive features of institutional characteristics of the ELDO should be mentioned. Firstly, despite close association with military programs, the civilian nature of launcher development was explicitly laid down in the Convention. It implied that governments should not bring military personnel or officers from the defense ministries as their representatives and should not use military budgets as a contribution to ELDO. The delegates, therefore, were usually mixed representatives from the Ministries of Foreign Affairs and other ministries relevant to the industry. Secondly, the annual budget of the ELDO should be approved by a 'special two-thirds majority', which meant that the decision should be approved at least by five Member States whose contributions added up to at least 85% of the total. The rule of 'special two-thirds majority' was also applied to the decision for programs in the technological development and production phases. This rule suggested that Britain, France and Germany were allowed to have veto power on programs and budget, in light of the share of financial contribution fixed in the Convention (Britain 39%, France 24%, Germany 19%, Italy 10% and Belgium and The Netherlands 17%), and the decisions for programs and the budget therefore required approval from all three Member States. Finally, national governments were solely in charge of allocating industrial contracts. The ELDO Convention stated that its secretariat had authority to place contracts only "in agreement with the government of the Member States in whose territory the work is to be carried out" (Article 16–2). In short, national governments were granted the power to control over financial as well as technological issues, and there was very little role for the ELDO secretariat to play. This rigid institutional structure made the ELDO as "victim to steeply rising costs to completion" (Whyte 1989) in latter half of 1960s.

The ESRO consisted of ten Member States. Norway, the only country in the initial eleven European countries gathered in Paris and London, decided not to join in the ESRO on the ground of financial constraints. Although the Norwegian scientists were very active in their attempt to persuade their government, the latter was not convinced that science alone could be enough to justify huge expenditure for space. For the Norwegian government, "ESRO itself was never important enough to make any foreign minister decide to join without support of other national interests" because "there was not any unified scientific community behind ESRO as there had been a prestigious group of high-energy physicists behind CERN" (Collett 1995, p.112). In other words, the science logic coalition was relatively weaker than that of CERN, and therefore the Norwegian government could not find the logic of science convincing enough.

The ESRO budget was drawn by proportional contribution from Member States according to the net national income of up to 25% to protect excessive contribution of the UK. Unlike CERN in which the budget was adopted by a simple majority, the ESRO Council required unanimity for a three-year budget ceiling, and the two-thirds majority for annual budget and for contribution questions, in response to the demand from governments for tighter financial control. But in contrast, simple majority rule was introduced for the decisions on the contents and plans for programs in order to respect autonomy of scientists. The authority to manage technological and scientific programs was largely granted to the ESRO secretariat. This division of power between national bureaucrats and scientists for financial and programmatic issues would eventually invite many difficult questions in the future, but at this time, it was intended to protect as much autonomy of scientists and their logic of science as possible from government intervention driven by the logic of finance.

There were two other important aspects of the institutional arrangement of the ESRO. First, concerning the CERN experience, the COPERS (preparatory committee for the ESRO) proposed establishing several European research laboratories that were independent from national organizations and operational centers as central focal points for knowledge and expertise. The ESRO was expected to take a so-called 'Bottom-to-Top' approach whereby the ESRO became the only source of ideas and concepts of missions, which operated with a view to transforming these ideas and concepts into reality by providing hardware, software, service, analysis and publication of results (Bonnet 1993). The structure of the ESRO was expected to be very centralized and concentrated so that the role of national organizations and scientists would become much smaller. However, the ESRO Convention defined that the European research institutions should be small because national governments as well as national science communities "feared that a strong in-house staff would rapidly become a privileged elite with better resources than national teams, and so able to dominate the shape and content of the scientific program" (Krige 1994, p.4).

Second, influenced by the CERN model, no specific arrangement was made to 'balance' geographical contribution and distribution of industrial contracts in the ESRO Convention. Major contracts were subjected to competitive bidding and awarded to the most cost-effective offer. However, during the COPERS meeting, there were some demands from smaller countries and Germany to guarantee an industrial return from the ESRO programs (Fischer 1994, p.33). As a result, at the meeting in June 1962, the delegates agreed that "the Organization shall place orders for equipment and industrial contracts amongst Member States as equitably as possible, taking into account scientific, technological, economic and geographical considerations" (Krige 1993d, p.43). This agreement was adopted as a principle, but there was no detailed rule on how to distribute the contracts and in what proportion to the contribution.

The distribution of contracts was a crucial issue for the European aerospace and electronics industry at that time. Although the scale of the space sector was smaller than the defense or aircraft production, it was rich in potential new technologies and commercial prospects. In 1962, as a response to the establishment of the ESRO and the ELDO, an industrial organization, called Eurospace, was created by major companies in this industry, under the initiative of the French and British companies, such as *Société pour l'étude et la réalisation d'éngins balistiques* (SEREB), Hawker-Siddeley, and Rolls Royce. The primary purpose of Eurospace was to promote space programs which would bring more industrial contracts for the member companies. However, since most of the companies in Eurospace were nationalized companies during the 1960s, the activities of Eurospace were largely influenced by the national policies and strategies which tended to be diverse across Europe, as we will discuss below, and it was therefore difficult for Eurospace to take collective action for proposing alternative ideas and strategies for the ESRO and the ELDO, despite individual companies having close access to national decision-making.

For European industry, the primary interest was to promote the development of space activities in Europe and strengthen its international competitiveness. Yves Demeriac, the first Secretary General of Eurospace, said that:

> European industry has never considered space as a moneymaking activity. [Its] main initial motive was to improve its technology so as to remain competitive in world markets. Space was a means of forming or retaining qualified teams capable of delivering advanced items of equipment and also – perhaps above all – to manage the joint development of complex systems or sub-systems. ... The target for European industry is clearly to acquire prime contractor ability for all space applications systems (quoted in McDougall 1985b, p.191).

So the activities of Eurospace were thus based on the logic of technology as a springboard for future industrial and commercial competitiveness. However, Eurospace gradually gained a more significant role after the principle of *juste retour* (see below) was introduced.

The Emergence of New Activities in Space

While the European governments were preparing to establish two new organizations, the space activities of the superpowers went one step further. The American President John Kennedy gave a famous speech in 1961 announcing a plan to send people to the Moon within the decade. The speech implied that the US government would invest more resources into space development. Inevitably, European government as well as industry were very aware of the increasing 'technology gap' (McDougall 1985a), particularly in the launcher technology. Concerning the development in the satellite technology, the use of geostationary orbit (GEO) for satellite telecommunications became the name of the game. The GEO telecommunications satellites would enable the transcontinental communication, which might have big commercial potential, but required more advanced launcher technology to carry heavier satellites. The European governments had just begun the development of a Europa launcher under the ELDO framework, and it was not certain when it would be completed. On the other hand, the United States had already launched several satellites, including GEO satellites. Space in Europe began to experience *le défi américain* (Servan-Schreiber 1967) which became the buzzword among European space community in the 1960s.

Indeed, the US government was moving quickly to facilitate the development of commercial activities in space. In 1962, the US Congress approved the establishment of Communication Satellite Corporation (Comsat)[11] to promote and develop satellite telecommunications network for commercial use. In 1964, the International Telecommunications Satellite Consortium (Intelsat) Interim Agreement (subjected to be renegotiated in five years) was initiated by the US government and agreed by 13 countries and Vatican City, following the success of American experimental communication satellites: Telstar and Syncom.[12] The US Comsat retained 61% share against 30.5% of European share, which gave a commanding position for the US government to decide the distribution of contracts, technological development, and regulations and management of international telecommunications.[13] In June 1965, the first US commercial communication satellite — Early Bird (later renamed as Intelsat I) with the capacity of 240 telephone circuits and one television channel — was successfully launched.

The immediate European reaction against the creation of Intelsat was to establish *Conférence Européenne des Télécommunications par Satellite* (CETS) in 1963, in order to represent European policies and strategies in the Intelsat meetings. The CETS was a hybrid forum of representatives from ministries of foreign affairs, post and telecommunications (PTT), and industry. The first and foremost priority of CETS was to gain a favorable negotiating position, particularly on the subject of industrial contracts, *vis-à-vis* the United States in the proposed meeting to revise Intelsat Convention in 1969. Given the increasing 'technology gap' with the US companies, European companies were unable to win competitive bidding for Intelsat contracts. For example, British companies received less than 1.6% of the total Intelsat contract, despite its contribution of 7.41% in 1967 (Russo 1993a, p.18). The lack of technological capability and expertise for application satellites seriously disadvantaged the position of European governments in the Intelsat negotiations, and therefore, they were urged to form a group under CETS.

Crisis, Change of Policy Logics and Institutions (1965–67)

The period between 1965 and 1967 is remembered as a difficult period in many areas of European efforts. The French government demonstrated its political willingness in its 'empty seat' strategy in the EEC to oppose a higher degree of integration during 1965–66, and unilaterally declared its withdrawal from the military arm of NATO in 1966. Subsequently, European institutions were thrown into stagnation, if not a crisis, and the ESRO and the ELDO were not exceptions. Indeed both of these organizations were young institutions, and there was much uncertainty therefore about how these institutions would influence the decisions of national governments. As discussed above, the ELDO was standing on a very fragile balance of policy logics, whereas the ESRO had to face the emerging issue of the application satellite technology for telecommunications, which would alter the characteristics of the organization even before the Convention entered into force. In fact, both organizations experienced serious challenges and criticisms during this period.

Table 3.1   Membership of CETS, ESRO, and ELDO in 1965

	CETS	ESRO	ELDO (share in %)		CETS	ESRO	ELDO (share in %)
Australia			✓ (0.00)	Luxembourg	✓		
Austria	✓			Monaco	✓		
Belgium	✓	✓	✓ (2.85)	The Netherlands	✓	✓	✓ (2.64)
Cyprus	✓			Norway	✓		
Denmark	✓	✓		Portugal	✓		
France	✓	✓	✓ (23.93)	Spain	✓	✓	
Germany	✓	✓	✓ (22.01)	Sweden	✓	✓	
Greece	✓			Switzerland	✓	✓	
Ireland	✓			UK	✓	✓	✓ (38.79)
Italy	✓	✓	✓ (9.78)	Vatican City	✓		

Source: Charters of CETS, ESRO and ELDO (compiled by author).

British Policy Change and Crisis of the ELDO

From the beginning, the ELDO was standing on a fragile balance of policy logics, and the changes of the international environment in the early 1960s had great influence on the balance, particularly between Britain and France — the two financially, politically, as well as technologically, important countries. The first action was taken by the French government in 1965. Having realized the rapid technological development of the American launchers and satellite technology and the American unwillingness to use the US launchers for European application satellites, the French government was frustrated by the delay of the development of the ELDO programs, and it demanded more drastic measures to catch up with American technology. The French delegation in the ELDO proposed a new timetable to skip the first program (called ELDO A/S), and to proceed to the ELDO B program, based on French *Diamant* technology which would be able to carry heavy satellites to geotransfer orbit (GTO). While many governments were against taking risks in unreliable technology, the French government threatened not to pay its financial contribution to the ELDO beyond the summer of 1965 if the French proposals were not accepted.[14] The ELDO Executives — weaker than those of the ESRO — tried to find a compromise, but no government seemed to commit itself to the French proposal.

Meanwhile, the US government approached European governments with an offer for a joint 'scientific' project for sending probes to the Sun or Jupiter. The offer was that the American government (NASA) would provide the launch, tracking and collection of data, and grant exports clearance for satellite technology licenses for very low costs. Although NASA had been promoting international collaboration in space science for a long time, the American offer was intended not only to foster scientific cooperation, but also to intervene and discourage the process of European launcher development. Notably, the French government viewed this offer was "a way to 'divert' Europe 'from the essential economic benefits to be derived from space through the exploration of communication satellites'" (Sebesta 1996, p.16).

Nevertheless, it was a very attractive offer for some countries where the logic of science was preferred to other logics, such as Germany. The German government, as discussed above, took an ambivalent stance towards the ELDO programs from the beginning, because some ministries and scientists were very reluctant to commit themselves to such an expensive program which would exhaust the budget for scientific research (Fischer 1994). Also, the US offer was welcomed in the context of German foreign policy (Keck 1976).

In the end, Europe as a whole turned down the American offer, but some countries chose to collaborate with the US government individually. Although the American offer did not influence the European scientific program as such, it produced an unexpected consequence in that the ELDO Member States clarified their positions with regard to the launcher development. The European governments were separated into two groups; one believed that the American launcher would be available for commercial launches in the near future, and one did not. The former, particularly Britain, became increasingly unwilling to commit itself to the European program.

Nevertheless, the ELDO Ministerial Council in April 1966 began to discuss the French proposal and subsequently decided to proceed with the new program called ELDO-PAS (Perigee-Apogee System).[15] However, the agreement was not negotiated easily. At this meeting, the British delegation officially announced its discontent with the progress of the ELDO, and posed a serious question as to whether the ELDO's work was worth continuing in a situation where the American launcher would be available. They argued that the costs of the program had become four times higher than the estimate agreed in Lancaster House in 1961 and the ELDO technology had become increasingly obsolete since the American and Russian launchers became far more advanced. If Europe continued to develop its own launcher, they argued, it would be impossible to recover the cost through the sales of a launch service because the market was too small. British delegates were also frustrated because "[a]lthough the Blue Streak first stage operated successfully in every case, each attempt to launch a satellite was marred by malfunctions elsewhere in the system" (Massey 1986, p.228). Moreover, the British delegates felt that the gains from the ELDO program were not equivalent to the British contribution, and "[a]side from problems arising from the letting of contracts, the development and production of an advanced technology gave rise to difficulties as a result of differing abilities to meet deadlines and disparate levels of efficiency" (Pfaltzgraff and Deghand 1968, p.32). The British delegates were, in short, fed up with bad management and program failures.

This change in British attitude was triggered by new policies initiated by the Labor government under Harold Wilson. After the electoral success in 1964, the Labor government began a campaign, the so-called 'white heat of technological revolution',[16] which was aimed at transforming the British industrial structure into a more high-tech-oriented, commercially competitive industry. The government set up the Mintech (Ministry of Technology), and appointed an influential politician, Tony Benn, to be in charge of the policy of 'white heat'. The 'white heat' policy was to re-assess the cost-efficiency of technological investment and to re-evaluate the high-cost, high-prestige programs with poor commercial prospects, particularly those which had military characteristics. Tony Benn was very critical about the way in which the aerospace/defense industries were managed, and he paid particular attention to the launcher development because it took up a large proportion of the R&D budget. He believed that the ELDO program was too expensive to produce a decent commercial return, and therefore he strongly encouraged shifting the resources from the European program to purchasing the American advanced technology (Edgerton 1996).

Meanwhile, frustrated by the performance, and industrial and technological return, the British industrialists gathered at the meeting of the National Industrial Space Committee (NISC, later renamed as UKISC) in May 1966 and published a statement urging the government to shift the priority of the launcher program from the ELDO to the all-British program (Blue Streak-Black Arrow). In response to this proposal, the Labour government decided to inject a massive amount of funding into the national programs (Table 3.2), and to restart the Black Arrow project which successfully launched the PROSPERO scientific satellite in 1971.[17]

However, the British government announced at the ELDO Ministerial Council in July 1966 that it would remain within the ELDO framework because the ELDO Convention prevented any Member States from withdrawing until the Convention has been in force for five years or before completion of any program in which the Member State has agreed to participate. It was illegal for Britain to withdraw unilaterally. But in return, the British delegate demanded a reduction in its proportion of financial contribution and, though unwillingly, other Member States agreed to do so from 38.79% to 27%.[18] Nevertheless, as a result of the restart of the national program, the total amount of British spending for space activities increased in 1966 and maintained high-level spending in 1967 (Table 3.2).

The decision in July 1966 was received with resentment from other Member States, particularly from Belgium and The Netherlands. The Dutch delegate stated in the meeting that the British decision "had caused grave concern and bitter disillusionment" and "would deal a serious blow to possible future cooperation" (quoted in De Maria and Krige 1992, pp.129–130).

Table 3.2 British Space Expenditure 1964–1967 (in $ million)

Year	National	ELDO	ESRO	Total
1964	2.00	48.05	1.29	51.34
1965	5.20	32.81	4.34	42.35
1966	29.40	32.38	9.66	71.44
1967	30.70	22.94	12.25	65.89

Source: De Maria and Krige (1992) p.129.

In addition to the British 'problem', the Italian delegates demanded a guarantee of industrial return (at least 80% of its contribution) from the ELDO program, since its workload and allocation of contracts were not sufficient to meet its contribution. It seemed that there was no common goals or solidarity among the ELDO Member States whose policy logics were becoming more and more divergent.

While the ELDO stagnated mainly as a consequence of the British demands, the French government was seeking an alternative partner for the launcher development. President de Gaulle and his Foreign Minister Couve de Murville visited Baikonur, the Soviet launch site in Kazakhstan, for the first time as Western leaders, and signed the Franco-Soviet cooperation agreement in June 1966. Although the agreement did not include cooperation in launcher development, some Member States of the ELDO regarded it as a sign of the French distrust of its European partners, and suspected that the Franco-Soviet cooperation might undermine the troublesome collaboration in launcher development. Furthermore, the British government (Ministry of Defense in particular) became suspicious of the intentions of the French policy since France had just withdrawn from the military arm of NATO earlier in 1966 (Sheehan and McLean 1990, p.283).

With the reduction of British financial and moral commitment, the ELDO became more of a French-led organization. In fact, it seemed that France was solely interested in developing an autonomous European launcher. Britain has retreated to the background and Italy was concerned with the industrial return rather than with the success of launcher development. The ELDO's new program (ELDO-PAS, later renamed as Europa 2) and the new launch pad (Kourou in French Guiana) gave a 'French taste' to the ELDO.[19] However, the French demand for strengthening the ELDO Secretariat for coordination and planning to make it more efficient was not accepted by other Member States, and the inefficiency of the ELDO did remain unchanged. Following the July 1966 Ministerial Council, ELDO established SETIS (*Société pour l'Étude et l'intégration de Systèmes Spatiaux*) with 50 engineers from Europe-wide companies to assist the Secretariat. But it "was not accompanied by a grant to the ELDO of overall design authority powers, meaning that the Secretariat and SETIS had still to face a division of authority among national project managers for most parts of the Europa 2 program" (Madders 1997, p.119).

The fragile combination of policy logics between Britain and France was finally losing its balance. On the one hand, the logics of autonomy and technology drove the French government to catch up with the superpowers and to develop a European autonomous launcher to carry heavy satellites to geostationary orbit. On the other hand, the British logic of finance remained unfulfilled because of inefficiency and failures of the ELDO programs, even though the 'white heat revolution' at home was driven by the logics of technology and commerce. There was certainly a perception gap between Britain and France about technological and commercial potential of the European launcher and the American attitude toward Europe. The two governments went in completely opposite directions, and other governments were neither articulating nor reconciling their differences, but pursuing their respective policy logics. The Italian government pushed its logic of technology further and demanded a fair industrial return, and the German government could not play any role because of the failure of the German-sponsored third stage was the source of the problem for the progress of the ELDO programs. Belgium and the Netherlands were sympathetic to the French attitude and voiced their irritation toward Britain, but could not influence the strong British determination in this regard. The decision of Ministerial Council in 1966 gave a certain direction to the future activities of the ELDO, but it could satisfy neither the French logics of autonomy and technology nor the British logic of finance.

Disputes over Application Satellites

The CETS began its life with a struggle. Although the success of satellite telecommunications by the American satellites increased the commercial opportunities, there were some issues that cast doubts on satellite telecommunication system for Europe. First of all, there was no consensus on whether Europe needed to have its own telecommunications systems outside the Intelsat. The European PTTs, those of smaller countries in particular, were seriously concerned about the risk and cost-efficiency of satellite telecommunication, which would compete against their terrestrial cable network. They claimed that they had already renewed their terrestrial network after World War II, and they could no longer afford to invest both in satellite and cable. On the other hand, the PTTs of big countries, together with the ministries of industry and technology, found it important to develop their own technological competence in satellite telecommunications, because they thought that the long-distance communication traffic would increase in the very near future. Hence, they took the parallel approach to proceed with national programs independently while negotiating at European level.

There might be three reasons why governments of big Member States took this parallel approach. First, the governments of big countries wanted to develop commercially and militarily[20] potential technological expertise for their national agencies and companies to increase the international competitiveness as well as national autonomy in the commercial and military technology. Secondly, they considered that it would not be productive to create another European organization for application satellites, nor to renegotiate the status of the ESRO which excluded those programs from its mandate. Thirdly, they perceived the revenue generated through utilization of the telecom technology would be enough to pay off the investment.

The British Ministry of Defense, in collaboration with the US defense authorities, began to construct a military satellite system, called Skynet, in the mid-1960s,[21] with anticipation that the Skynet technology might be used for commercial civilian programs.[22] In the summer of 1966, the French and German governments separately began studies for the national civilian telecommunications satellites (named SAROS and Olympia, respectively), but since the two projects were quite similar in terms of technological requirements, they decided to fuse the two projects into a joint program called *Symphonie* in early 1967 to share the costs and risks. In 1968, the Italian government also decided to build its own national civilian satellite, called SIRIO, using technologies developed under the ELDO's test satellite programs (Collette 1992). The smaller countries were frustrated by these national programs which might widen the gap between the companies of the big and smaller countries.

What was more complicated was that there was no available launching vehicle for Europe to put satellites into GEO. The Europa launcher was still at the elementary stage and the pace of the progress was not encouraging. The European governments therefore had to rely on American launchers, and the US government was not willing to provide launching services for the European application satellites as it sought to maintain the dominance of the Comsat in Intelsat. In July 1966, the US National Security Council made a decision (NSAM 354) to provide the American launcher technology to the ELDO only if it was not used for (1) improving communication satellite capability; (2) nuclear missile delivery capability; and (3) transferring to third countries (Sebesta 1994a, p.24).

These institutional, technological, and political issues notwithstanding, the governments of big Member States put forward the question on whether to develop a European application satellite in the CETS meeting in November 1966. The meeting concluded that European countries should seek the commercial application technology, and the ESRO would be the most suitable framework to develop such capability, despite the legal constraints on application programs and the problem of membership (some CETS countries were not members of the ESRO). The ESRO executives received the conclusion of the CETS meeting with mixed feelings. On the one hand, the scientists were concerned about the introduction of application programs that might jeopardize the original development plan which had been already badly damaged during the first three years of its exercise, and vigorously opposed the CETS decision (Lévy 1993). However, the majority of scientists, on the other hand, accepted the CETS decision and encouraged the change of the ESRO's priority, because they expected that it would imply more efficient use of capital resources, more industrial contracts which would restore the balance of contract distribution among Member States, more attraction for competent engineers to work in the ESRO instead of national institutions, and more political attention to the ESRO's work. Furthermore, the scientists recognized that it was difficult to justify satellite development and expensive launching cost only for the purpose of scientific research.

The difficulty that European governments faced to move on to development of application satellite was arouse out of the institutional constraints and mismatch of policy logics. The ESRO, strongly associated with the logic of science, was not regarded as an appropriate organization, but European governments could not find institutional alternatives. This institutional setting shaped the policy logics of

Member States. The British decision to develop Skynet was driven by its logics of military, (national) autonomy, and technology. The Franco-German Symphonie program was driven by the logic of technology, as a step toward the logic of commerce, whereas the Italian claim for industrial return was driven by its logics of technology and autonomy. The changes of national policy logics were the forces for changing the institutional constraints of the ESRO, and the ESRO scientists began to realize that the logic of science alone was no longer appealing to decision-makers. Although there was resentment among some scientists, the majority of them recognized the need to form alliances with other policy logics for the survival of the logic of science, and they finally welcomed the decision of the CETS.

Introduction of the Principle of juste retour

The increasing appeal of the logics of technology changed the perception of policy-makers toward the ESRO's activities. The smaller Member States in particular began to realize the technological gap between their industry and that of big Member States, and to become concerned about the imbalance of the distribution of industrial contracts involving commercially potential technologies. In the first two years, the ESRO management team preferred the rule of competitive tender, and took geographical balance into account when several bidders were competing in acceptable margins. However, the criticism from industrially ambitious countries, which had been unsuccessful in winning contracts, such as Spain and Italy, gave rise to dissatisfaction for this management rule, and a huge gap emerged in industrial returns as a result of it (see Charts 3.1 and 3.2).[23] They found that their industries were not benefiting from the membership of the ESRO (and to some extent the ELDO in the case of Italy) in relation to their contributions, and they were frustrated that their contributions went to the benefit of strong and competitive companies in Britain and France (Bondi 1993). By the end of 1967, the Spanish delegate threatened to withdraw from the ESRO if some rules were not made to guarantee industrial return. As a response, the ESRO executives encouraged the European space industry to form consortia, such as MESH, STAR and COSMOS (Table 3.3).[24] These Consortia were not the ideal way to solve the problem for several reasons. First, there were not enough companies in smaller Member States to join all three consortia. For example, the most competent Spanish engineers were concentrated in CASA (Construcciones Aeronauticas SA) which belonged to COSMOS, so that if other consortia received contracts, there would be very little technological and industrial benefit for Spain. Secondly, the companies found it difficult to accumulate technological expertise if the contracts constantly provided the opportunity to develop certain technology. For example, telecommunication satellites were developed mainly by MESH (OTS, ECS, Marecs etc.), but COSMOS also received some programs such as Intelsat V and Franco-German TDF/TV-Sat. On the one hand, the MESH companies stated that they were specialized in telecom and it would be cost-efficient if they received the contracts, but on the other hand, the COSMOS companies stated that it would be unfair to concentrate high-potential programs to the same set of companies. Thirdly, there was a question of technological duplication. Although consortia encouraged technological transfer for avoiding duplication within the same consortium, there was almost no technological transfer between consortia. Finally, the major companies were not satisfied to receive prime contractorship on a rotational basis. Although the formation of consortia helped to distribute contracts to smaller and weaker companies to a large extent, it did not satisfy everyone.

Table 3.3   Major European Consortia

	MESH	STAR	COSMOS
History	Oct. 1966: created Dec. 1969: Fiat joined	1969: created as EST* Sep. 1970: restructured as STAR	1969: created as BAC Consortium* Nov. 1970: restructured as COSMOS
France	Matra	Thomson-CSF, SEP	Aérospatiale
Germany	ERNO	Dornier	MBB, Siemens
UK	Hawker Siddeley	BAC*	Marconi*
Italy	Fiat	CGE-FIAR Montedel-Laben	Selenia
Others	Saab-Scania (S) Fokker (NL)	Ericsson (S), Contraves (CH)	ETCA (B), CASA (E)
Tech. Cooperation	TRW System (USA)	Hughes (USA)	Aeronautic Ford (USA)
Major Programs	TD-1A, Spacelab, OTS, Marots/ Marecs, ECS, Telecom 1 (F), Hipparcos	Geos 1 and 2, ISEE-B, Space Telescope, ISPM, Giotto	Meteosat 1 and 2, Intelsat V (Ford), Exosat, TV-Sat/TDF (F-D)

*   Marconi was in STAR (EST) and BAC was in COSMOS in 1969 and swapped their places in 1970.
Source: Palacios (1978, p.25), ESA (1984, p.213).

The governments that were not satisfied with the 'consortia solution' proposed an alternative solution; the principle of fair geographical return, or *juste retour*. The concept of *juste retour* was, in short, a guarantee that companies located in certain Member States would receive the contracts in the same proportion as Member State's contributions. If a Member State contributed 20% of the budget, the companies in the Member State would receive 20% of the contracts.[25] The question of introducing the principle of *juste retour* was on the table of the ESRO Council since 1965, but large countries, particularly France and Britain, were vigorously against the idea. They argued that the principle of *juste retour* would undermine international competitiveness of European industry, and it was totally unacceptable to be 'penalized' for having competitive industry. The conflict between big and smaller countries became deeper in the mid-1960s, and the ESRO's new Director-General, Hermann Bondi took the initiative to mediate the two sides. In November 1967, the ESRO Member States concluded an agreement which included the following points: (1) by 1971, each Member States should have at least return coefficient of 0.7 (70% of contribution); (2) ESRO had the right not to award contracts to a most competitive offer, if it was unfavorable for geographical return; but (3) the competitive criteria should be favored if it encouraged an association of companies; and (4) tender could only be accepted to improve geographical distribution if its price was not more than 10% higher than the most competitive bid (Krige 1993d).

Charts 3.1 and 3.2 show the gradual convergence of coefficient in the beginning of the 1970s as an effect of Bondi initiative. Although some Member States which did not reach the coefficient of 1 continued to demand industrial and financial compensation, the principle of *juste retour* was indeed effective to satisfy those complaining Member States. The principle of *juste retour*, as a policy norm, settled well into the institutions of European space collaboration. What was also important was that the transnational feature of the ESRO which derived from characteristics of the logic of science was seriously damaged by the demand for fair industrial return by national delegations who were driven by the logics of technology and commerce.

Chart 3.1   Evolution of Coefficient 1965–1977 (Part 1)

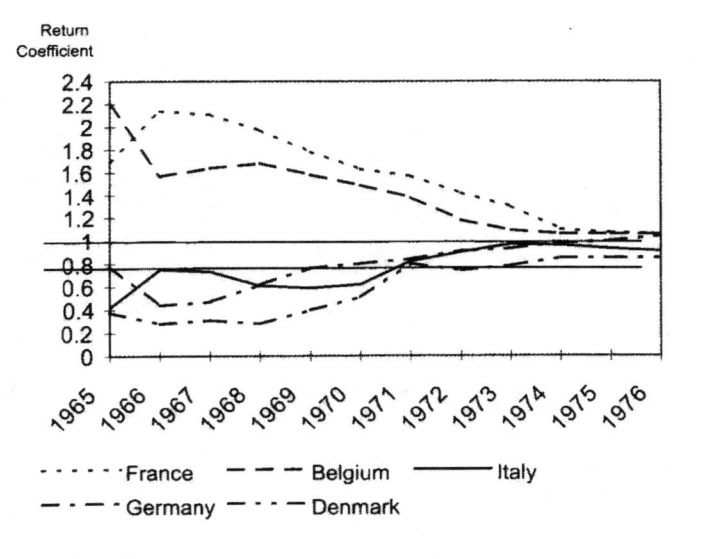

Source: Palacios (1978, p.28).

Chart 3.2   Evolution of Coefficient 1965–1977 (Part 2)

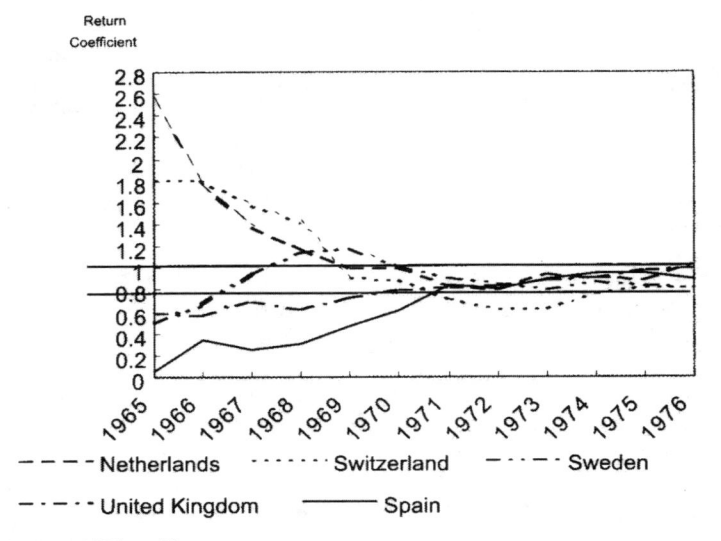

Source: Palacios (1978, p.29).

Policy Logics in 1965–67

The institutions of European space collaboration began to settle down during this period, but not as initially planned. The ESRO, supported by the logic of science, has gradually lost the enthusiasm and transnational characteristics as the logics of technology and commerce emerged. Big Member States in particular were driven by the logic of technology, together with the logic of commerce, to catch up with the development in the US for commercially useful technology, while smaller Member States were also driven by the logic of technology so as to ensure their access to the ESRO's technological programs. Obviously, these Member States were interested in the commercial potential of these programs, but their primary concern was to develop technological expertise, and therefore, the logic of technology was at the forefront of the policy logic for them. The conflicts over the application satellites and industrial return influenced the institutional development of European space collaboration. On the other hand, the ELDO was almost torn apart by the French logic of (European) autonomy and the British logic of finance. It is also important to mention the role of the US influence. In the first place, a rapid technological advance and successful application of space technology in commercial programs were strong pressures for European governments to define their policies towards space collaboration.

Muddling Through (1968–70)

Standing on a fragile balance of policy logics, the institutions of European space collaboration needed to be adjusted to the circumstances and to accommodate different policy logics. However, reconciling those policy logics was not an easy task. The European space organizations still had to face a difficult time.

A European Space Policy? Establishing the ESC and the Causse Report

While there were crises over European space collaboration, European governments began to blame the ways in which the European space programs were managed. The idea that Europe needed a coherent space policy was shared among the ESRO and ELDO Member States, especially since the ESRO programs, which were the only potential customers for the ELDO program, were actually changing, the ELDO also had to change its strategy to provide a launch service for application satellites in order to justify the current program. In order to discuss a coherent policy for space, the Member States of the ELDO, ESRO and CETS formed the European Space Conference (the ESC) in Paris in December 1966.

The first task of the ESC was to draw a draft of a single European space policy. Jean-Pierre Causse, the Director of Brétany Space Centre of CNES, was entrusted with the task of drafting a report on the options for European space collaboration. The Causse Report, submitted in December 1967, contained several new ideas on how Europe should manage space programs. First, the report acknowledged that science programs themselves were not sufficient reason to justify the existence of the ESRO and its expenditure, and recommended the inclusion of the application satellite in the ESRO's activities. Secondly, the report stressed that the application satellites and launch vehicle programs were crucial for Europe to maintain international competitiveness, particularly against the United States. But at the same time, the report also expected that these programs would strengthen the position of Europe in the collaborative programs with the US. Thirdly, the report suggested that Europe could develop Direct Broadcasting Satellites (DBS) without violating Intelsat agreement, since DBS was not included in Intelsat agreement. The DBS program was also encouraged by a new organization of TV broadcasters around European countries, the European Broadcasting Union (EBU), so that the ESRO did not have to persuade national PTTs which were skeptical about European satellite telecom programs. The idea of a DBS program was quickly approved by CETS and EBU as Eurafrica (CETS-C) satellite. Finally, the report recommended the creation of a single European organization for space. Causse himself expressed that the launcher development had to be coordinated with satellite programs, or *vice versa*, and it was inefficient to separate launcher and satellite program in different organization (Carlier and Gilli 1994, p.90).

The ESC meeting was scheduled to open in Spring 1968 to discuss issues raised by the Causse report, but it was actually held after a six months delay because the ESRO and the ELDO had serious problems, and the Member States were not willing to participate. In the ESRO, tensions between Italy and other Member States were mounting. Despite the Bondi initiative on the principle of *juste retour* which would be effective from 1971, the Italian delegation, who were deeply dissatisfied by the distribution of contracts and the escalation of cost of the Thor-Delta (TD) satellites, announced that it would block the council decision on the 1968 budget if its contribution to TD programs could not be reduced to 11.72% of the original cost estimate (Russo 1992b, p.26).

The situation in the ELDO seemed more hopeless. In April 1968, Britain expressed its disappointment with the two recent launch failures and expressed its unwillingness to undertake any further financial commitments, in spite of the reduction of its share from 38.79% to 27% in July 1966. In July, Italy joined Britain in expressing its dissatisfaction with the new plan called 'T8/A' which was proposed by SETIS to ensure minimum investment in technological development for Europa 2 (ELDO-PAS) development. Italy regarded that the 'T8/A' proposal would inevitably reduce the Italian share of industrial contracts, despite the fact that other Member States' share would increase. France and Germany, on the other hand, became desperate to find a breakthrough, since the US government gave an ultimatum that NASA would launch Franco-German Symphonie as an experimental satellite, which implied that Symphonie could not be used for commercial transmission of communications (Curien 1987, p.49).

The impact of the American refusal to provide a launch service for commercial purposes was significant for the German space policy community. As Fischer (1994) pointed out, there had been significant diversity of opinions on whether to develop expensive European launchers or to rely on cheaper American ones, but the American refusal eliminated the latter option. Since the Symphonie program was the highest priority for Germany in the mid-1960s, it was unacceptable for the space policy community to accept that Symphonie would not be launched. The German government could not find any options but to commit the ELDO programs more than ever. German policy logics were now shifted from the logics of technology and finance to that of autonomy. The policy logic shift of the German government has certainly influenced the balance of logics in the ELDO. ELDO was now divided into two camps of policy logics: the Franco-German logic of autonomy and the Anglo-Italian logics of finance and technology.

The Causse report was ambitious and optimistic in the time of mutual suspicion and conflict of national policy logics. Although few adjustments were made in 1966–67, the Italian government, driven by the logics of technology and commerce, became the most dissatisfied Member State both in the ESRO and the ELDO, and blocked any decisions unless its demands were accepted. The innovative Causse report was forced to be put back on the shelf until Member States could agree to discuss about it. Nevertheless, the vision that the Causse report proposed was certainly regarded as a desirable alternative, and provided a framework of the future discussions.

Saving European Collaboration: The ESC Bad Godesberg Meeting

Despite a series of crises and confusion, the European governments, particularly France, Germany and the Low Countries, were still committed to collaboration and were desperately seeking a way out of the disorder. The representatives from Belgium (J. Spaey) and the Netherlands (J. Bannier) launched attempts to rescue European collaboration in November 1968. Spaey used a traditional approach to convince Italy to stay in the ELDO by negotiating with the French and German delegations to offer Italy a bulk of workload (the apogee motor) of Symphonie. However, Italy was not satisfied with the offer and maintained its position to demand a reduction of its contribution to the ELDO. On the other hand, Bannier, the Dutch Minister for Science, proposed in the ESC meeting at Bad Godesberg that European space collaboration under these circumstances could only be possible with the '*à la carte* system' in which each country could decide on a case-by-case basis to participate.

The Dutch proposal marked a turning point in the institutions of European space collaboration. Before the proposal, there was a general understanding that all member states had to participate in every program. This was the fundamental reason for separating the ESRO from the ELDO because some countries did not want to participate in launcher development. Moreover, there was a general understanding that if countries decided to participate on an *à la carte* basis, it would harm the development of European industry since the government might not guarantee companies to receive contracts constantly, which would damage the development of a particular technology or types of models. Furthermore, some countries were afraid that *à la carte* participation would grant more power to big Member States because programs may not be brought to fruition without the advanced technologies of these countries.

Initiated by the Dutch proposal, the ESC meeting at Bad Godesberg in November 1968 produced several important agreements on disputed issues. The first issue was the organizational arrangement for future European space collaboration. Member States agreed to form a single European space organization for basic programs with the option of opting out of the launcher program. Britain, with other non-launcher countries, was satisfied with this decision, because it believed that it would have the opportunity to exit from the ELDO commitment. Although other Member States agreed on the possibility of the British opt-out from launcher, they still wanted to keep Britain, which might launch its national satellites with the American launcher, as a customer of Europa 2. Thus, the ESC placed the condition that Britain (and other countries which opted out from launcher development) would not be required to purchase the European launcher at more than 125% of the cost of an equivalent non-European launcher if the European launcher became available.

However, the ESC meeting could not find a means of developing an application program. The main reason was, although the Bad Godesberg meeting suggested the possibility of British opt-out from launcher development, the financial arrangement for the ELDO after the British withdrawal was not yet defined, as a result of which there was an ambiguity with regard to the extent to which British resources would be available. The decision on an application program (Eurafrica) had therefore to wait for the re-arrangement of the ELDO budget.

Exit from the Mess

Long enduring crises in European space collaboration seemed to be easing its way in 1969. Following the decision at Bad Godesberg, the question of British and Italian contributions in launcher development was finally settled in the ELDO Ministerial meeting in April 1969. France, Germany, Belgium and the Netherlands jointly expressed their commitment to complete Europa 1 and 2 programs (none of previous flights was successful yet), and agreed to shoulder the shortfall of the British and Italian share on the new plan in which Britain and Italy were not interested. They also agreed to begin a study for a new launcher which would not use the Blue Streak as the first stage. The success in breaking the deadlock was largely due to the French commitment with support from Germany and the Low Countries. Persuaded by CNES, the French government decided to provide sufficient resources to cover the gap after the British retreat; in return they would initiate a new program. The decision in April 1969 showed not only the French willingness to develop the European launcher for a commercial satellite, but also that the moment had arrived for turning over the leadership in European space development from Britain to France.

Although the ELDO Ministerial council sorted the financial arrangement which enabled Britain to have sufficient resources to invest in an application satellite, the ESRO and CETS had a new problem regarding the customer. The development of Eurafrica satellite was planned to start in March 1969, but EBU became critically doubtful for the prospect of the launcher availability of Europa 2 or the possibility of launching the satellite by American rocket. Moreover, EBU also began to doubt the cost-effectiveness of having a broadcasting satellite since it was planning to replace its terrestrial networks. In November 1969, the EBU Administrative council concluded that DBS would be more expensive than the terrestrial network, and therefore it would not invest in satellite development.

However, quite fortunately, European PTTs re-emerged as a potential customer for an application satellite. Initially PTTs were skeptical about proposals for the regional satellite telecommunications system, but increasing demand for telephone services, technological reliability through Intelsat programs, and commercial success of Intelsat services changed the policy environment for PTTs requiring a reconsideration of the potential of regional satellite systems. Furthermore, the result of the negotiation of revision of the Intelsat Convention in 1969 favored the regional telecommunication system so that there were no legal barriers for European PTTs to operate a regional system. For the ESRO, the change in the attitude of PTTs was a real breakthrough for application programs. In July 1970, the ESC meeting in Brussels officially decided to begin two programs — one experimental satellite, later to become the Orbital Testing Satellite (OTS), and a follow-on major satellite, later to become the European Communications Satellite (ECS).

Institutions and Policy Logics during the 1960s

The institutional frameworks for European space development began to settle its shape at the end of the 1960s. The initial enthusiasm of science logic coalition for space research soon retreated behind the strong logic of technology with the support of the logic of commerce, particularly with regard to the prospects of an application satellite. As discussed above, many Member States had the logic of technology as the primary policy logic to promote application satellites and to introduce the principle of *juste retour* because their first objectives were to ensure access to European technological programs which may not be produced in their own countries. A fragile balance of policy logics for launcher development was beginning to take shape under a strong willingness of the French government to have a European autonomous launcher.

These processes of institutional formation were strongly influenced by external factors. The extremely rapid pace of technological development of the superpowers, the success of Intelsat and the emergence of satellite applications, and the American refusal to provide a launch service for European application satellites helped to shift national policy logics to similar positions. The German policy logic, through its Symphonie program, converged with the French logic of (European) autonomy, whereas the British and Italian negotiating position tended to favor a reduction of financial commitment. However, the Anglo-Italian convergence was not motivated by the convergence of their core policy logics, since the British policy logics were based on the logic of finance for a launcher and the logic of commerce for application programs, whereas the Italian logic was based on the logic of technology. At the end of the 1960s, the Franco-German logic of autonomy attracted other small countries and began to shape the institution of European space collaboration in their favor.

Nevertheless, the Anglo-Italian convergence made a certain impact on the shape of institutions. Italy's insistence on receiving industrial contracts induced the Bondi initiative in 1967 to introduce the principle of *juste retour*, and the British discontent with the ELDO's performance led to the creation of a European Space Conference and pulled out the idea of *à la carte* participation. In short, the institutions of European space collaboration were changing to accommodate the difference in the policy logics of Member States. Although the turbulence within the organizations of European space collaboration was not completely over, the future seemed much brighter.

Post-Apollo Programs and Package-deal

While Europe was struggling to proceed with the launcher and satellite developments, the superpowers had reached the highest point of their 'space race'. In July 1969, Apollo 11 had landed on the surface of the Moon, marking the finest hours of American history of space development and the end of space race. However, soon after the great success, NASA and the American space community met a problem of 'Aftermath of Apollo'. During the 1960s, NASA enjoyed strong political and financial support, and became a huge public institution, but the level of support inevitably decreased to a large extent after achieving its objective. The first priority for NASA was to maintain the level of funding and employment under these circumstances. It was imperative for NASA to keep creating new programs and objectives to attract political attention, and in this context, NASA began its campaign for the post-Apollo programs.

In the beginning, NASA had promoted a permanent human presence in space as a core concept of the post-Apollo programs, meaning a permanent Space Station, manned Space Shuttle as a transport system to Station, nuclear rockets to increase launching capacity, and a Space Tug which would tug satellites from low Earth orbit (where the Space Shuttle would release satellites) to geostationary orbit. For NASA, it was important that the post-Apollo programs should be a manned space program in order to maintain the technological capability, developed under the Apollo programs, and attract public attention (Heppenheimer 1997; McCurdy 1990; Mark 1987). During this campaign, NASA began to use the European situation to threaten the US policy-makers that Europe was undermining the monopoly of satellite launchers. NASA also claimed that a substantial cooperation with Europe in the post-Apollo programs, particularly the Shuttle program, would undermine European effort to have its own launcher.

In February 1969, Thomas Paine, then the NASA Administrator, suggested to newly elected President Richard Nixon that cooperation with Europe in the Shuttle program would "help [European] avoid wasting resources on obsolescent developments" (quoted in McCurdy 1990, p.101) and, as a result, Europe would rely on US launchers. Indeed, the American policy-makers thought that there would be other advantages to having Europeans in post-Apollo programs, such as restoring the leadership which was damaged during the Vietnam War, reducing the pressure of technology gap accusation, and securing political support from Congress. Hence, although the proposals for cooperation in the post-Apollo programs had little relevance to the problems of Europe relating to its satellites and launcher programs, NASA made a strong case that cooperation with the United States would provide vital technological knowledge and extensive experience in space operation.

European Reaction: Autonomy or Technology?

The American offer certainly induced a strong European reaction. It was the first time that the United States had given serious consideration to share advanced space technology and program management, albeit with some conditions. From the European point of view, the offer was an attempt to undermine current programs in the ELDO. The French government in particular reacted fiercely. Michel Debré, the Minister for Defense, claimed that dropping European autonomous launcher "would have meant leaving space and the exploration of planets to the Americans and the Russians", and he was determined that "if France had to go ahead alone, I would find sufficient resources through my own ministerial budget" (Carlier and Gilli 1994, p.40) to build a national launcher. In March 1970, Pierre Aigrain, *Delegue General* for scientific and technical research, submitted a report to recommend a reorientation of French space policy with regard to the American offer. The report concluded that the construction of a launch vehicle with European partners was inevitable if France did not wish to let the Americans monopolize space telecommunications (Ministère du Développement Industriel et Scientifique 1970). The French decision-makers took this report seriously, and the Interministerial Council chaired by President Georges Pompidou decided to adopt the report as the government strategy for space, despite strong opposition from the Ministry of Finance in May 1970.

At the European level, a joint ESRO/ELDO working group chaired by Jean-Albert Dinkespiler, the ESRO Director of Programs and Planning, and Jean-Pierre Causse was set up to prepare the European position to the US offer. The working group took an ambivalent position: it suggested, on the one hand, that cooperation with the US would be valuable in terms of technology and subcontracts, but on the other hand, any existing programs should not be altered by participating in the post-

Apollo programs, and Europe should have sufficient independence to take full management responsibility.

Based on the report, the Fourth ESC was held in July 1970 to discuss the matter further at ministerial level. The question was focused on whether Europe should continue building its own expandable launcher or should participate in the post-Apollo programs. From the beginning there was a general understanding among many Member States that Europe preferred the Space Tug because it was a major technical challenge requiring expertise in robotics and cryogenic fuels. Eurospace, the industrial association, organized a symposium in September 1970, and concluded that it was interested in the post-Apollo programs, although there were a variety of opinion among industries. For example, British companies put priority on post-Apollo over Europa 3, whereas French electronic and aerospace companies were unanimously skeptical about the American offer (Sebesta 1995, pp.17–20).

European governments also faced a dilemma. On the one hand, participating in the post-Apollo programs, which meant abandoning the ELDO program, would result in technological dependence. But on the other hand, the possible technology transfer would strengthen the industrial and technological base and increase the level of employment because of the new workload. In the meeting of ESC held in November 1970, the Member States focused on three issues. Firstly, the Member States wanted a full partnership rather than a mere subcontractor position. They demanded full access to technological and managerial expertise, a prime contractorship for a substantial part of the program, and a role in designing and developing the program. Some Member States, Italy in particular, insisted that Europe should be involved in every stage of development and management, even though European governments shoulder a smaller portion of the program.

Secondly, the amount of money asked by the Americans was twice as much as Europe budgeted for Europa 3 whose estimated cost was some $550 million (Sebesta 1994b, p.328). It implied that Europe would not be able to commit to both the post-Apollo programs and Europa 3, because of the scale of the costs. Member States were still divided on whether to choose a European own launcher or the American program. The British delegate expressed its confidence that NASA would provide a launch service on an *ad hoc* basis, even if Europe did not participate in the post-Apollo programs, whereas the French delegate demanded the guarantee of service if Europe decided to drop its Europa 3 program.

Finally, NASA, in order to attract European participation, suggested that it would not oppose the provision of launch services for satellites with 'peaceful purposes'. However, with regard to the launch of European commercial satellites, President Nixon declared that the US would launch other countries' satellites only if Intelsat made a favorable recommendation asking the US to provide launch assistance. This policy implied that Europe needed to overrule the US Comsat's power of veto by a two-thirds majority of 77 Intelsat Member States.[26] In fact, the French and German officials found the US policy as *de facto* veto to launch Symphonie as an operational satellite (Sebesta 1996, p.29).

The ESC meeting did not produce a common platform of negotiation. Although there was a strong French determination for developing Europa 3, its policy logic of autonomy was not shared with other Member States, especially Britain. The

European space collaboration was, again, at a critical stage in which the difference of policy logics hindered collective decisions.

US Policy Change and German Interest in Spacelab

While the Europeans were struggling to reach a common position for the post-Apollo programs, there were certain moves on the other side of the Atlantic. Firstly, there was a significant change in the culture of NASA. During the Apollo period, NASA had never been worried about the cost or implications of the program, but under the low political and financial support, it had to make a feasible economic justification to promote the post-Apollo programs.[27] Due to this low level of support it was forced to narrow down the range of options that NASA might take. It was indeed impossible to have a Space Station at this stage, and therefore the focus of the post-Apollo programs shifted to the Space Shuttle because the Shuttle was technically the difficult part of the programs. It would be harder to build the Space Station without proper cargo and human transportation, and more importantly, it was expected that the Shuttle would stimulate public imagination and eventually increase support for a Space Station.

Secondly, in order to secure the political support, NASA had to make a political deal with the US Air Force (USAF). The USAF was a major customer of satellite launches, and it had its individual space program. NASA wanted them to join on board the post-Apollo programs, but in order to do so, it had to make certain concessions. NASA offered the USAF that it would not only pay the cost of development in full, but would also pay to build all operational Shuttles, even though the Air Force would have full use of two out of four of the Shuttle fleet, whereas the USAF would contribute only by providing its political support and guaranteeing to launch its satellite by Shuttle (Heppenheimer 1997, p.255). This involvement of military changed the nature of the post-Apollo programs and the relationship with other countries. The Space Tug, the most favorite program for Europe, was pulled out from international cooperation because it would handle military satellites, and the USAF did not want share such military information with Europe (Bizony 1996, p.49). The USAF also wanted to cooperate with Europe through 'clean interface', meaning that they did not want Europe to be an integral part of the development but a relatively peripheral component which would be completely detached from the main body of the Shuttle.

Finally, there was a change in NASA administration. Thomas Paine, an enthusiast for international cooperation, resigned in September 1970 and was succeeded by James Fletcher. Fletcher had to face, from the beginning, a significant opposition from politicians about bringing Europeans into the Shuttle program. They considered that the Shuttle was a revolutionary technological achievement and there was no reason to share such state-of-the-art technology. At the same time, in a context of *détente*, the US Executives became more interested in cooperation with the Soviet Union in the Apollo-Soyuz missions, since it offered an opportunity to learn the Soviet manned-space technology. There was also a growing sentiment among politicians that the US launching policy should be more restrictive to other nations' satellites because of increasing competition in satellite communications. Therefore, Fletcher had little option with regard to cooperation with Europe.

The change in the US position was more discouraging for Europe, especially for France, since the Shuttle was less appealing than the Space Tug, and there would be no significant sharing of technological and managerial expertise. Under this condition, the only part left for Europe was the so-called 'Spacelab' which was a scientific laboratory loaded on the Shuttle cargo bay. The 'Spacelab' was not an independent system in terms of life support and power generation system, but it was definitely a 'clean interface' program. The only advantage of this program seemed to be that it would be cheaper (estimated $150–250 million) and would not disturb the Europa 3 project.

However, the German, and to some extent the Italian governments expressed their interest in the Spacelab program. There were several reasons for Germany to be interested in the Spacelab program. Firstly, since the beginning of German space development, there was considerable interest in manned-space activity and a reusable shuttle. Eugen Sänger, a famous rocket scientist and former advisor for Ministry of Transportation, was the leading figure of such projects, and many German scientists and engineers were influenced by him to a certain extent.[28] Secondly, there was strong lobbying by the US government through diplomatic channels, and the German executives were concerned as to the consequences of their relationship with the US if they did not join Space Shuttle program. Thirdly, the Spacelab was of relatively little cost compared to the Space Tug program which was estimated at about $500 million. Fourthly, a strong lobbying was done by groups of scientists who wished to have access to microgravity research. The United States and Soviet Union had considerable experience in microgravity research during the 'space race' period, while Europe was left out from those ground-breaking experiments. Finally, NASA estimated that it would purchase at least 12 Spacelab units in the future. It was a significant amount of contract which would strengthen the technological base for space infrastructure.

In retrospect, these expectations were not met with reality. NASA procured only two Spacelab units, and the cost of each flight became far greater than expected, so that many scientific experiments were squeezed out to compensate the Spacelab expenditure. And worst of all, the scientists became skeptical about the usefulness of the Spacelab, because of the costs and low frequency of flights (Russo 1997a). Since the Spacelab was funded and developed only by Europe, and completely detached from the Shuttle development process, it was as if Europe was a subcontractor developing with its own money. Therefore, it was often said that the Spacelab was "Europe's most expensive gift to the people of the United States since the statue of Liberty" (McCurdy, p.102).

The ESRO Reform: Introduction of 'Optional Participation'

While European countries were discussing the question of the post-Apollo programs, the ESC meeting in July 1970 also discussed the question of the European launcher as well. Despite the German interest in the Spacelab, France, Germany and Belgium stood up to promote the new launcher program: Europa 3. It was designed as a two-stage (instead of three-stage Europa 1 and 2) launcher to carry heavier satellites since Britain and its Blue Streak no longer participated in the ELDO in the Europa 3 program. However, Italy did not accept the new concept which would consequently reduce the industrial contracts to its industry. In the meantime, the ESC could not agree on the reform of the ESRO. France and Belgium strongly demanded to restructure the ESRO to become more flexible for an application program, as new ideas for application programs such as aircraft navigation and meteorology had emerged from the early 1970s. But the governments of smaller countries, Denmark in particular, made clear that they did not wish to jeopardize science programs and to increase expenditure for the ESRO. Frustrated by these oppositions, France threatened to veto the three-year budget of the ESRO, which should be adopted unanimously.

As the Bondi initiative saved European collaboration from falling apart in 1968, a new report submitted by the Committee of Senior Officials, a creation of the Bad Godesberg meeting, produced an idea to break the deadlock in the negotiation. The report, known as the Puppi report, was built upon previous reports (the Causse and Bannier reports), but two new elements attracted attention. First, the report recommended that Europe should invest not only in telecommunication satellites, but also other areas of applications (navigation and meteorology), and the Member States should be allowed to participate in the programs on a case-by-case basis, while the scientific and R&D programs should be mandatory. Secondly, Europe should adopt a set of organizational principles for a consolidated organization that would be based on the ESRO with the ESC as its own Council to make political decisions. Financial contribution for the single organization should be based on GNP, but the industrial contracts should be allocated under the principle of *juste retour*.

The Puppi Report was supported by a new political climate in Europe. In May 1971, French President Pompidou and British Prime Minister Heath met in London to agree over British entry into the EEC, and the French and British officials had a lengthy discussion about space issues in a friendly atmosphere (Lévy 1984, p.83–84). The change of the position of British delegation toward the ESRO also brought a different approach to the negotiation. The British delegate used to be organized by Science Research Council consisting of scientists and bureaucrats, but since the mid-1971, the Ministry of Industry joined the delegation in response to the increasing importance of an application program. The change in the structure of British delegation certainly contributed to the process of transformation of the ESRO.

Indeed, these changes produced a positive result in the ESRO Council in July 1971. France, Germany, Britain and Italy all agreed to begin studies for application programs for navigation and meteorology alongside telecommunications, and they decided to participate in all programs (in other words, they did not opt out from any of these programs), and agreed to pay contributions according to the proportion of GNP. Although some Member States, Denmark in particular, expressed its unwillingness to participate in any of these programs, such a unilateral position would have less repercussion in the negotiation since the ESRO could decide programs without the consent of Denmark due to the introduction of the *à la carte* system. The ESRO Council in December 1971 finalized the arrangement for application programs: all Member States except Denmark would participate in Aerosat (air navigation satellite); Denmark and Spain opted out from Meteosat (meteorological satellite); and Denmark, Spain and the Netherlands decided not to participate in Orbital Testing Satellite (OTS), a modified version of CETS communication satellite program.

What was remarkable in this ESRO Council meeting was the first 'Europeanization' of national project. Since 1968, the French space agency, CNES, has been studying the possibility of satellite weather monitoring as a national program. However, having shifted resources to launcher development, Meteosat was not able to attract sufficient national funding, and some people in CNES began to consider withdrawing from the ESRO in order to shift the budget for science programs to meteorology. The French delegation to ESRO was put in a very difficult situation: they argued that if Meteosat was not 'Europeanized', France would not pay the ESRO contribution from 1972 in order to shift resources to the 'national' Meteosat program. Other Member States thought it was blackmail, and did not appreciate the idea of sharing the costs of a national program. They argued that if Meteosat was Europeanized, the work had to be done at ESTEC — one of the ESRO's technological centers — instead of the CNES Toulouse Center. The question of transferring facilities, technology, personnel and industrial contracts was the major issue in the negotiation, but François-Xavier Ortoli, French Minister for Research and Industry, was not easily convinced to shift the resources to Europe because the CNES labor union, which gained influence in the events of 1968 and 1970 wage dispute, was strongly against the transfer of the program completely to ESTEC (Lévy 1984, p.86). The decision was eventually made in the ESRO Council in March 1972 that Meteosat should be Europeanized: ESRO was given the responsibility of developing, launching and managing a first series of pre-operational satellite, and responsibility for operation was supported by both CNES and ESTEC.

The other interesting outcome of the Council was about the design of OTS. Since the Eurafrica project, France, Germany and Italy were in a fierce battle to promote their national programs as models for new satellites, in order to have a leading role in the commercially potential program. They all convincingly argued that their accumulated technology and expertise through Symphonie and SIRIO programs were available, and the ESRO should take advantage of it in order to save development cost. Even Britain submitted a plan to launch a national satellite called UKATS (UK Application Technology Satellite, later renamed GTS, Geostationary Technological Satellite) which only existed on paper. At the end of discussion, the ESRO secretariat took an initiative to 'go European' which meant that the ESRO directly asked industry to design a new satellite. The plan, which industry brought to the ESRO, was sufficiently advanced in terms of technology, and satisfactory for all Member States from a financial point of view (Collette 1992; Russo 1994). Indeed, the OTS program was so well-performed that its design was succeeded by other telecommunications programs such as Marots (Marecs) and ECS.

The success of the reform of the ESRO in the early 1970s was due to the changes of policy logics and political environment. First, the Puppi Report was submitted to provide a vision and a framework for the reform. Particularly, the stress on 'optional participation' or the '*à la carte system*' liberated the ESRO from being hostage to a unilateral claim from a Member State. Second, British accession to the EEC and a subsequent Anglo-French summit helped to smooth the talk between France and Britain. Britain was still a very influential Member State, and it was crucial that the

British government took a decision to support the development of commercial application within the framework of the ESRO. Thirdly, although the French negotiating position was strongly influenced by the CNES labor union and budgetary constraints, the French government was determined to promote the 'Europeanization' of Meteosat, and eventually they were able to convince the Toulouse Center to accept the transfer of the development center to ESTEC.[29]

Nevertheless, it should be noted that the introduction of the rule of optional participation, the concept of Europeanization, and fierce competition for the leadership of commercially potential programs were all signifying the importance of 'national policy logics' in the ESRO. The initial logic of science – and its European characteristics – was completely taken over by national policy logics of technology and commerce.

Towards Single European Organization: The Package-deal

To a large extent, the American offer to European governments to participate in post-Apollo programs disturbed the unstable balance of policy logics between Member States of the ELDO. But further and more serious damage was done by the failure of the European launchers. The first flight of Europa 2 in November 1971 blew up in the middle of the flight, and disappointed all Member States especially Germany whose enthusiasm for European autonomous launcher development was fading away in favor of the American Shuttle. The ELDO Council immediately asked Robert Aubinière, long-serving Director-General of CNES and incoming ELDO's Secretary-General, to report the cause of the failure of the ELDO from a managerial point of view: the report was submitted in June 1972. It pointed out that the core problem of the ELDO was that there was no technical authority in the Secretariat, and therefore the management of any program was always restricted under strong demands from Member States concerning the industrial return. Moreover, the ELDO structure for the allocation of contracts failed to encourage the exchange of technical information, and no one in the ELDO could take responsibility for that. With the disadvantages of the ELDO structure in mind, the report concluded that Europa 2 was not worth being continued.

The failure of Europa 2 and the Aubinière report certainly discouraged Germany and Italy along with Britain from the launcher program. In March 1972, the German government even suggested canceling Europa 2 and 3 programs altogether and to participate in the post-Apollo programs. France and Belgium were the only two countries still remaining interested in the European launcher program. The French President Georges Pompidou urged the German Chancellor Willy Brandt to support the development of Europa 3 at the Franco-German summit in July 1972, but Brandt argued that the priority was on Spacelab instead of Europa 3, and that Germany could only support Europa 3 if France supported Spacelab. Under these circumstances, the CNES Launch Vehicle Division began a study to find an alternative launcher model from mid-1972, just in case Europa 3 was cancelled. The model was tentatively called L3S (*Lanceur 3ème Génération Substitut*) which, as the name suggested, was developed as a substitute for Europa 3.

Having realized that it would not be possible to attract other Member States to launcher development, the French representatives took a dramatic step in the ESC meeting in December 1972. First, the French Minister of Industrial and Scientific Development, Jean Charbonnel, proposed L3S to replace Europa 3, under the condition that the CNES would pay 60% of the costs and, in return, have managerial authority. The German government, on the other hand, indicated that it would favor the construction of Spacelab, and would pay up to 50% of the development cost. It made the point clear that if France supports Spacelab, then Germany would prepare to take part in L3S program. Britain, jumping on the bandwagon, demanded a commencement of a new application program for maritime telecommunication (MAROTS). Britain made a point later (March 1973) that it would support L3S program on the condition that France participated in MAROTS and the responsibility for L3S inertial navigation system, which was a militarily important system, was given to the British firm, Ferranti (Carlier and Gilli 1994, p.97).

Table 3.4   National Contributions for Major Programs

	L3S (Ariane)	Spacelab	Marots	Total Expenditure (MAU)
France	62.50%	10.00%	12.50%	272.05
Germany	20.12%[1]	52.55%	20.00%	251.50
UK	2.47%[2]	6.30%	58.50%	72.44
Italy	1.75%[3]	18.00%	2.30%	63.66
Belgium	5.00%	4.20%	1.00%	32.24
Spain	2.00%	2.80%	1.00%	16.79
The Netherlands	2.00%	2.10%	-	13.89
Switzerland	1.20%	1.00%	-	7.53
Denmark	0.50%	1.50%	-	6.48
Sweden	1.10%	-	-	4.08
Others[4]	1.37%	1.55%	4.70%	13.38

1   Expressed as a fixed sum of DM320 million.
2   Expressed as a fixed sum of 11.25 MAU.
3   Expressed as a fixed sum of 5 billion Lire.
4   Sponsoring countries were liable if they could not find contributing country.
Source: Madders 1997, pp.167–168.

Subsequent to this meeting, the ELDO Council held in April 1973 decided to cancel Europa 2 because Germany declared that it would not pay any more for Europa 2 except its rundown cost. The decision eventually led to the dissolution of the ELDO since L3S was integrated as the ESRO project, and therefore there was no substantial program for the ELDO without Europa 2. The eventful history of the ELDO came to an end without succeeding in putting a satellite into orbit.

The decision was confirmed in the ESC meeting at Brussels in July 1973. After a lengthy discussion, L3S (renamed as Ariane in October 1973), Spacelab, and Marots were adopted as ESRO special projects. The meeting also decided that the financial responsibilities for these programs were given to the sponsoring countries — France for L3S, Germany for Spacelab, and Britain for Marots — and the prime contractors should be chosen from these countries in return. In the case of L3S, CNES was entrusted for overall management and development. And with regard to the cancellation of Europa 3 and *de facto* dissolution of the ELDO, the ESC was ordered to set up a committee to draft a single European Space Agency.

Conclusion

The beginning of European space collaboration coincided with the 'space race' between the superpowers. Such an external environment had shaped and limited the choices of national policy logics and institutional arrangements at European level. In the beginning, the idea of European collaboration in space was inspired by the scientists who had successful experiences of collaboration in CERN and drove national policy logics toward the logics of science. However, the question of launching capability brought different national logics into space development: the British logic of finance, the French logic of technology and commerce, and the German and Italian logic of technology. Thanks to division of work between the ESRO and ELDO, the ESRO could be based on a coherent policy logic of science, but as its activities expanded, the other logics, namely the logics of technology and commerce, emerged to play a role in the ESRO's decision-making process, which eventually led to a series of budgetary difficulties. On the other hand, the ELDO, which stood on a fragile balance of policy logics, experienced consecutive failure, bad management, and as it went along, the Member States turned their backs against unsuccessful and poor institutional performance.

One conclusion that can be drawn from the discussion in this chapter is that the stability of programs depended on a coherence of policy logic. While the ESRO stagnated due to the crush of policy logics, the programs proved unstable and unsuccessful. Once the policy logics of Member States were converged into the logics of technology and commerce in the development of application satellites, then programs were successfully carried out. However the convergence of policy logics could not happen without significant institutional changes. The introduction of the principle of *juste retour* and optional participation made it possible to proceed to the ESRO's programs under a complicated mixture of policy logics. The package deal, an extreme form of optional participation, was indeed the final answer to end the crush of national logics.

The ELDO was also a good example as to how incoherent policy logics undermined the stability of a program. Because the policy logics of Member States were so diversified and divergent, the ELDO had to choose an awkward system of three nationally-developed stages, and that caused a lot of trouble in terms of program management, which was never solved until its dissolution.

Two external forces played significant roles. On the one hand, the commercial success of telecommunications programs by the American government and industry changed the policy environment around space development. The European governments recognized the widening gap of technological competence, and therefore, they aimed to achieve a higher technological level in order to compete for commercial programs. However, their objectives were seriously constrained by the American decision not to provide a launch service for operational satellites, and eventually led European governments, particularly the French, to strengthen its logic of autonomy.

Another important factor in the process of institutional change was the leadership, or norm entrepreneurship, of a few distinguished individuals. Nothing was more important than the role played by Edoardo Amaldi and Pierre Auger, with the support of Massey in the beginning of European space collaboration. Also other personalities in charge of the ESRO and ELDO management had influenced the course of institutional development. Jean-Pierre Causse, Hermann Bondi, Theo Lefèvre, and Robert Aubinière were individuals who have mobilized their ideas and efforts to find a middle ground of different national policy logics under certain institutional arrangements.

As far as the movement of European integration was concerned, European space collaboration provided little inspiration. Ruling out the Euratom model and choosing the CERN model separated two movements, and two 'international' organizations had lives of their own. National governments were jealously protecting their national industry and decision-making authority for space in their hands. In other words, Europe was an option instead of a *necessity* particularly for big countries during the ESRO and ELDO years.

Notes

1   Satellite launch is constrained by the rotation of the Earth and relative distance to the objects in space, therefore spacecraft has to be launched within a certain period of time to maximise the efficiency of the rocket. This is called a 'launch window'.

2   Prof. Reimer Lüst, who was Chairman of the Scientific and Technical Committee of ESRO and later became Director-General of the European Space Agency, identified five individuals (Club of Five) who were most influential in the process of setting up European space collaboration: Edoardo Amaldi, Pierre Auger, Hendrik van de Hulst, Freddie Lines and Sir Harrie Massey (Lüst 1984).

3   Euroluna was a proposal to develop an Apollo-type programme to send a probe to the moon.

4   Blue Streak itself did not have satellite-launching capacity, but was being used as the first stage. Black Knight was developed as an upper-stage of Blue Streak.

5   The Helios US-German programme was a cooperative solar probe project from the late-1960s to the early 1970s. It had nothing to do with the French-Italian-Spanish military satellite Helios programme in 1980s-90s.

6   The importance of this military technology was even multiplied by the success of the French nuclear test in the Sahara Desert in February 1960.

7   This meeting is also famous for the Concorde supersonic aircraft agreement.

8   In this study, I use Germany for Federal Republic of Germany unless there is no specification.

9   Krige suggests that at one point: Thorneycroft had permission to accept up to a 60% share of the project, and he was prepared to spend up to £42 million. On the other hand, the original Blue Streak-Black Knight was estimated to cost £50 million ... (Krige 1993c, pp.27–28).

10 La Vaillée (1984) argued that "Belgium has vigorously defended the need for a coherent space programme on a sufficiently large scale to guarantee the independence of Europe in a field rich in subsidiary benefits" (p.96).

11 Comsat was jointly owned by US communications carriers such as AT&T, ITT and RCA, and by private investors. Although it was a 'private' corporation, it was given the signatory status of Intelsat.

12 The first experimental satellite, Telstar, was launched in 1962, but it was injected into low elliptical orbit, so that the time to communicate through satellite was limited. Syncom series was, on the other hand, launched in 1963 and orbited in geostationary satellite, which provided stable communications for 24 hours.

13 The membership grew to 48 of which Comsat held 55% and Europe held a 27.5% share in 1966. It became a 63–country organisation with a 52.6% Comsat share and a 26.6% European share in 1968. Currently 143 countries are the members of Intelsat and the European share (28.50%) has overtaken the Comsat share (10.83%), though the latter still is the largest shareholder (Russo 1993a, p.12; Intelsat 1999).

14 It is interesting to note that the French government took a completely opposite attitude towards the risk of advanced technology in the ESRO and ELDO. In the case in the ESRO, the French government did not want the British-German proposal for high-risk technology for the LAS programme, but in the case in the ELDO, it wanted a new design and technology for a new launcher. Nevertheless in both cases, the French claims were favoured for its industry.

15 Perigee and apogee are a lowest and highest point of orbit. PAS concept was to equip motors to kick satellite at Perigee to bring it into geostationary orbit.

16 The slogan was publicly expressed in the 1963 Labour Conference in Scarborough by Wilson. Wilson was strongly influenced by the Association of Scientific Workers, an association of left-wing scientists. To see how British left-wing science logic coalition with 'norm entrepreneurs' such as Alfred Robins and Hugh Gaitskell developed its position in Labour politics, see Horner (1993).

17 The Black Arrow programme was cancelled when the British government decided to take part in the Ariane programme.

18 To compensate this reduction, Germany shouldered 27% from 22%, Belgium and Netherlands 9% from 5.5% together, and Italy 12% from 9.78%.

19 In July 1966, the ELDO Ministerial Council decided to move the launch pad from Woomera, Australia to Kourou, French Guiana, despite strong opposition from Australia. Since Australia lost its reason to remain as a Member State of ELDO, it withdrew from it.

20 Soon after the success of the first experimental satellite, the US government launched the Defence Satellite Communication Systems (DSCS) for military purpose in 1963.

21 Although SKYNET 1 was built by the American firm (Philco Ford), the SKYNET 2 satellites which were launched in 1974 were developed under the prime-contractorship of British company: Marconi (Hayward 1996).

22 As an immediate result, the British companies received the contracts from NATO to develop military satellites.

23 Sweden was an interesting exception. In 1967, Saab-Scania won a contract for the telemetry, tracking and command system for TD1A satellite. If it was not awarded, Sweden might have joined the group of unsatisfactory countries (Stiernstedt 1984).

24 The form of consortia emerged as a practical habit among European companies in mid-1960s, and finally settled down to three consortia with fixed partnership around 1970. These consortia loosely existed after the introduction of the principle of 'juste retour' and the establishment of the ESA until beginning of the 1980s.

25 In reality, it was not possible to distribute contracts in exact proportion of contribution, so that the concept of 'coefficient' became the heart of the debate. See the argument below.

26 The voting rights in Intelsat were distributed according to the share. At this point, American Comsat had more than 50% of the total share, which meant natural veto power for Comsat in simple majority voting. However, Intelsat Member States could overrule American veto if two-thirds of Member States were against the American vote.

27 NASA even hired a consulting firm, Mathematica, to produce a thorough economic analysis (Mark 1987, p.49).

28 One example is that when Germany proposed a reusable rocket in mid-1980s, it was named after Sänger.

29 The experience of Europeanization of Meteosat had important implications in the case of the Europeanization of the SPOT satellite. See next chapter.

Chapter 4

From Ariane to Columbus: The Logics of Autonomy and Technology in the Early ESA Years

After a long and difficult struggle to establish a stable institutional framework during the 1960s and early 1970s, Europe finally found a feasible institutional arrangement that satisfied the wide diversity of national policy logics. The foundation of this institutional arrangement was largely reflected in the institutions of the new single European organization, the European Space Agency (ESA). Unlike the experiences of ESRO and ELDO, in its first decade ESA seemed to be steadily carrying out new programs and those programs produced good results. However, Europe found itself again in a difficult position in the middle of the 1980s, because of the American proposal for the International Space Station (ISS).

This chapter seeks to analyze the interaction between the new institutions of European space collaboration and the reformation of national policy logic from the mid-1970s to the late-1980s. It considers, first, the way in which the institutions of European collaboration were defined by the ESA Convention, particularly in terms of the relationship with national programs and articulation of different national logics. Then it focuses on the effects and consequences of American offers for ISS programs and how the policy logic of Member States changed. This chapter, in contrast to the previous one, puts more emphasis on how European institutions shaped the strategies and policy logic of Member States of ESA and, consequently, the outcome of negotiations at the European level, as we assume that the institutions under the ESA framework were established and relatively stabilized. It will also pay attention to the process of institutional development at national level, since European decisions had a significant impact on the formation of national space policy institutions.

Establishing the European Space Agency

The implementation of the decision to begin three new programs as a 'package-deal' and to establish the new European Space Agency (ESA) at the 1973 ESC Brussels meeting was hardly secured amidst the changing political and economic environment in Europe. First of all, the oil crisis following the decision of OPEC countries to quadruple the oil price in 1973 caused a significant increase in the prices of high-tech materials and a highly inflationary economy. It was thought that the estimated cost of new programs, particularly Ariane and Spacelab, would be too excessive to maintain the political and financial commitment of the sponsoring governments of the two programs, France and Germany. Given the experience of ELDO and ESRO, budget overruns would be considered the first reason for the failure of a collaborative program.

More importantly, the results of elections held in some European countries in 1974 cast doubt on the future of the 1973 agreement. The Schmidt government replaced the Brandt government after the election in May of 1974, and Hans Matthöfer, who had little enthusiasm for long-term space policy, took over as Minister for Science and Technology. More seriously, Valery Giscard d'Estaing who was newly elected as French President in May of 1974, had been known as a space-antagonist while he was the Minister of Finance during the Pompidou presidency. The Ariane launcher — the central program of the 1973 'package-deal' — seemed to be at risk because Giscard d'Estaing had strongly protested against it.

His central concern was that the expenditure for Ariane was motivated solely by French and European autonomy, and it would be more economical for Europe to buy launch vehicles as well as application satellites from the United States (Lévy 1984). He and the new Minister for Industry and Research, Michel d'Ornano, ordered a moratorium on Ariane development and a review of French and European space policy. They even considered cooperating with the Soviet Union, on the basis of the bilateral treaty of 1966, to use Soviet vehicles for satellite launch, which was ultimately declined by the Soviet authorities. While some European governments, particularly Belgium, protested quite fiercely over the decision of Giscard d'Estaing to suspend the Ariane program, Germany decided to wait for the conclusion of the French review, which meant that Germany might possibly reduce its commitment not only to Ariane but Spacelab, depending on the outcome (Geens 1984).

With support from the French Ministry of Defense, Ministry of Foreign Affairs and a majority of the space industry, CNES officials went on a "'crusade' to defend Ariane" (Carlier and Gilli 1994, p.42). At the end of 1974, the Ministry of Industry, responsible for studying the launch market and cost-efficiency of Ariane, concluded that it was essential to continue the Ariane program on two conditions: renegotiating the ESA Convention to be more encouraging for 'Europeanization', i.e. to transfer national programs to ESA; and significantly reducing the national programs, the Diamant in particular (Lévy 1984; Carlier and Gilli 1994). The reduction of the national budget and increasing Europeanization of national programs were resented by many CNES engineers who would cause a greater problem in 1976 (see the section below on the SPOT program).

For some non-ESRO/ELDO Member States, the shift to a single European agency was a good opportunity to reconsider their membership, but the only country that officially applied was Ireland. Irish scientists and industrialists saw this as an opportunity to strengthen their weaker high-tech industrial base, though it was difficult to convince financial authorities in Ireland where space industry was almost non-existent, with no comparable technological expertise in this area. However, the Irish government somehow "could see the sense of the contribution that would arise in favor of development of high-technology industry and also of the possible emergence in due course, based on these benefits, of a real space activity" (Manahan 1984, p.91), and accepted membership of ESA in 1976.

Other possible candidates, Austria and Norway in particular, did not submit their applications to ESA, largely due to financial constraints, despite their status as

ESRO observers. In Norway, for example, industrialists and the Ministry of Foreign Affairs — in light of its application to the EEC — made a strong case for joining ESA, while scientists found that the consequences of staying out of ESRO had not been too harmful. Its Andøya Rocket Range and Tromsø stations were used for various scientific experiments in upper-atmospheric research using sounding rockets. Although the referendum of 1972 rejected Norway's accession to the EEC, the Ministry of Foreign Affairs continued to persuade relevant ministries to be in favor of membership in ESA, while ESA Member States expected Norway to join in order to reduce their financial shares. However, the National Council for Scientific and Industrial Research (NTNF) as well as the Ministries of Industry and Finance concluded that the industrial return would not be satisfactory in relation to the financial obligation, and space research would jeopardize other research projects, particularly in that time of economic downturn and tight budgets (Collett 1995). Norway, in fact, opted out of ESA, but maintained its relationship with the organization, and eventually participated in the Marecs program because of the pressure from ESA Member States, particularly Britain, to join the program in order to share the cost. This *ad hoc* cooperation was soon to be abandoned for two reasons: first, the Norwegian government wanted to participate in the decision-making process as long as it was participating in the program; and second, the increase in oil prices brought a fortune for Norway — it became a net-exporter in 1975 — and space technology, particularly remote sensing and data analysis technology, became important for exploiting its natural resources. Norwegian industrialists again pressed the government hard to change its policy. This time there was no reason for the government to oppose the idea of joining ESA (Landmark 1984). Eventually Norway became an Associate Member in 1981, and a full Member State in 1987, together with Austria.

Thus, the ESA Convention was adopted by eleven countries, Belgium, Denmark, France, Germany, Ireland, Italy, The Netherlands, Spain, Sweden, Switzerland, and the United Kingdom, during the seventh and last ESC meeting in Brussels in April 1975 (the Convention came into force on 30 October 1980, but ESA began its *de facto* operation in 1975). Technically, the ESA Convention was a successor to the ESRO Convention, but there were important changes in the rules and procedures of space collaboration in Europe.

ESA Convention

The ESA Convention is largely based on the ESRO Convention, adding important institutional developments during the 1960s and early 1970s with one new article (Article VII on industrial policy) and five Annexes. We shall examine some of its important aspects and changes.

Coherence of activities The Convention sets up four purposes for ESA in Article II: long-term policy, activities, coordination, and industrial policy. The first purpose was inevitably necessary for the new Agency because of its optional participation mechanism and the principle of *juste retour*. The introduction of these two rules implied that ESA would become an agency for accommodating incoherent and *ad hoc* cooperation for the patchwork of programs driven by national policy logics.

Thus, the Convention had to make sure, in the first place, that there would be integrity and coherence in ESA's programs based on long-term policy (LTP). In order to maintain coherence, the Convention granted the Director-General (DG) authority to plan the LTP, to initiate new programs, and to implement them.[1] Although Member States do not necessarily adopt the DG's draft on LTP, the authority given to the ESA Executive is much more significant than that of ESRO.

The second purpose, elaborating and implementing activities, laid out a strong emphasis on application programs. It sent a clear message that European space activities no longer concentrated on scientific activities as ESRO did, but on applications. Nevertheless, science programs were considered mandatory and Member States were obliged to contribute according to their proportion of GNP. As in the ESRO Convention, the ESA Convention intended to minimize political intervention from Member States by giving more power to the Executives to initiate and execute programs which could be approved by the Council by a simple majority. However, Member States demanded that the Executive should not be given too much decision-making power in the area of financial expenditure for science programs. Thus, as in the ESRO Convention, the decision as to the level of resources for the coming five-year period still requires unanimity (Bonnet and Manno 1994, p.28).

The other important point is that both mandatory and optional activities should serve "exclusively peaceful purposes" (Article II). The clause on peaceful purposes was also in the ESRO Convention, but it was more important for ESA since the latter included launcher development activities which still had a close link with missile development. The smaller countries, particularly the neutral countries such as Sweden and Switzerland, strongly insisted that the 'peaceful purpose' clause be inserted to ensure that ESA would not develop Ariane in order to support military activities, while the big countries, France in particular, did not have any difficulty accepting it. However, given the nature of 'dual use technology', a distinction between military and civilian uses for technology was hard to establish. Three programs inherited from ESRO could possibly be used for military purposes: meteorological data from Meteosat; navigation signals from Aerosat; and the Ariane rocket for launching military satellites. In fact, the last case was contested when Britain decided to launch its military communication satellite (Skynet 4) by Arianespace. ESA Member States generally agreed, nevertheless, that the concept of 'peaceful purposes' meant developing 'non-military' technology, i.e. the ESA should not deliberately develop space technology for military purposes. Therefore, the use of Ariane to launch military satellites was not an infringement of the ESA Convention, because it was not deliberately developed for this purpose (Madders 1997, p.185).

Europeanization   One of the new features introduced in the ESA Convention was the positive encouragement of 'Europeanization' (or 'internationalization' in the text). Concerning the substantial activities at a national level during the 1960s and 70s, the Convention obliged Member States to announce their national programs and encouraged the individual countries to offer them to ESA as collaborative programs in order to avoid unnecessary duplication and competition between ESA and national space agencies (Annex IV). Therefore, the exchange of information, facilities, and personal was strongly encouraged when not inconsistent with national security or third-party arrangements. Indeed, the ambitions of the Convention go beyond coordinating the European space program and national programs, to encompass "integrating [national programs] progressively and as completely as possible into the European space program, in particular as regards the development of applications satellites" (Article II-c). The experience in 1973, when Ariane, Spacelab, and Meteosat programs were integrated into European activities, provided some examples of how Europeanization should proceed, but some Member States, France and Germany in particular, were not entirely convinced that all national programs should be integrated. Nevertheless, the formal requirement gave an additional impetus to the process.

The other aspect of Europeanization is the preference for a European launcher. From their experience with the Europa programs, some Member States, particularly France, demanded it be put in the text that ESA and Member States give preference to Ariane. Although Ariane was widely accepted as the next generation launcher and basic technologies were proven in the successful French Diamant program, there were some Member States, Britain in particular, who were skeptical about the reliability of Ariane. As in the decision of the ESC meeting at Bad Godesberg in 1968, the British delegation demanded that they should not be obliged to use Ariane for every satellite launch. After long negotiations between France and Britain, the Convention stated that ESA and Member States should grant preference to Ariane "if this does not present an unreasonable disadvantage" compared with other available launchers at the envisaged time "in respect of cost, reliability and mission suitability" (Article VIII-1). Unlike the Bad Godesberg decision, there was no explicit benchmark for what constitutes 'unreasonable disadvantage' which might be a potential source of conflict (Massey and Robins 1986, p.239). However, the success of the Ariane program reduced the likelihood of conflict over giving preference to Ariane.

Industrial Policy of ESA

Perhaps the most significant departure from the ESRO Convention was the introduction of an industrial policy clause in the main body of the text of the ESA Convention. As we saw in the last chapter, the industrial policy of ESRO, which was based on the principle of competitive bidding, was completely distorted by the introduction of principle of *juste retour*, adopted to satisfy strong demands from some Member States and to save the organization from crisis. The space industry in the majority of Member States was still in its infancy, and there were important differences in the level of industrial development between larger and smaller countries. Indeed, all the Member States wanted to protect their national industries. The discussions of the Industrial and Contract Policy Subgroup, which was responsible for drafting the rules and procedures of industrial policy for the Convention, were based entirely on the principle of the rule of *juste retour*. The Member States recognized that there were significant differences in European industry and that there was a need for the principle of *juste retour*, but the question was posed whether this was a means or an end for industrial policy. For some countries, it was simply the means to fix the imbalances in industrial capabilities which would be converged at some point through *juste retour*, and therefore the principle should be applied for a limited period of time (Krige 1993e). On the other hand, some small countries, particularly Belgium and Sweden, demanded that the rule should be implemented as rigorously as possible in return for participation in major optional programs (Stiernstedt 1995, p.34). Thus, as Duran (1993) argues, Article VII of the Convention came to contain "fundamentally contradictory objectives" (p.73): the Agency tried to reinforce European industrial competitiveness through the use of competitive methods, while optional participation and *juste retour* allowed governments to intervene in the development of industry.

Article VII of the Convention, in detail, states that the industrial policy of ESA shall be designed in particular to:

1–a. meet the requirements of the European space program and the coordinated national space programs in a cost-effective manner;

1–b. improve the world-wide competitiveness of European industry by maintaining and developing space technology and by encouraging the rationalization and development of an industrial structure appropriate to market requirements, making use in the first place of the existing industrial potential of all Member States;

1–c. ensure that all Member States participate in an equitable manner, having regard to their financial contribution, in implementing the European space program and in the associated development of space technology;

1–d. exploit the advantages of free competitive bidding in all cases, except where this would be incompatible with other defined objectives of industrial policy — contradiction between juste retour and international competitiveness.

Right from the start, the term 'cost-effective' puts Article VII in question. We all know that 'cost-effective' means more than just the cheapest price available. Sometimes it is interpreted as 'value for money', but as George van Reeth (1995), former Director of Administration of ESA, argues, "value depends for a major part on individual judgments" (p.102). Given the complex interaction of the differing policy logic of the Member States, how could it be possible to determine the proper 'value' of the program? Perhaps in retrospect, the term 'cost-effective' was interpreted as 'the ESA Executive has to give the best possible management effort to minimize the development cost and to maximize the outcome of the program'. Indeed, the Executive achieved that goal quite successfully in the programs during the 1970s and early 1980s, particularly the Ariane program, despite surging inflationary economic conditions.

The second objective, improving worldwide competitiveness by encouraging rationalization of the industrial structure, was also interpreted in many ways. In general, there seemed to be two ways in which ESA and European industry might considerably improve international competitiveness through rationalization. First, European governments could increase the size of the market by providing additional funding for more programs, while restructuring industry through mergers and acquisitions to gain economy of scale. The American companies — the major competitors in the space market — received an enormous number of contracts through US defense procurement as well as big civilian programs such as the Apollo project. There was no way for European governments to match the size of American public procurement, and, therefore, it was necessary to concentrate on developing the industrial structure to maximize the use of resources. In fact, major restructuring had been going on at a national level during the 1970s in European countries. Nord- and Sud-Aviation merged into Aérospatiale in 1970 in France, Hawker-Siddeley and British Aerospace Corporation merged into British Aerospace in 1977 in Britain, while ERNO merged with VFW in 1969 in Germany. However, these 'national champions' could not reach the size and level of American space industries unless they were merged into 'European champions'. This was not conceivable at the time of the 1970s (Hayward 1986; 1995; Vernon 1974), particularly given the constraints of the principle of *juste retour*.

The other way to achieve the objective was specialization. Given that European industry was not comparable to American industry in terms of size and scale, it would be possible to improve its competitiveness through specializing in particular technology or applications. In fact, the ESA Executive sought a way to concentrate certain technologies in a small number of companies, and some of them were successfully specialized, in particular a technology such as solar panels or radar sensors, at the expense of creating a monopoly in Europe. However, the companies in smaller countries in particular had difficulty specializing in a particular technology because of the ESA rules on optional participation and the principle of *juste retour*. From the company's point of view, optional participation — where government could take part on voluntary basis — did not guarantee continuity for contracts in specific technologies, and the principle of *juste retour* would bring contracts involving technologies in which the company may not have expertise. Indeed, some Member States, Spain and Belgium in particular, were enthusiastic about developing a comprehensive space industry, rather than a specialized one. They spread their resources across various programs and their national industry was forced to shift its resources into diverse areas of research. Of course, such an industrial policy contributed to moving European industry out of its infancy, but it did not immediately contribute to improving the international competitiveness of European industry as a whole.

Nevertheless, it should be noted that the concept of improving international competitiveness was strongly emphasized in the context of autonomous European capability in space. The first Director of Planning and Future Programs of ESA, André Lebeau, wrote in the first year of *de facto* operation of ESA that the importance of the industrial policy of ESA "is the creation of an independent European capability in space applications. Independence here does not mean isolation or refusal to cooperate, but refusal to accept uncontrolled dependence" (Lebeau 1976, p.3). This suggests that the logic of autonomy was the key driving force behind at least one of the concepts of ESA industrial policy.

The third objective, equitable participation in relation to financial contributions, or the principle of *juste retour*, had already been implemented during the ESRO years, but the definition of 'equitable participation' needed to be specified in the new

Convention. First of all, Annex V of the Convention states that the target coefficient is to achieve a return of 1 – the value of a contract has to be 100% of the contribution – and that ESA shall intervene if the coefficient of certain Member States goes below 0.8, instead of the 0.7 that had been decided in 1968 in ESRO. These rigid rules of industrial return would inevitably reduce the margin of flexibility in industrial contracts and could increase the possibility of creating an inefficient industrial structure in Europe. The other important question was whether the coefficient should be calculated by overall return or by programs. Since optional programs allow Member States to participate and contribute voluntarily to programs, the calculation of return became a very complex issue, particularly when a company in a Member State not participating in a program received a contract for that program (Imbert and Grilli 1994). Thus, the Convention adopted the principle of overall industrial return, not a return per program, philosophy. Article II-1 of Annex V only states that "within each optional program ...", particular *preference* shall be given to industry and organizations in the participating States" (emphasis added), instead of exclusive obligation. However, in practice Member States demanded that a coefficient of 1 be achieved during the 1980s, hence the principle of overall industrial return became unconvincing for those Member States which received less in contracts than 100% of their financial contribution. Thus the procedure for contract distribution became more oriented towards return per program calculation (Dondi 1980).

The concept of equitable participation also posed a question on the 'equitable voting rights' of participating states in relation to their contributions. Article XI-6–a defines that each Member State "have one vote in the Council" on matters in which they take part. The concept of 'one state, one vote' was contested by some countries, particularly the big ones, which claimed that programs should be decided by those who pay through proportional voting rights (Lafferranderie 1988). The introduction of the so-called 'double two-thirds majority' procedure – which means that a decision has to be taken by two-thirds of all participating states which shall include at least two-thirds of contributions to the program (Annex III of the Convention), insofar as decisions to start a new phase or to terminate a program – was a response to those claims. However, the principle of 'one state, one vote' remained the central voting system, because there was a sort of *de facto* leadership of the major contributing states, and it would be impossible to implement programs without acknowledging the demands of the big countries. In other words, there was no need for a proportional voting system since Member States participated in programs on a voluntary basis through the 'optional participation' framework.

The fourth objective – use of competitive bidding where compatible with other objectives – also seemed a difficult objective to reach, because the principles of *juste retour* and optional participation opened up the road for big companies to take subcontracts. Small companies in Member States, the big countries in particular, were under significant competitive pressure to get subcontracts in ESA programs, since big companies in the same countries were not always the recipients of the prime contracts due to the rotation system within the industrial consortium or the sponsorship of the program. Therefore, big companies were forced to play the same role as small and specialized companies (van Reeth 1995). Even when a big company received the prime contract, small companies in the same country suffered because the prime contractor would take as large a share of the work as possible within the limits of geographical return (Müller 1989). On the one hand, it helped to create a strongly competitive environment even under the principle of juste retour, but, on the other, it tended to produce an unfair and unstable market environment for smaller companies.

To sum up, the purposes and rules of ESA industrial policy proved to be ambiguous and contradictory, due to the fact that the Convention rested on a compromise between the diverse policy logics of the Member States. However, the lack of integrity in industrial policy provided a certain flexibility for Member States and the ESA Executive to interpret the Convention on a case-by-case basis, and in the end, they were able to avoid possible conflicts between different policy logics. Until the late 1990s, the industrial policy was largely accepted by the majority of the Member States because of this flexibility and a steady increase in the ESA budget that helped European industry improve its competitiveness. Nevertheless, the principles and practices of ESA industrial policy would be challenged again when the commercialization of the space market became a more important game in the late 1990s (see next chapter).

The Effect of ESA Industrial Policy on European Space Industry

Even though the practices of juste retour and optional participation began during the ESRO years, the formal implementation of them as ESA industrial policy had a gradual effect on the shape of the European space industry. The most significant impact was the expansion of political intervention in the awarding of prime contracts. The introduction of optional participation gave national delegations the opportunity to nominate the prime contractors for the programs they sponsored. Prime contractor is the most attractive contract for a company since it is the most profitable part of program development and enables the company to develop management experience in complex projects, in addition to garnering prestige and influence over European industry. However, because of *juste retour*, the prime contractors could expect to receive less than 20% of total contract value, which is too small a share to achieve an efficient prime-sub contractor relationship. It was far less than prime contractors in the United States, which generally received about 50–60% of the value of contract (Müller 1989).

The new ESA industrial policy has influenced the pattern of industrial behavior to a large extent. Consortia were gradually dissolved and political intervention became a more significant factor for determining prime contractors and the promotion of specific technologies. Through the first ten years of ESA operation, the industrial policy settled into a more programme-to-programme based organization, while distribution of contracts was getting closer to a coefficient of 1. However, a fundamental contradiction in industrial policy, competitiveness and equitable return, remained unsolved for a while.

Organizational Structure of ESA

The ESA Convention defines a very simple organizational structure for ESA. It consists of two principal organizations, a Council as the only decision-making body, and an Executive led by the Director-General (DG). Article XI and XII define the procedure and responsibilities of these bodies.

Council and supporting bodies The Council, the decision-making body, consists of the representatives (senior officials from space agencies or relevant government ministries) of Member States with full voting power and representatives from Associate Member States and (since the late 1980s) the European Commission. Compared to the ESRO Convention, the voting procedure was much simpler and more straightforward. Apart from the financial arrangements (level of resources) for mandatory programs[2] which is still taken by a unanimity[3] – as in the ESRO Convention – and the general budget which is adopted by a two-thirds majority, most decisions are taken by a simple majority, including the adoption of new programs, both mandatory and optional.[4] This simplicity in voting procedure is largely due to the separation of decision-making for optional programs from the Council. Since some Member States may not take part in optional programs, the decisions will not be made in the Council but by Program Boards where only the participating states attend and vote for certain programs by unanimity. In addition, for mandatory programs, the simple majority rule was retained from the ESRO exercises to protect the autonomy of scientists.

As far as policy coherence is concerned, the Convention suggested that the Agency could hold Council meetings at the ministerial level to establish a long-term policy for European space activities. However, the Convention put forward a very ambivalent definition of ministerial meetings. The only reference to them is in Article XI-8-b – the Council shall elect a chairman for a meeting when it meets at ministerial level – and there it lacks explicit definition and procedures. Part of the reason for this is that it was assumed that the majority of the responsibilities of the Council would be dealt with by the Council at delegate level. The institutionalization of optional participation and the principle of *juste retour* by the ESA Convention provided a sense of relief for the Convention drafters (mainly from national administration and space agencies) in that there would be no more political struggle over contributions and industrial returns, the major subject at ESC meetings (Loosch 1993). Nevertheless, the history of ESA proved that such predictions by the Convention drafters were wrong, and the Council at ministerial level has become a regular feature of decision-making for LTP since 1985. The lack of formal definitions and procedures notwithstanding, the practice of Ministerial Councils became well-institutionalized in the context of the ESA decision-making process to supplement the lack of coherence and political weight in the Convention.

The role of Director-General and Executive One of the lessons learnt from the experience of ESRO and ELDO was the importance of the role of the Secretariat (Executive in ESA jargon) in trying to ensure the integrity and coherence of the programs and long-term policy. The officials who came from ESRO to draft the ESA Convention insisted on increasing the responsibility and competence of the Executive, while the representatives of the Member States were against it. At the end of the negotiations, the representatives, recognizing the importance of the Executive, conceded to some extent and agreed that the roles of Director-General (DG) and Executive should be expanded, although the ultimate decision-making power remained with the Council.

The most important addition to the power of the DG was the right of initiative. Although ESRO DGs took initiatives occasionally in cases of procedural deadlock or budgetary crisis, the ESA DG was given formal recognition and authority to be the mediator in times of crisis. More importantly, the ESA DG was granted exclusive authority to initiate long-term policy and relatively autonomous power to initiate programs.[5] Although the Member States have the ultimate power to alter a proposal from the DG on long-term policy or programs, it is less common that the Council rejects or dramatically amends the proposal. In other words, the right of initiative gives the ESA DG more autonomy to shape the grand design of ESA policy. The ESA DG was also given the power to draft agendas for the Council meetings, at both delegate and ministerial levels. As many studies on agenda-setting claim, the power to set agendas gives an "initial crucial veto point in the policy process at which [DG] can exercise [its] power, either to make policies happen, or to prevent anything from happening that would diminish the well-being" (Peters 1994, p.9). The rights of initiative and agenda-setting gave the ESA DG significant control over the decision-making process, albeit without formal voting rights.

Nevertheless, it is also true that the ESA DG was required to carry on close consultation with the Member States in order to formulate long-term policy and Council agenda. His proposals had to be approved by the Member States, and without their accord, he could not obtain the financial resources to execute his plans. Therefore, one should be careful not to overestimate the rights of initiative and agenda-setting granted the ESA DG.

Summary

To a large extent, the ESA Convention spelled out the rules and practices developed during the later stage of the ESRO and ELDO years. The principles of *juste retour* and optional participation were again strongly supported by the smaller countries within the logic of (national) autonomy and technology in order to protect their industries, while the big countries became increasingly selective about their participation in programs, compensating the lack of programs at the European level with national programs. The new institutional framework under the ESA Convention was, in short, adjusted to accommodate the differences in national policy logic.

However, there were some new features added to the institutions of European space collaboration. The concept of 'Europeanization' and the strengthening of the Executive to maintain the coherence of programs were introduced in the Convention to prevent the ESA from becoming a confederation of programs, rather than a collective body for activities. This new set of institutions, it was hoped, would function to create a sense of European solidarity in space activities and lead to further 'integration' of programs. We shall see how this new institutional framework shaped the policy-making and implementation of programs in the early period of ESA operation (1975–85).

Early Programs of ESA

The European Space Agency began its life with a busy schedule of programs carried over from the ESRO years. Science programs, such as the ISEE (International Sun/ Earth Explorer) and IUE (International Ultraviolet Explorer), both in cooperation with NASA, were crammed into the laboratories of ESTEC, while new optional application programs — Ariane, Spacelab, Marots, as well as OTS, Aerosat and Meteosat — were lined up to be developed under the new Agency. Such a high volume of programs and workloads added more complexity and difficulties to ESA management, which was occupied in coping with the new rules and procedures of *juste retour*. It is not my intention to explain the details of these programs, but to provide an overview of how the ESA Executive and Member States managed to take advantage of the new institutions.

Science Program

Perhaps it was the scientists who had to cope with the change in institutions the most. The logic of science was no longer to be the priority for many Member States, and the institutional and financial protection that ESRO had provided faced possible weakening as a result of expanding the role of the agency. For scientists from big countries in particular, the weakened status of the logic of science in ESA encouraged them to look for national programs. By the mid-1980s, there were more national scientific programs than ESA programs, and scientists from big countries were not wholeheartedly involved in ESA programs, unlike those from smaller countries without a national space program or agency. In order to attract the half-hearted scientists and unwilling Member States for increasing the level of resources, SSAC (Space Science Advisory Committee) produced a report stating that European programs under ESRO/ESA had been less expensive than those under national space agencies, and that the European programs were efficient, though the rule of *juste retour* was mitigating that efficiency (ESA 1978, pp.24–25).

The other problem for the young Agency was the question of resources. The funding for science programs remained at the same level as the ESRO budget (or even less, taking inflation into account). Moreover, an expected increase in launch costs due to the use of Ariane and the expansion of the scope of research to include microgravity research would mean that the distribution of resources for existing disciplines might be reduced significantly. Serious funding constraints forced national delegations and scientists to reconsider the balance of resource distribution among disciplines. Under such circumstances, the ESA Director of Planning and Future Programs André Lebeau asked the Space Science Advisory Committee to undertake a discussion on a long-term strategy for scientific activities in 1977. SSAC then proposed to the Council that it increase the level of resources for mandatory programs in the light of the emergence of new disciplines, but the Council in June 1979 could not reach an agreement, largely because of strong opposition from France and Britain. The French space community tended to prefer national programs and cooperative programs with the United States and the Soviet Union, so the increase in the ESA budget for science would mean that the resources would be diverted to an unfavorable destination. On the other hand, British scientists considered that the level of resources should not be increased because of the difficult economic situation in Europe, although they favored a European program. Britain even argued that it would not be possible for ESA to commit to every field of space science, and therefore, ESA should leave some sub-fields within each discipline to the United States or the Soviet Union. The smaller countries, notably Belgium, Denmark, The Netherlands, Sweden, and Switzerland, argued favorably for the SSAC proposal since their science programs depended heavily on ESA programs (Russo 1997b, pp.14–16). Despite the protests from the smaller countries, the ESA procedures require unanimity for decisions concerning the level of resources, and at the end of the debate, the mandatory budget did not increase as SSAC expected.

Horizon 2000

Frustrated by the financial constraints, European scientists as well as industrialists increased their pressure on the ESA Executive to guarantee a certain frequency of programs to develop research and technical expertise for industry. They threatened ESA that both scientists and industry "would abandon space activities unless medium-sized programs were to be undertaken by ESA every year" (Bonnet and Manno 1994, p.36). However, the Member States were not even attempting to achieve the required unanimity to meet the demand from scientists and industrialists in the beginning of the 1980s. The breakthrough came through an interesting collaboration of ESA Executives and scientists to develop an ambitious plan to reflect the expectations of the scientists, which was later called 'Horizon 2000'.

Horizon 2000 was a long-term strategy plan looking twenty-years ahead with four 'cornerstone programs' and a cluster of programs to maintain a balance between disciplines (ESA 1984b). The beauty of this strategy was to mix large and small programs to respond flexibly to contingencies and scientific evolution. The 'cornerstone' programs were typical 'multi-purpose' programs which would serve several disciplines, whereas the smaller missions were focused more on the needs of particular disciplines (see Figure 4.1). It also strategically used international cooperation to reduce development costs so that they fit within realistic budgetary limits. Neither ESA nor ESRO had a plan of this kind with a long-term vision and commitment within given limited funding, and in this sense, it was revolutionary to conceive such a well-structured plan.

The ESA Executive immediately endorsed the plan with full support. Erik Quitsgaard, the ESA DG, guaranteed that the plan would be on the table at the second Ministerial Council[6] in 1985. Surprisingly, the Member States unanimously agreed to raise the level of resources for the next five years to meet the requirements of Horizon 2000.

One possible explanation for the behavior of the Member States was, of course, that the structure of the plan convinced them that the programs were feasible within the financial requirements. But it can also be explained by the mood of the Ministerial meeting in 1985, held in Rome, which was quite high-spirited because of the proposal of new programs to participate in the International Space Station (see below). The positive feelings toward the logic of (European) autonomy — often referred to as 'the spirit of Rome' — might have influenced the process of decision-making in favor of Horizon 2000. The plan was also discussed in the Council (at delegate level) in 1988 for the third-year review of the five-year period, but again the Member States agreed to continue Horizon 2000 for another five years without any changes. The position of Britain in this process was particularly interesting. Since the Council required unanimity for approval of the third-year review, Britain had veto power over the continuation of Horizon 2000. Just a year before the meeting, Britain had famously exited from all European manned-space programs (Hermes, Ariane 5, and Columbus: see below) for financial and political reasons, and many expected the same would happen with the ambitious Horizon 2000 plan. The British delegation conditioned its endorsement on the outcome of a general review of the management of the Science Program, which was conducted under the chairmanship of the German scientist Klaus Pinkau. The review concluded that there was no fault in the management, and eventually, Britain voted for approval of a 5% increase above inflation for Horizon 2000 for the next five years (Bonnet and Manno 1994, p.66).

The success of Horizon 2000 was a good example of how the ESA institution worked in the 1980s. The clash of the principles of finance and science was resolved through the positive attitude of the scientists and initiative of the ESA Executive to persuade those Member States whose policy logics were inclined toward the principle of (European) autonomy. With some luck in timing, the science program became revitalized to move forward, at least until the mid-1990s.

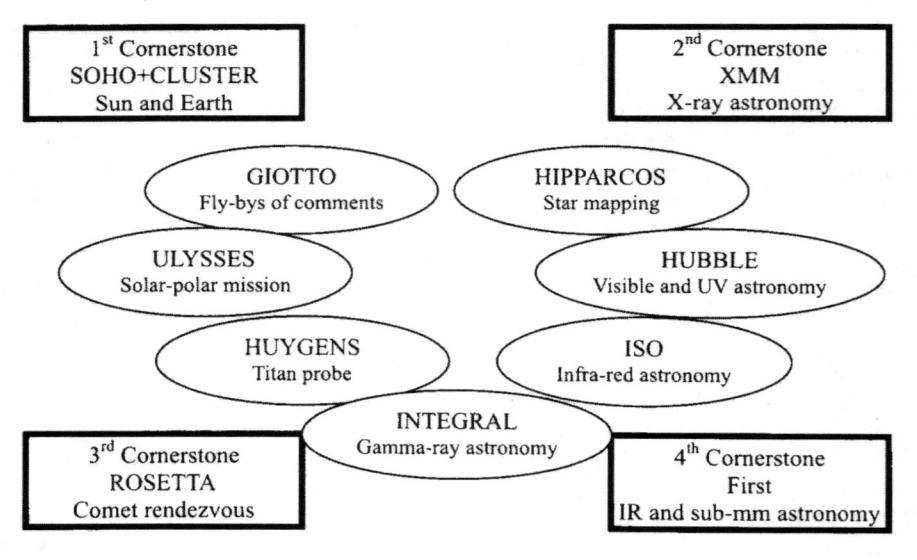

Figure 4.1   Horizon 2000

Optional Programs: Ariane and Arianespace

Participation in optional programs was considered, at least theoretically, as a device to free ESA from political conflict, because the governments were able to participate only when they wished to, and to contribute as much as they chose. However, it did not guarantee that a program would be successful. In different cases, there were several factors that made the process of programs development difficult.

Nothing was more important than the success of the Ariane program for the ESA of the 1970s. Not only was Ariane the largest program, but also its success was also imperative in order to have access to space for application satellites. For CNES, which assumed the responsibility for managing the study phase, failure was an intolerable option. At the beginning of 1976, nevertheless, the program seemed to be experiencing its first problems. CNES insisted on maintaining its role in the production phase, while Germany preferred to delegate the production to industry rather than CNES in order to strengthen the commercial competitiveness. Even before the first launch, a group of representatives from ESA and national space agencies were in disagreement whether to develop beyond the first series of experimental launches,[7] and CNES was forced to re-evaluate the possibility of commercial use of Ariane. The major problem was the institutional difficulties in ESA and CNES to promote commercialization. Certain participating Member States in the Ariane program regarded ESA as a research and development agency, and they were also concerned about the risks and costs of producing a launcher for commercial purposes without any concrete orders from customers. Under these circumstances, the Director of Launch Vehicle for CNES, Frédéric d'Allest, proposed in December 1977 a solution which was to separate commercial activities from the functions of ESA, and set up a commercial company under the close supervision of agencies and industry (d'Allest 1995). The company became known as Arianespace, of which CNES, 36 European companies participating in the production of Ariane and 13 banks held shares, and d'Allest himself became the chairman.

The big potential customer at this point was Intelsat. It was preparing to launch a new series of satellites, Intelsat V, in the early 1980s, and the American Atlas-Centaur and Space Shuttle were already making a move to bid for it. In April 1978, the ESA Council, equipped with the ideas of d'Allest, took the risk of ordering procurement for the production of a series of launch vehicles beyond the existing six without having obtained a firm contract with Intelsat (Creola 1984). Fortunately for Europe, Intelsat was convinced of Ariane's reliability and capability, even though it was yet under development, and selected Ariane as the Intelsat V launcher in 1978. Ariane was successful even before the first launch!

The first launch was a big Christmas present for all the people who were involved in space development in Europe. On 24 December 1979, Europeans saw for the first time a successful three-stage heavy satellite launcher of their own. In fact, Ariane was not only a good launcher, but also a very advanced one made without any help from outside Europe. The American authorities refused to agree to a technical assistance contract between Martin Marietta and Aérospatiale, and restricted the technology transfer to a Swiss consortium responsible for the fairing system which covers the payload container (Carlier and Gilli 1994, p.163). Not only was it an endogenous European effort, but also some of the technologies in the Ariane program were world-class. Ariane was the first application in Europe to use liquid oxygen/liquid hydrogen technology, and NASA, which was struggling with the development of the Space Shuttle, asked to license this technology to manufacture the Space Shuttle's main engines (Creola 1984, p.33).

Ariane was not only commercially and technically successful, but also administratively an outstanding program. First of all, the deadline for launching the first vehicle was set for the end of the 1970s in order to meet the requirements of the Intelsat V contract, and the actual flight took place just a week before the deadline. It was in fact the first major program to meet its original deadline. Secondly, the Ariane program kept within the estimated budget even with the high inflation during the 1970s. France was already committed to pay up to 35% of cost overruns, but if Ariane went beyond this mark, even France would not be able to support the program, and indeed, the program did not break the mark (Bignier 1995). The secret of this success, compared in particular to the ill-fated Europa programs, may be found in the strong central management structure delegated by CNES. Unlike the ELDO management, CNES was able to design a technologically coherent program and to manage efficiently the selection of contractors according to their competence within the constraints of *juste retour*. It conferred strong management authority and structure over contractors and a common understanding of the content of the work of each contractor (d'Allest 1988, p.167). One symbolic, as well as substantial, example of CNES management was the selection of Ferranti. This British company was selected to develop the guidance system because of its strength in Blue Streak, although from the point of view of *juste retour*, selecting a company from a low-contributing country was a politically difficult decision. However, as we discussed above, the ESA Convention allows the selection of a contractor from a non-participating or low-contributing country even if it upsets the balance of industrial returns. CNES took advantage of this rule and gave preference to the logic of technology over the logic of finance.

Aerosat

During the 1960s, air traffic across the Atlantic Ocean increased dramatically and raised concerns for governments on both sides of the Ocean. Air traffic was controlled mainly via a ground operational system that was inefficient and expensive because there were many areas over the Atlantic that the ground navigation system could not cover. The idea of navigating aircraft via a signal from a satellite was welcomed by the American and European governments from the start. For European governments, it would not only increase the safety of air navigation, but also present an opportunity to develop expertise in telecommunication technology and to cooperate with the US in the application program. European governments, represented by ESRO, were already in contact with NASA, the US Department of Transportation and relevant American authorities in 1969, and ESRO signed an MoU (Memorandum of Understanding) in August 1971 with the American Federal Aviation Authority (FAA)[8] to develop two out of four satellites, and to share the cost of launch, administration, and operation. It was also decided that the satellites should be owned jointly by Europe (as a group) and the US, and be managed by the Aerosat Council in which both the US and the Europeans would have one vote (which immediately means that each side has the veto power in the Aerosat Council).

However, the Aerosat program was thrown into chaos because of surging oil prices and subsequent funding problems in 1974–75. The US government became increasingly reluctant to contribute to the program. At the same time, in addition to the cost problem, European airline companies and civil aviation control authorities began to question the usefulness and cost-effectiveness of Aerosat. They proposed using other telecommunication satellites (OTS and Marots) for navigation to reduce the cost. But the final damage was done to Aerosat when the US Department of Defense (DoD) which had been developing its own original military navigation satellite system (Global Positioning System, better known as GPS) announced that the signal from Navstar — GPS satellites — would be available for civilian use subject to some conditions. The DoD claimed that the satellites were developed and would be operated under military budget, and GPS would be totally under the control of the DoD. It implied that the navigation service, vital to air traffic safety, would be unilaterally shut down for military reasons when the US became involved in a military conflict. Loss of control by civilian and European authorities was, for European governments, not the preferred solution, but under the circumstances it was considered a better choice than not having any navigation satellites at all. Nevertheless, the question of military control over a civilian-use navigation system (GPS) continued to be questioned by the European authorities, who would initiate a new satellite navigation program called Galileo in the 1990s (see chapter 7).

Spacelab

Unlike the success of Ariane, Spacelab — the twin in the 'package deal' of 1973 — was not blessed with glory. It was a successful program technologically, but commercially and financially a failure. Not only inflation during the 1970s, but also technical changes, deadline slips, and an uneasy relationship with US authorities and companies had a large impact on the cost of Spacelab development, which had risen to almost 1 billion US dollars, against the 250 million estimate. While the Space Shuttle program was struggling because of technical difficulties and intervention by the Department of Defense (see previous chapter, also see Bizony 1996; McCurdy 1990), Spacelab also had to adjust to the changes in the Shuttle program, which caused further difficulties for European agencies. Despite these managerial problems, cooperation with the US went remarkably well. European (mainly German) industry did not hesitate to count on support from American industry. A German industrialist, Hans Hoffmann, recalled that "we were the people who 'learned lessons from Skylab'", and made the "decision to engage quite a number of consultants from McDonnell Douglas and TRW" (Hoffmann 1995, p.44). NASA helped to sort out any delicate technical problems at every stage of development.

However, the good relationship with the US did not offset the development cost. NASA had projected that the potential uses of Spacelab would be seriously lower than what they had expected in the early 1970s, and the US government decided to add only one additional Spacelab to what it was obligated to buy (one unit), at a cost of $128 million (Logsdon 1991, p.12). ESA Member States, particularly Germany, were devastated by the decision since they had planned to recoup their development costs through the sale of Spacelab to NASA.[9] Furthermore, ESA was not able to afford use of the system because of the high cost of Shuttle launch fees and experiments. NASA and ESA co-funded only one program, Spacelab-1, in 1983, and subsequently launched two Spacelab missions in 1985, while Germany funded its own national mission using Spacelab (D-1) in 1985, in order to stimulate the utilization of Spacelab (Sebesta 1997). However, the Challenger explosion in 1986 had a huge impact on the Shuttle program, and the Spacelab was not used until 1991. Although a technologically advanced spacecraft, Spacelab was not exploited to its maximum performance.

The experience of cooperation for Spacelab with the United States held many lessons for Europe. Firstly, cooperation tended to reflect the balance of power in terms of technology. ESA was put in a secondary role at every stage of development because of the limits of its technical expertise. The cooperation went smoothly in practice because Europeans acknowledged their weakness and accepted the junior role, but deep inside policy-makers' and engineers' minds, they recognized that this technical dependency would jeopardize their ability to control and manage a cooperative program. Secondly, the Spacelab experience taught Europeans to elaborate utilization plans and marketing strategy. The tragic sales record underlined the weakness in forecasting the potential use and cost analysis for the Spacelab utilization program by its own, and to depend on the American forecast. Of course, the American Shuttle was the only customer for Spacelab, and the utilization program was largely defined by NASA, so there was little room for ESA to predict and control what would happen with the utilization program. But it can also be said that European participation in Spacelab was driven by the logic of technology promoted by Germany, and there was less concern for commercial returns from the sales of Spacelab. Finally, the experience of Spacelab taught the structure of cooperation. The post-Apollo program was an American program, and it was difficult for Europe to escape the influence and consequences of American decisions. ESA could not participate in the decision-making process at NASA on the Shuttle program since Americans wanted to have a 'clean interface' in terms of finance and decision-making. ESA Executive and Member States learned that this structural dependence and lack of participation in decision-making would not be a favorable structure for cooperation. In other words, the Member States recognized that the logic of (European) autonomy should be the key policy logic even for cooperative programs.

Policy Logics of Early ESA Programs

Both scientific and optional programs were particularly important in the process of shaping the institutional path of the European Space Agency. Horizon 2000 was a significant achievement in bringing the attention of scientists to ESA, and recuperating the status of the logic of science in the ESA operation. By the same token, the success of the Ariane program proved that optional participation and delegating managerial competence to the sponsoring country was an appropriate approach to a difficult and complex program such as launcher development. It was also a confidence boost for European engineers that they could complete a technologically advanced program without outside help, and, more importantly, the success of Ariane brought autonomous access to space and 'non-dependence' on a US launcher. On the other hand, the two cooperative programs with the United States, Aerosat and Spacelab, were both unsuccessful in many aspects. Under a surging inflation, the cost of Spacelab quadrupled over the estimate, and Aerosat was left to be taken over by the American military GPS system.

These experiences impressed upon the European space community that European space capability had come to a point of departure from American technology, and hence promoted a debate on whether Europe could be — and should be — more autonomous in making decisions, even in the cooperative programs. The logic of (European) autonomy thus came to the center of this debate and began to influence European programs. The new ESA institutions, particularly the optional participation framework, made the decision-making process much easier, so that those Member States which did not share the same policy logic — notably Britain — did not have to be in conflict with the logic of autonomy. However, it should be noted that the rising policy logic of autonomy did not necessarily mean that European countries were more 'integrated' in European programs. The logic of autonomy in this context should be interpreted as a 'non-dependence' on the US, rather than a positive sense of 'European identity'. In fact, as we see below, some Member States shifted the focus of their application programs from European to national programs. Here, again, the institutional aspect, the optional participation, played a big part in the story.

National vs. European Program: Telecom Satellites

Satellite telecommunication was already a part of daily life in the 1970s, and the commercial prospects for services as well as satellite production were increasing all the time. The evolution of Intelsat and, more importantly, the success of Ariane encouraged ESA Member States to develop a telecommunications satellite (Telecomsat). However, the larger countries preferred to develop their expertise through national rather than European programs. This shift to national programs made it more difficult for the smaller Member States to accumulate the technical expertise for telecomsat, also vital to their national industry.

H-Sat/Olympus

In 1975, the ESA Executive proposed a powerful and sophisticated telecomsat program, H-Sat. Responding to an expected market growth, H-Sat aimed primarily to provide Direct Broadcasting Satellite (DBS) technology. European industry as well as the European Broadcast Union (EBU) took the initiative and approached ESA with the proposal that Europe needed to capture a sizeable market share before other countries caught up with the advanced European technology developed under the Eurafrica project. National governments, convinced by the argument from EBU and industry, became enthusiastic about the new program and committed to provide considerable government funding. The competition among industry to get contracts for the H-Sat program was, even under the principle of *juste retour*, quite fierce, since each competing company figured they could recoup the development costs through subsequent sales of satellites (Müller 1989, p.44).

The French and German governments (and industries) were particularly interested in the H-Sat program. They argued that H-Sat should be exempted from the rule of *juste retour* because of its significance and implications for the future of industrial competition in Europe, and the distribution of contracts should be decided according to competitive bidding. The ESA Executive, in consultation with industry, estimated that French and German industry would constitute more than 60% if the contracts were distributed according to industrial competitiveness.[10] Although the ESA Executive tried to maximize the industrial return for smaller countries, the estimate fell far below their expectations. For these countries, the proposal from the ESA Executive was not acceptable since they regarded H-Sat as a big opportunity to join the most profitable business, one in which they had failed to set foot through OTS and ECS programs. In reaction to the fierce criticism from the smaller countries, the ESA Executive proposed two alternative programs, one less efficient program with a greater share of work for smaller countries and another which included a follow-up program that would provide them a larger share of work. The first alternative was strongly supported by the smaller countries, but the big countries, particularly Germany, were totally dissatisfied. It was not only an inefficient and less attractive program, but also a much more expensive program with little work share for Germany. As a leading country in broadcast satellite technology, the German government decided to withdraw from the H-Sat program and 'go-it-alone' in March 1978, since the costs were expected to be recouped through commercial profits, and German industry did not have to share its advanced technological expertise.

For the smaller countries, the withdrawal of Germany from H-Sat was a huge blow to the program technologically and financially. Belgium and Sweden strongly protested against the German unilateral withdrawal from the H-Sat program, since the German government had promised its commitment in the ESA Council. In order to avoid criticism, the German government tried to bring France — also resenting the change of proposal — into the same camp in order to override the Council decision. However, the French government was in the middle of negotiations with other European countries to promote the production of Ariane, and it preferred not to upset the other delegations by withdrawing from H-Sat (Carlier and Gilli 1994, p.236). Pressure came also from inside the French space community when Télédiffusion de France (TDF) claimed that it was no longer in favor of the concept of H-Sat since the costs had risen beyond the level of potential benefit. The French delegation had lost their main reason for committing to H-Sat and decided to leave the program. France joined Germany to co-develop a twin program of TDF (French) and TV-Sat (Germany).

Without the major contributors and technologically advanced countries, the remaining Member States had to face difficult choices. On the one hand, the program seemed to have become much less efficient and technologically mediocre, so would not be competitive in the satellite market and, therefore, would not justify the investment. But on the other hand, it would be a complete waste of funding to stop the program. In the end, Britain, Italy and The Netherlands, with support from the Associate Member Canada, decided to go on with the program using more simplified and less expensive technology, and a fair balance in work share (L-Sat, later renamed Olympus). Retrospectively, H-Sat/Olympus showed the negative side of optional programs where the leading countries opted out of the European program because of strong demands by smaller countries. The story of H-Sat/Olympus indicated that there were wide gaps between national industries, and they were driven by the logics of (national) autonomy and technology, although they shared the logic of commerce. The clash of national policy logics made the French and German governments decide to withdraw from the program despite the institutional constraints.

TDF/TV-SAT

France and Germany had already developed their technical competence for telecomsat through their national programs. Germany had DFS Kopernikus and DFS-1 and 2 satellites in order to secure the telecommunication infrastructure between West Germany and West Berlin. On the other hand, France had developed its own national telecommunication satellites, Télécom 1 and 2, to ensure communication between mainland France and its overseas departments. One particular interesting feature of the Télécom program was that it was promoted not only for civilian purposes but also for military use. The French Ministry of Defense was not sufficiently enthusiastic about space communications because of the costs and reliability, but the Télécom program provided an opportunity to establish a communications infrastructure without investing too much money in development. The Ministry of Defense, in cooperation with CNES, developed a system called Syracuse, which was put on Télécom satellites alongside civilian payloads.

After withdrawing from the H-Sat program, the French and German governments decided to collaborate on separate but identical programs developed by the same group of companies. They established a consortium of six companies called Eurosatellite GmbH based in Munich in 1978.[11] The contributions (and contracts) were shared between Germany (54%) and France (46%) under prime contractor Messerschmitt-Bölkow-Blohm (MBB) for TV-Sat 1/2 and TDF-1, while Aérospatiale was awarded the prime contract for TDF-2 (Collins 1990, p.112).

The TDF/TV-Sat program was thus launched with full expectations, but the program soon faced a serious challenge. GE Astro Space Division of the US announced the provision of a set of satellites called Astra for the private European broadcasting operator SES (*Société Européenne des Satellites*), which was one of the target customers for TDF/TV-Sat. The Franco-German program was troubled by delays and schedule slides and was losing ground in the competition with Astra. By mid-1986, the companies in the Eurosatellite consortium realized that they needed some government support to protect, at least, the French and German markets. The French and German governments encouraged viewers to buy smaller dishes which could only receive the TDF/TV-Sat signal, but soon both governments faced mounting pressure from America to open their domestic markets for free competition. Moreover, the French government was also in confusion after the defeat of the Socialists in the 1986 election. Jacques Chirac, the new right wing Prime Minister, revoked the franchises for the TDF satellite, and Gérard Longuet, the Minister for Posts and Telecommunications, cast serious doubt on the reliability and operability of TDF. The Chirac government decided in 1987 that it would commit much less for TDF follow-on programs, so that industry should find its own resources, and unless industry could find resources for follow-on programs, the first satellite, which was fully funded by the government, would be launched as an experimental satellite. French industry somehow managed to finance TDF-2 — although the funding was not sufficient to upgrade the technology, so that the satellite was virtually identical to TDF-1 — and TDF therefore began commercial operations when it was launched in 1988. However, it ended in total failure because the frequency allocation was not sufficient to provide services, due to the lack of political support (Carlier and Gilli 1994, p.238). In the end, TDF was used only on an experimental basis for distribution of digital high-definition broadcasts.

German TV-Sat experienced more humiliating consequences. TV-Sat was already under serious criticism and few in the German government supported the program. The first satellite was eventually launched in 1987, but the satellite could not function properly because of abnormality in its solar panel. The satellite was a complete failure not only commercially, but also technologically. The whole investment, about 390 million DMs, was completely wasted.[12] On the other hand, Astra, which won the contract for SES, was successfully launched in December 1988 and the subsequent series continue to provide DBS broadcasts all over the European continent.

The disastrous results of the TDF/TV-Sat program underlined a complex issue in the commercialization of space activities and the role of ESA and national governments. It can be said that if Germany and France had collaborated at the ESA level, and had not spent too much time in political negotiations, there would have been a chance for the European satellite to win over DBS. If ESA had been able to concentrate their resources and technical expertise on one system, instead of two — Olympus and TDF/TV-Sat — the chances of building a competitive system might have been greater. However, through the experience of TDF/TV-Sat, the French and German governments and space agencies realized that telecommunications technology had matured and political intervention may have become inefficient for promoting programs. In fact, after these, European governments lost some of their enthusiasm for telecommunications programs, and industry began to emerge as the central actor in finance, research, and development in this area.

The telecommunications programs were a particular focal point of the clash of different policy logics. ESA began with the success of OTS and ECS, but soon after these initial programs achieved their goals, the big countries began to shift their attention to national programs in order to strengthen their own industrial capabilities. The logic of commerce played a big part in this movement, but the smaller countries also shared the same policy logic. They too wanted to develop their national capabilities — perhaps more than the big countries because they were technologically behind. The clash between the big and smaller countries was eminent in the H-Sat program, and both Olympus and TDF/TV-Sat ended up without any commercial success. The Member States gradually recognized that political intervention could only produce fruitless conflict among Member States, and the role of government in commercially competitive programs became less important. Perhaps, as Marsh (1991) argued, the patchy contracts through optional participation and the principle of *juste retour* were not adequate to improve industrial competitiveness in the global market, and such fruitless contract battles may have weakened whatever advantages Europe enjoyed, as we have seen in the case of DBS.

Earth Observation Programs

The US Landsat program, the first civilian program, opened up a new frontier for space activities: Earth observation (EO). The US had already started military surveillance from satellites through the Corona program (Day 1998, Pebbles 1997), and initially Earth observation was regarded mainly as a military activity. However, the success of the Landsat program encouraged European scientific and academic use of remote sensing data, and furthermore, the impact of Landsat data on the 1973 Arab-Israeli conflict was so significant that some in the United States demanded restriction of EO data distribution outside the US (O'Cornell *et al.* 2001). Some European governments, therefore, became interested in developing an EO program for Europe, and France in particular took the initiative.

SPOT

The French space agency, CNES, began its study in 1970 for an EO satellite program which would be used not only for scientific use, but for more application-oriented uses such as agriculture, resource management, environment, cartography and so on. However, the *Institut Géographique National* (IGN), collaborating with CNES as cartography and geography experts, preferred an observation system by aeroplane instead of satellite, and CNES agreed with IGN to set up a formal organization for EO activities, *Groupement pour le Développement de la Détection Aérospatiale* (GDTA). GDTA originally aimed to promote aerial observation, while not ruling out observation by satellite. CNES, along with its GDTA activities, carried on its study of the EO satellite and its application programs, and submitted a report to the government in 1976 with a recommendation to develop a space platform for EO activities.

CNES, as obliged in the ESA Convention, put forward the idea of an EO satellite program, SPOT (*Satellite Probatoire d'Observation de la Terre*),[13] in the ESA Council to discuss the possibility of Europeanization of the program. ESA had been engaged in a study of EO technology, and the majority of Member States preferred a radar satellite to the SPOT optical satellite because of the weather conditions over the European continent.[14] The German government in particular made explicit its position that it would not make any contribution for optical sensor technology. Other European governments, with the exception of Sweden and Belgium, found that they could not afford to pay for another program under the heavy strain of the expenses for Ariane and Spacelab while Landsat data could be purchased at a lower price (Carlier and Gilli 1994, p.220).

Meanwhile, the situation within CNES became restless. The creation of the European Space Agency and the shifting national resources for big European programs inevitably squeezed the budget for CNES. National programs such as Diamant were cancelled because of budget cuts under Giscard d'Estaing's redefinition of space policy (see above). The Europeanization of SPOT was considered to further damage CNES's own program. Worse, the Ministry of Research and Industry proposed to lay off a hundred CNES staff members to balance the budget. This proposal led a long CNES strike at the Toulouse Space Center where most of the application research was conducted, and concluded by replacing both the Chairman and Director General and withdrawing the proposal for the reduction of staff. CNES as well as the French government realized the depth of the resentment towards ESA in Toulouse and decided to withdraw SPOT from ESA to give CNES the responsibility for developing the whole program (thereby SPOT sometimes referred to as Satellite Pour Occupé Toulouse; interview with CNES official, 27/11/97).

Political considerations for developing SPOT forced CNES and the French space policy community to reorganize the objectives and justifications for the program. First of all, the logic of technology, which drove the program in the first place, was not enough. It was debated that France should have all technological expertise (sensors and platform system which are quite different from the telecomsat platform), but it was not necessarily a justification for a national, instead of European, program. Secondly, the logic of science was not the driving force. The Landsat data was fairly useful to the scientific community (and a lot cheaper than developing its own satellite), and if France wanted to develop one, it would be more appropriate to develop it as a mandatory ESA program. Thirdly, the logic of autonomy, which might be the most appealing, was also weak, since Landsat data distribution did not exclude the French or the European scientific community, so that there was no situation such as existed in the case of launcher development. Fourthly, the logic of finance was quite strongly in favor of reducing the program budget under the severe economic conditions that followed the oil crisis. Therefore, the two remaining policy logics, military and commerce, were the pillars of the argument CNES advanced to protect and justify the program.

CNES, though not responsible for military programs at this time, argued that the potential for military use of EO satellites and the problem of exclusivity of American intelligence would soon become a problem of gaps in information, and therefore it was necessary to develop the technological expertise for EO satellites. On the other hand, CNES recognized that the Landsat data users would pay more for better satellite images (Landsat images were not well-appreciated in Europe because of their poor quality), and argued that the commercial sale of SPOT data would recoup some of development costs. Thus, in 1982 CNES created an affiliate, as it did for Ariane, called Spotimage for the marketing and promotion of SPOT data. These two policy logics finally convinced policy-makers in France to promote SPOT as a national program with minor contributions from Sweden and Belgium (4% each).

Helios

On the other hand, the military implications of SPOT data became ever more important. Although the resolution of SPOT data was not adequate for tactical use, many experts in arms control found that the SPOT data was useful for verification of arms control treaties and crisis management[15] (for examples, see Jasani 1987,

McLean 1992b, Parker 1992). However, French military authorities (Ministry of Defense, *Délégation Générale d'Armement*, and *Secrétariat Général à la Défense Nationale* under the Prime Minister) were not particularly enthusiastic about developing a satellite exclusively serving military purposes. From 1977 to 1982, the French MoD conducted research on military reconnaissance satellites using SPOT technology, called SAMRO (*Satellite Militaire de Reconnaissance Optique*), but the idea was shelved because of considerable doubts about its effectiveness on the part of the military and space communities and financial difficulties arising from the development of the military telecomsat, Syracuse. On the other hand, French politicians under the Mitterrand Presidency announced their willingness to exploit SPOT within the common European defense structure. The French government began its campaign to revitalize WEU by giving it responsibility for arms control verification via satellite, particularly since the American President Reagan had announced an ambitious Strategic Defense Initiative (SDI), which would lead to US domination of military space activities (WEU 1984). At the same time, the pressure to promote military programs on the part of industry, Aérospatiale and Matra — prime contractors for the SPOT program — in particular, was rising after the cancellation of the SAMRO project (Dauncey 1994, p.263) to compensate for the huge gap with the US industry, which would receive a significant amount from the SDI project.

Under these circumstances, the French Minister for Defense, Charles Hernu, decided to start a new study of the military reconnaissance program, Helios. His decision was driven by the fact that independent military reconnaissance and intelligent systems were required for the *"logique de puissances nucléaires"* (Grouard 1989, p.24), and the French government felt that it needed more intelligence capability for the on-going conflict in Chad (McLean 1992a; Paolini 1987). The French military officials, on the other hand, were not happy with the decision since they were not willing to spare their resources for a reconnaissance satellite program, and asked the government to consider an alternative to reduce the financial burden of the program. France was already in negotiations with Germany when they were planning to develop SAMRO as a part of wider Franco-German security cooperation (Friend 1991; Heisbourg 1998), but since the German government was not at all interested in an optical satellite system, it was extremely difficult to convince the Germans to join the program (Paolini 1987).[16] On the other hand, Italy and Spain, which shared the same interest in observing the Mediterranean and Northern Africa, emerged as potential partners in place of Germany. They were content with the specifications of the Helios program, and decided to participate in the program to a limited extent (Italy and Spain contributed 14% and 7% respectively).

The interesting aspect of this 'multinational program' was the ways in which they shared responsibility. Obviously, the contract for Helios was distributed according to the share of the contribution but so too in the share of the allocation of data distribution. Italy and Spain had exclusive rights to so-called 'shutter control', which meant they could take images anywhere they wanted to, and those images were used exclusively by the countries that had ordered that particular data. In other words, the Helios was acting as a 'national' satellite, even though it was developed 'multinationally'. The Helios arrangement was further complicated when France demanded that the satellite should be controlled from the CNES Toulouse Space Center without the attendance of Italian and Spanish personnel, so that Italian and Spanish military officials had to send orders to French officials to acquire the imagery. This episode tells us how difficult it was to jointly develop and operate a military program even among European countries with similar strategic interests (Coudy *et al.* 1988; Fleury 1987).

Summary

As a pre-developed technology, the policy logics for EO satellite programs among ESA Member States were quite complex and diverse. The failure of the Europeanization of SPOT showed the difficulty of convincing European partners to become involved in a new technology, and even within France the program was not driven by single coherent policy logic. Both SPOT and Helios were not just *grand projets* to show off the technical achievement and greatness of French independence, but were also driven by other factors such as the labor dispute at the CNES Toulouse Center and the American SDI initiative. And as a consequence of these historical contingencies, the policy logic which drove SPOT was mainly the logic of commerce, whereas Helios was driven by the logic of autonomy (and autonomous nuclear power) with little support from military officials who were more driven by the logic of finance. But in both cases, French industry played a role in increasing government spending for satellite programs through the logics of commerce and technology. Hence, this mixture of different policy logics within the French policy-making process resulted in a rather strange form of 'multinational' collaboration with other European partners (Belgium and Sweden for SPOT and Italy and Spain for Helios). The differences in policy logic, again, created two programs at the European and national levels, but unlike the Olympus/TDF-TV-Sat case, European countries benefited from having two satellite systems because of their different technological specifications.

Space Station Programs

Having been successful in various areas of space activity, particularly in the launcher, the European space community became more confident in its technological achievement. For some Member States of ESA, particularly Germany and Italy through their Spacelab involvement, the next step for European space activities would be the development of manned space capability. More than a year before US President Reagan announced his intention to start the International Space Station (ISS) program, in January 1983 the ESA Council adopted a plan called the Space Transportation System Long-Term Preparatory Program. The study was aimed to develop an idea for a new launcher system beyond Ariane 4, and the possibility of carrying astronauts to a space platform which would be used for commercial exploitation of space (Harrison 1987, p.48). The fact that ESA had already begun its study for an autonomous space platform prior to the American invitation is often ignored, but it is therefore important to note that ESA was already moving forward in the development of autonomous manned space capabilities.

Nevertheless, President Reagan's State of the Union Address in January 1984 and the subsequent official invitation to participate in ISS had an impact on European governments (for the process behind the American decision, see Mark 1987; McCurdy 1990). Although ESA had already begun its study of a manned space program, the Member States were cautious, if not skeptical, about the intentions of the US Administration. From their experiences with the Symphonie, Aerosat, and Spacelab programs, the sense of caution was widely shared by most of the ESA Member States. For NASA, the major objectives of the international invitation were, first, to share the cost, but "not at the expense of losing control over development and management of the facility once in orbit" (Hayward 1993, p.336), and second, James Beggs, then NASA administrator, believed that international participation would support and justify ISS before a Congress not in favor of funding the project (Bizony 1996). But to the European governments, these American intentions were not sufficient to guarantee equal participation and autonomous European decision-making capability. The ESA Executive, together with the Member States, began to evolve a plan for European participation in ISS towards the end of 1984, and the Long-Term Plan (LTP) was submitted to the Council. Since the plan involved a significant increase in the ESA budget, it was not possible to make a decision at the Council level, which consisted of representatives from the space agencies and national administrations. Hence, the ESA Executive called for a Council meeting at the ministerial level for the first time since 1977[17] to discuss the LTP in accord with Article XI of the ESA Convention.

Rome Ministerial Council in 1985

The Ministerial Council held at Rome in January 1985 marked a historical turning point for European space collaboration. First and foremost, ESA manifested its political intention to develop an 'autonomous' civilian space system. Apart from military space capability, manned space technology was one remaining area of space activity in which European space community lacked capability. Although Spacelab provided certain technology for a life-support system and microgravity research environment, Europe lacked a vehicle to carry astronauts into space. The decision at the Rome meeting to begin a study for the development of Ariane 5 was not only a technological program, but also a "commitment to maintain and develop independent European capabilities in space" (ESA/C/LXVII/Res.2 (final), 31/1/85). This idea was evidently developed through European experience in the Spacelab program, which was, after all, dependent on the American Shuttle program. Raimer Lüst, the Director-General of ESA, stressed that ESA needed to develop autonomous capability in all key areas, because "long-term cooperation is therefore only possible between partners with equal rights" (Lüst 1987, p.17).

The concept of 'independent capability' was also driven by other political and institutional reasons. From past experience, particularly with the Aerosat program from which the US government decided unilaterally to withdraw (see above), ESA learned that the MoU (Memorandum of Understanding) was regarded as a binding agreement in Europe, while it was regarded as a semi-formal confirmation of understanding without legal binding power in the US. For the US government, the agreement would not be 'legally binding' unless the Congress adopted it as an international treaty, and therefore an agreement based on an MoU would not guarantee the budgetary commitment over which Congress had the final authority (Hayward 1993). In other words, the ISS project would always be under scrutiny by Congress, and could easily be subject to budget cuts or, in the worst case, cancellation. Given the considerable skepticism in Congress, inconsistency in funding was a big concern for Europe, and therefore developing 'independent capability' was necessary to protect the European project from American unilateral decisions.

Indeed, the concept of 'independent capability' and a shared uncongeniality toward the American attitude around the time of the invitation to Europe to the ISS project produced a strong sense of identity among the participants of the Rome meeting. The atmosphere was often described as the 'spirit of Rome' — a mixture of enthusiasm for the new program and ambition for European autonomy in space. The mood of Rome can be best described in the words of the British Minister for Space, Geoffrey Pattie:

> We believe that Europe must ultimately aim for a comprehensive range of autonomous facilities. This means that sooner or later Europe must have not only its own manned space capabilities but also the means of access to and from orbit (quoted in Madders 1997, p.298).[18]

In retrospect, it is ironic to see Pattie's expression of his enthusiasm for autonomous and manned space capability, which his successor, Kenneth Clarke, denied completely in the space of two years.

Pattie's enthusiasm was not only generated by his preference for European autonomy, but also because he was "keen on getting a place for [his] country somewhere in one of the programs closely related to what [he] knew [British] industry wanted to have" (House of Lords 1987, p.207). He took the initiative to create a central government agency to deal with space policy, and to study further options for British participation in the ESA programs proposed at the Rome meeting. The British National Space Centre (BNSC), led by former ESA DG Roy Gibson, was entrusted to coordinate each department's policies relating to space into a single strategy, and more immediately, to conduct a study of the advantages and disadvantages of British Participation in ESA LTP programs (see chapter 7). Pattie's initiative was certainly a big leap in the institutions of British policy-making process, in which the central focus of strategy had been missing.

The study, called the Space Station Utilization Study, was submitted to the government in 1987. A number of expert panels were established, each representing a particular discipline within the space sciences who might benefit from a space station or associated unmanned platforms.[19] Emphasis was placed upon the remote sensing opportunities provided by a polar platform, reflecting the already considerable investment in this area by the Government. The team of representatives from governmental bodies such as the Department of Trade and Industry and the Natural Environment Research Council specifically asked to consider the consequences of not participating in the program (Harrison 1987, p.50), largely because the Thatcher government had decided that the space budget should be frozen, based on its review of science spending in 1987. Pattie, who was supposed to fight against this decision, was sacked from government after the general election in June 1987, and replaced by the more space-skeptical Kenneth Clarke. As a young agency based on a fragile coalition of departments without enthusiastic support from minister, the BNSC could not have the power to influence either the government's decision or the new minister's direction (interview with former BNSC senior official, 22/5/98).

In parallel to the Space Station Utilization Study, BNSC DG Roy Gibson made an initiative to draft a National Space Plan, which aimed to lay out the strategic direction of British space policy for the next ten years, particularly in the matter of the ESA LTP program. The draft was submitted to the government in mid-1986, but the government ignored the plan and took no action (Gibson 1988, p.76). The initial enthusiasm and optimism had left the BNSC during 1986 and early 1987, and the British delegation had to attend the next Ministerial meeting at The Hague without any specific plan or instruction but with a space-skeptical Minister.

The Hague Ministerial Council in 1987

The British policy shift notwithstanding, the Council meeting at the ministerial level at The Hague in November 1987 was filled with an atmosphere of enthusiasm. The disastrous failure of Space Shuttle Challenger in January 1986 cast doubt on the reliability of the Shuttle as the sole transportation system to carry crew and equipment to the Space Station, which in turn provided additional justification for developing an autonomous European spaceplane based on the French Hermes design. Furthermore, the demand from the US DoD to use ISS for military purposes was regarded as an infringement on the concept of the 'exclusively peaceful purpose' of ESA. The ESA Member States claimed that they were prepared to 'go it alone' if the US government decided to use the ISS for military purposes (McCurdy 1990, p.102). This question of military use, again, added justification to the development of the Columbus Man-Tended Free-Flyer (MTFF) module, which could be detached from the ISS and could carry out European experiments autonomously. The mood in the Hague meeting was also inspired in favor of European autonomy and further integration of activities at the European level by the agreement on the Single European Act in 1986.

The British delegation, led by the Minister for Trade and Industry, Kenneth Clarke, but without BNSC DG Roy Gibson, who had resigned his post just before the Hague Ministerial Council knowing that the British decision was not going to be the same as his (interview with former BNSC DG, 22/5/98), was an exception to the euphoric mood at the Hague meeting. Although the British delegation had no specific plan or strategy, Clarke had a strong belief that manned space programs were not value for the money. A few months before the Hague meeting, Clarke made it explicit that the ESA LTP "[were] grandiose, not well targeted and do not provide for enough industrial and commercial participation" and therefore "[i]t is no good arguing ... that any money spent on any space program is justifiable when it reaches the considerable sums arrived at by the European agency" (HC Debate, 28/10/87). He was determined that the proposed manned space programs were optional programs, hence there was no need to jump on the bandwagon if he did not see any scientific or technological advantage for Britain. Moreover, he was aware of French leadership in the ESA LTP programs, and he thought it was wrong that France should determine that the central thrust of ESA be turned to manned space programs (HC Debate, 12/11/87).[20]

Thus, at The Hague meeting Clarke opened his argument by criticizing the logic of autonomy in ESA's Long-Term Plan as "about catching up with the US and the Russians" and claiming the increase in space spending for manned space programs would "cripple our industries rather than enhance their competitive potential" (*Space* 1988 no.1 p.54). He announced that Britain would not participate in any programs related to manned space and would concentrate its spending on the Columbus unmanned polar platform. He also attacked the programs as being too driven by the logic of technology "largely led by engineers and enthusiasts who want to work towards a totally autonomous European position in space, particularly concentrating on manned space flight" which might lead "to huge escalation of cost and also, in [Britain's] opinion, lead to some loss of certainly industrial and commercial, and to some extent scientific objectives as well, in favor of just getting into manned space flight to emulate rival superpowers" (House of Lords 1987, p.194). For him and the British government, the logics of finance and commerce, and the logic of science to a lesser extent, should be the basis for the strategy of European space collaboration.

The major driving force behind the British decision was the logic of finance. Prime Minister Thatcher clearly explained the British policy in the House of Commons: "It is quite correct that we have not been able to find the considerable amount of extra expenditure that was requested" for participating in ESA LTP programs, and "therefore we shall continue our subscription to the European Space Agency, but at present we are not able to find more money" (HC Debate, 23/7/87). Furthermore, Clarke stressed that the government was exploring the possibility of encouraging the private sector to invest in the government program (see, for example HC Debate, 12/11/87 and 13/1/88).[21]

On the other hand, the British government emphasized that the criteria for decision-making in space programs should be more commercially oriented. The British government decided to take the leadership in the polar platform in the Columbus program because of "British Aerospace and the other companies which are interested" (House of Lords 1987, p.198). Nevertheless, the logic of commerce was not given the highest priority. For example, British industry had hoped for a 15% share in the Columbus program to secure the leadership and prime contract for the polar platform, but the British government only allowed 5.5%, insufficient to claim the leading role in the program.[22] Most of the 250 million pounds for the Columbus program would be funded from the existing budget, and very little (11 million pounds) was added for the Columbus program for one year (*Space* 1988 no.3). In addition, the decision not to fund the Ariane 5 program represented the lack of a clear strategy based on the logic of commerce. The industry clearly expressed its demand for Ariane 5 participation. Michael Marshall, the chairman of the Parliamentary Space Committee, stated after the Rome meeting that "British Aerospace and other parts of British industry have a current interest in increasing the United Kingdom equity stake ... we should all welcome that kind of increased participation in an undoubted European success" (HC Debate, 25/7/85). But Clarke made a decision not to participate in Ariane 5 simply because it was designed to carry astronauts, so that additional costs would be added to the program to ensure their safety. Clarke himself admitted that his decision was made "[b]ecause ESA is leading us in one direction we have all been reacting to ESA somewhat and taking the advice of industry too late" (House of Lords 1987, p.197) and therefore, he said, "[his] next step has got to be to discuss with the companies interested in Ariane what we do now in the light of the decision" (*ibid.*, p.195). In other words, the decision to opt out of Ariane 5 was derived from Clarke's dislike — one might call it an obsession — for manned space programs without serious consideration of the demands from industry, and therefore we can conclude that the primary policy logic behind the British decision in 1987 was not the logic of commerce, but the logic of finance.

The same principle applied for the scientific programs. Although Britain supported the new ESA strategy for the scientific program Horizon 2000, in the Rome Ministerial Council in 1985, Clarke crossfired by turning down ESA's request for a 5% annual increase in its mandatory science budget up to 1992, calling instead for a thorough review of this as well. He argued that the science budget had already had a 27% increase in real terms in the three years to 1989, and did not require an immediate further raise (Collins 1990, p.168). His argument paid very little consideration to the scientific merits of Horizon 2000, even though he repeatedly emphasized that scientific — together with technological and economic — benefit should be the criteria for selecting space programs (see, for example, *The Times* 29/10/87).

The British decision at the Hague meeting was fiercely criticized in and out of Britain. The Select Committee on Science and Technology in the House of Lords conducted a comprehensive investigation on UK space policy before and after the Hague meeting.[23] The report, published on 17 December 1987, shared the view with the government that man in space was an expensive and hazardous activity, and it was "not necessary to put a European in space independently of the Americans" (House of Lords 1987, p.63). However, the Committee expressed its concern that the decision to opt out completely from the manned space program, particularly Ariane 5, would have significant consequences. The government responded that it viewed Ariane 5 as a commercially inadequate program, and as long as the UK committed to unmanned programs of ESA, UK industry would not lose its competitive edge (House of Lords 1988).

Despite all the criticism, the British decision to opt out of the manned space program and to place priority on financial discipline and commercial benefits became the basis of the British space policy until today (interview with former Minister for Space, 21/4/98). The policy driven by the logics of finance and commerce was unpopular in and out of Britain in 1987, but, as we will see in the next chapter, the dynamic geopolitical and politico-economic change in the late 1980s to early 1990s proved that the British decision was not too outrageous (Lord Reay 1991).

The British decision to opt out of three major programs — Ariane 5, Hermes, and Columbus MTFF — generated the problem of the reallocation of the share of contributions. The Member States except Britain had to decide either to reduce the size of the programs or to increase their proportion of contributions. The financial deficit had to be shouldered particularly by the countries sponsoring Ariane 5, Hermes and Columbus — France and Germany. The first big question was the German willingness to support Hermes. The German government had already decided to commence study on the Sänger program, a two-stage horizontal take-off and landing vehicle named after German space engineer Eugen Sänger, which was based on studies in the fields of space systems and supersonic transport systems over the previous few years (Högenauer 1988). The total cost was estimated at USD 12 billion over 20 years, which would represent a considerable proportion of the space budget. After the decision to choose Hermes as a European program at the Council meeting in June 1987, the German government engaged in a big debate as to whether to participate in the Hermes program or to place priority on Sänger. In November 1987, a few days before The Hague meeting, German Minister for Technology Riesenhuber announced that Germany was prepared to contribute to the Hermes program if the total ESA spending program were reduced by 15 to 20% (Collins 1990, p.167). The ESA Executive and the Member States, particularly France, had to accept the offer in order to keep the Hermes program alive. However, the condition that Germany tried to impose upon the ESA LTP was quite severe, and as a result, the estimated cost proposed at the Hague meeting became quite "ambitious and unrealistic" (interview with DLR senior official 15/6/98).

On the other hand, the French space community, as well as politicians, were quite happy with the outcome of the Hague meeting. Both the Socialist President and the Right-wing government strongly supported the concept of 'independent European capability' and French commitment in the Ariane 5 and Hermes programs. Alain Madelin, the Minister for Industry, commented in the press briefing after The Hague meeting that "to go into space you will no longer need a Soviet or American passport — a European passport will do" (French government press release, 10/11/87). But French policy logic was not only driven by the logic of autonomy. There was also serious consideration of the technological development, at least in the CNES and the community of space engineers. Herbert Curien, then the President of CNES, argued that manned space technology would be the space technology of the next century because manned presence in space would make satellite and space station repair possible, and that would reduce the cost of developing and operating satellites. However, the idea was deeply intertwined with the logic of autonomy. In order to develop 'European' technology, Curien argued, ESA Member States had to have free access to the ISS and a reasonable system of co-ownership and co-decision making structures (Curien 1985).

French policy logic in the Hague decision was, therefore, dominated by the logics of autonomy and technology; however, French scientists could not enjoy the decision as much as the engineers and politicians. The French *Académie des Sciences* published a report concerning French space policy in March 1988, expressing that there were many tasks which could be done by robots, and it would be wrong to invest heavily into manned space technology to achieving space spectaculars. The report warned that the financial distribution should not be distorted by the political ambition for autonomy, and it would be irresponsible to sacrifice scientific research (*Académie des Sciences* 1988). This strong criticism seemed to be a reflection of the anxiety of the space science community that space science would be further marginalized. Scientists shared a sense of understanding that the establishment of ESA had already pushed science into marginal activities, but they feared further political intervention in scientific activities for the protection of 'politically important' programs.

Policy Logics for ISS Participation

The invitation to participate in the ISS project was certainly an époque-making moment in the history of European space collaboration. The Member States, apart from Britain in The Hague meeting, decided to commit to an unprecedented scale of spending for space development. It seemed the agreement on such large-scale programs was made possible as a natural consequence of the maturity of European space capability, but it was not so natural as it seems. First of all, the agreement was only possible because the proposed programs were optional programs. The institutional arrangement allowed Member States like Britain to stay out of the programs, and the rest of the Member States were able to proceed without fear of a veto by one country. Secondly, the politicians in the sponsoring countries, France and Germany, were deeply committed to the programs for one reason or another. The French government was strongly motivated by the logics of autonomy and technology for access to space, whereas the German government was driven by the logics of technology, commerce, and science for manned presence for microgravity experiments and the logic of autonomy which the German government learned from its experience in the Spacelab program. Thirdly, although the programs aimed to achieve 'independent European capability' in civilian space activities, the programs were originally national programs, not 'European' programs like the OTS program (see previous chapter). In other words, the role of the ESA Executive in the process was limited to that of a coordinator, rather than a central player. Finally, the decision was accepted as a 'package deal' between France and Germany to approve the Hermes program in return for a reduction in the total cost of the programs.

Having said that, these factors also permitted the neglect of an important warning expressed by the British delegation. Indeed, the ESA LTP was very ambitious and unrealistic in terms of financial arrangements, and lacked sensible analysis on the economic and commercial aspects of the programs. In other words, the Member States except Britain put too much emphasis on the 'Spirit of Rome' and the logics of autonomy and technology and neglected the financial and commercial consequences. The lack of such consideration would soon become the seed of problems for European space collaboration in the 1990s.

Conclusion

If we compare the policy logics adopted by national governments and the decisions made in the Rome and The Hague meetings to the ESC decision in 1973, we may find interesting aspects of the development of European space collaboration during these 10 to 15 years. First of all, both decisions were induced by the American invitation to participate in their programs — post-Apollo and ISS — and European governments reactions to them, but there was more emphasis on European autonomy in 1987. Of course, the decision to begin the Ariane program was driven by the logic of autonomy, but this time, Germany joined the French camp to promote an autonomous European program because the German government discovered the importance of maintaining decision-making power and autonomous capability in transatlantic cooperation through its bitter experience in the Spacelab program. Secondly, both decisions were taken as a kind of package deal, but the circumstances were quite different. In 1973, the package deal was a necessity to break through the series of crises, but in 1987, the decision was made smoothly within the existing institutional arrangement. Optional participation saved the European process from the crisis that it had experienced in the 1960s.

However, what became obvious during these years was that the Member States developed their strategies based on their own domestic industrial, financial, and political concerns. Although the ESA Executive had been given the power to initiate programs and to provide coherent long-term plans, those plans were mostly dominated by 'Europeanized' national programs such as Hermes. In other words, European strategy became a mere aggregation of national programs, and the leadership of sponsoring countries became more important than the European collective efforts. The telecommunications and Earth Observation program cases were good examples. The conflict over the H-Sat/Olympus and TDF/TV-Sat programs tells us that ESA institutions did not become the obvious choice for big countries, particularly when a program had high stakes. However, the unsuccessful result of Olympus and TDF/TV-Sat also tells us that the 'go it alone' option would not be the best option if Europe could concentrate its resources into one program. The other important aspect of the story was that the gap between larger and smaller countries widened during this period. Although program management and leadership in the decision-making process were dominated by the big countries, smaller countries also enjoyed benefits from the single European agency through optional participation and the principle of *juste retour*. Some smaller countries, Spain in particular, had developed their national industry through European programs which would never have been possible with a national program alone.

Space science activities were somehow an exceptional area within the ESA program. The privileges granted under the ESRO period were protected as a mandatory program. Although there were some problems with a lack of political and financial attention, the innovative Horizon 2000 plan enticed not only European scientists but also policy-makers to revitalize European activities.

In short, European space collaboration in the 1970s and 80s was a period when the logic of autonomy at both the national and European level emerged as the dominant policy logic, and this policy logic often intertwined with the logics of technology and commerce (and in the case of the British decision in 1987, the logic of finance).

Notes

1   The ESA Executive has created a new Department of Planning and Future Programmes, and named André Lebeau, former Assistant Director of CNES as the director of the department as well as vice-DG of ESA (Lebeau 1979).

2   In the ESRO and ELDO Convention, the term 'level of resource' meant total sum of programme budget, but in the ESA Convention, it only means the contribution to the mandatory program because optional programs have their own legal arrangement and financial envelopes.

3   There is no reference in the Convention to consensus or constructive abstention voting, and therefore, the decision has to be taken by explicit 'yes' votes from all participating Member States. However, the Council occasionally took decisions by consensus when it was difficult to have explicit 'yes' votes from all Member States (Loosch 1993).

4   Unanimous decisions are required for the determination of the level of resources, review of the level of resources at the end of the third year of each five-year period, Europeanization of national programmes, amendment of the Convention, and accession of new Member States. A two-thirds majority is required for changing mandatory programs, recommendation to Member States about harmonization of technology development, approving general budgets and financial arrangements, adopting Staff and Financial Regulations, and technology transfer to third countries.

5   For mandatory programs, the ESA DG has exclusive authority over mandatory programs while Member States may take initiatives to commence optional programs as they 'Europeanize' their national programs.

6   The ESA Ministerial Council was held just once in 1977 to formally approve de facto operation of ESA. The second Ministerial Council was indeed the first substantial Ministerial meeting.

7   In the primary agreement in 1973, there were six experimental launches carrying ESA satellites. There was no governmental or commercial contract proposed beyond these six launches.

8   Australia, Canada, and Japan were also signatories of MoU as user countries.

9   It was estimated that NASA would procure 12 units by the end of the 1980s.

10 The estimated distribution of workload was as follows: France 32%, Germany 30%, UK 10.3%, Italy 9.8%, Sweden 5.9%, Belgium 5.1%, Switzerland 3.4%, Netherlands 1.5%, Denmark 1.3%, Spain 0.7% (Müller 1989, p.44).

11 AEG, ANT Nachrichtentechnik and MBB-ERNO of Germany, Aérospatiale and Alcatel-Espace of France and ETCA of Belgium.

12 The German government was only able to recover 95 million DMs from insurance (Collins 1990, p.116).

13 It was later renamed Satellite pour l'Observation de la Terre without changing the abbreviation.

14 The advantage of the radar satellite is that it would be operational over cloudy skies or even at night, but radar technology is much more difficult to interpret; however, optical satellite data can be handled quite easily.

15 The Chernobyl disaster in April 1986 gave a chance for SPOT to make itself available for disaster monitoring, and this experience reinforced the usefulness of SPOT images in security management (Colucci 1987).

16 Germany pursued the development of radar reconnaissance technology via civilian programme by sponsoring ESA's European Remote Sensing Satellite (ERS) series.

17 The Council at ministerial level in 1977 convened a meeting to formally recognize the establishment of ESA before the ESA Convention entered into force. Thus, the meeting in 1985 was the first substantial ministerial meeting to discuss substantial strategic issues.

18 Pattie's enthusiasm for space can also be found in his article (Pattie 1985).

19 The Columbus programme consisted of two segments. One was a free-flying manned space laboratory which would be detachable from ISS, and the other was an unmanned space platform in the polar orbit for Remote Sensing activities. The latter was proposed by the British government, whereas the former was promoted by Germany and Italy.

20 He also said that spending an additional 200 million pounds a year "on a project to put Europeans – probably Frenchmen – into orbit by the year 2000" would not be justifiable (HC Debate, 25/11/87).
21 This policy direction has continued under the Labour government since 1997 (see chapter 6).
22 Eventually, the polar platform was detached from the Columbus programme as the Envisat programme to which Britain contributed 22% and received the prime contract for Matra Marconi Space.
23 The report was published a month after the meeting, and therefore the recommendations took the form of criticism of the government's decision in the Hague meeting.

Chapter 5

European Space Collaboration in the Post Cold War Era

The institutions and policy logics of European space collaboration, despite their relative success and stability, were put under strong pressure to change and adjust to the new international and domestic political, economic, and technological circumstances. Three major factors influenced the context of policy-making for space in Europe. First and foremost, the end of the Cold War changed the international security structure and the concept of 'defense'. During the Cold War, the aerospace industry depended on stable government procurement and financial support for military R&D. The end of the Cold War put the industry, not only in Europe but also all over the world, into a situation where industrial restructuring was thought to be the only way to survive. Although the European space industry did not heavily depend on military procurement, this geo-political structural change had direct and indirect effects.

Secondly, as a consequence of the end of the Cold War, the German reunification and further integration of Europe, particularly its economic and monetary integration, changed Germany's priorities for public spending. The budget for space activities, particularly big programs such as the International Space Station (ISS), were reconsidered to match government priority to meet the financial criteria set by the Treaty of the European Union, better known as the Maastricht Treaty. Even for Member States which decided not to immediately join the Economic Monetary Union (EMU) and single currency, such as Britain, the pressure to reduce space spending became stronger.

Thirdly, also as a consequence of the end of the Cold War, the American space industry restructured at a very quick pace. More than 30 aerospace companies had merged into a handful of companies in the first 5 years of the 1990s. It was thought that the concentration of industry would give American companies more competitiveness, and indeed they became more aggressive in the international space market. Finally, the development of a commercially potential market for space activities, namely telecommunications and launch services, brought private actors into this government-dominated sector. European governments, as well as other governments, had to find a new concept and role for government in space activities which were growing more and more commercially oriented.

The European governments had to face the changed circumstances and adjust their policy logics accordingly. National and European institutions had been developed under particular circumstances to accommodate different policy logics, but they seemed to be inadequate vehicles for supporting the transformation. Particularly, the traditional orientation of space industrial policy — protection of national industry through the principle of *juste retour* and 'national champions' —

grew increasingly obsolete in the face of commercial competition in applications programs and launch services both with American industry, which had achieved an overwhelming scale through consolidation, and with emerging Russian and Chinese industries.

This chapter seeks to analyze how European governments have reacted to the structural changes in international space activities, and what the consequences of the responses were. In the space of a decade or so, the European governments found that space activities needed a completely different policy orientation. The programs for participating in the International Space Station (ISS) had become too heavy a burden to meet the tight financial constraints, as European governments realized the need to take action to strengthen competitiveness of European industry in the face of intensifying competition with American industry.

In seeking an explanation for the process of changes in policies, this chapter will focus on the process of convergence of national policy logics at the European level, and the way in which European governments incorporated new concepts into the European policy-making institutions. In order to do so, this chapter displays the two important changes during the 1990s: European participation in ISS programs; and industrial restructuring and the question of European consolidation as opposed to the concept of 'national champions'. At this moment, the changes are in evolution, and therefore, it would be impossible to undertake a conclusive examination of the subject. However, it should be stressed that the intention of this chapter is to understand the nature of and driving forces behind these changes of policy logics and European institutions.

Financial Constraints and Manned Space Programs

The impact of the changes, the financial constraints in particular, immediately influenced the most expensive programs — the programs most vulnerable to budgetary pressure — manned space programs. The German government, concentrating its financial resources on restructuring former East Germany after reunification, was not able to keep to its commitment to space infrastructure programs. The other governments also followed the same path because of fiscal pressures on them arising from the need to meet the criteria to join the single European currency.

Emergence of a Stronger Logic of Finance

It was ironic that it fell to the newly created German space agency, DARA, to formulate the German position for the Munich Ministerial Council held in November 1991. DARA had been established in 1989 to propose, promote and implement German space policy, especially in relation to strategy for manned space programs. However, as soon as DARA was established, it plunged into a completely contradictory situation where it had to formulate a policy to reduce the cost of programs, and to prevent, instead of promote, further development due to the financial crisis associated with German reunification (Hobe and Spude 1991). In the face of these challenges, DARA proposed, in the ESA Council meeting prior to the

Munich Ministerial Council, a radical alteration of both the concept and cost of the Columbus Man-Tended Free-Flyer (MTFF), which had already exceeded the cost target set out in The Hague meeting. It was clear by then that the German commitment to the logic of autonomy was gradually losing ground to the logic of finance.

Another piece of bad news from the US added to the already depressed mood in Europe. Following the Challenger disaster, the White House appointed Norman Augustine, then the CEO of Martin Marietta, to head an independent inquiry into NASA's affairs. The report of December 1990, known as the Augustine report, stated that the Space Shuttle and Space Station absorbed a considerable amount of funding which should have been used for other projects. The report gave the highest level of importance to science and Earth observation, including environmental monitoring, and judged that the Space Station was too big, too complicated, and too expensive (House of Representatives 1990). Based on this report, the small but powerful Appropriations Committee of the House of Representatives voted to terminate Space Station funding in 1991, though the decision was subsequently overruled by a vote on the floor of the House of Representatives (Bizony 1996; Hayward 1993). European policy-makers regarded this incident as an opportunity to legitimize their claim for European autonomy (Quilès 1991, p.14). However, they also became more insecure about the future of the Space Station program as a whole, and began to worry that it would not be worthwhile to invest in Columbus if there was no Space Station (interview with DLR official, 4/6/98).

Under these circumstances, the Ministerial Council made painstaking decisions. First of all, the resolution reaffirmed the principle drawn up at The Hague meeting — European autonomy in space — and preserved the concepts of the Columbus Free-Flying module and Hermes spaceplane. However, in practice the Member States sought cooperation with Russia, which had far more advanced experiences on manned space flight, to reduce spending at the expense of the logic of autonomy (interview with ESA official, 12/5/98). Finally, tight 'political' monitoring was introduced. The cost overrun during the previous few years was already convincing political leaders to doubt the management competence of ESA, national agencies and industries. Thus it was agreed, in principle, to hold annual meetings at ministerial level to "evaluate the progress made by the programs under way" and to "consider the impact on these programs of changes in the world political context" (ESA/C-M/XCVII/Res.1 (final)).

Although the outline of the Munich Ministerial Council did not seem different from that of The Hague meeting, the underlying policy logic had changed to a certain degree. Germany's shift in policy was considered, at that time, a temporary measure due to the unusual circumstances brought on by reunification. However, a more fundamental change was taking place at various levels of policy-making for space.

Autonomy vs. Finance

For some governments, the French in particular, the outcome of the Munich Ministerial meeting was a setback to the plan for European autonomy, and the

French government urged other European governments to demonstrate their determination and commitment to the decision made at The Hague.

In May 1992, the German government signaled that it was not only going to slice Columbus into two elements — polar platform and Space Station module — but it was also giving up the concept of 'free-flyer' and reducing it to 'permanently attached module'. While the German government was making this painful decision, the French government was also under pressure to give up its pet project — Hermes. Although the French government strongly advocated that Hermes was still a realistic program, it did not make sense to the German government unless it could reduce the overall costs as well as its contribution to the Hermes program (interview with former CNES DG, 18/5/98). At the same time, if a decision on Hermes could not be reached, France and the other Member States supporting the program would withdraw their support from the overall plan (Creola 1991, p.291).

The Director-General of ESA, Jean-Marie Luton, had to step forward to reconcile the differences between France and Germany. His idea was to introduce a new concept of 'autonomy through cooperation'; this meant that studies on space transportation should be conducted jointly with NASA and, if possible, in cooperation with Russia. The Long-Term Plan proposed at the next Ministerial Council in Granada in 1992 by the Director General was filled with words such as "a strong and credible partner" with a good "balance" and "coherence" to improve "cost-effectiveness", while Europe should maintain its identity and objective and obtain maximum benefit from these fora of cooperation (Luton 1992a).

The Ministerial Council which took place in Granada, Spain in November 1992 proved to be merely a formal occasion to acknowledge the difficulties existing among ESA Member States. The outcome of the meeting hung on the edge of the balance between the French policy logic of autonomy and the German logic of finance. Although the reduced Columbus program and the ESA-Russian Hermes elements were approved, there were technical, financial, and political uncertainties. First of all, the future of the International Space Station (ISS) as a whole was not at all clear. Secondly, the situation in Russia was far from stable. No one knew whether the Russian government was willing to — or capable of — maintaining its huge space industry. Thirdly, there was uncertainty over the concept of 'Europe'. The referenda on the Treaty of European Union (Maastricht Treaty) were held in Denmark and France a few months before the Granada Ministerial Council, and the results were disastrously damaging to the image of 'Europe', including its space activities. Ministers and heads of space agencies were uncertain if their national parliaments would accept the decision which emphasized the concept of "European autonomy through cooperation" and a costly project in the name of Europe. And finally, even as the Maastricht Treaty was under attack, the financial arrangements for the single European currency were regarded as further constraints on the already-declining space budget of the ESA Member States.

Defeat of the Logic of Autonomy

For a short period of time after the Granada meeting, European programs for manned space seemed to have better prospects. In 1993, the new American administration under Bill Clinton issued a formal invitation for Russia to join the

ISS partnership, and the US Congress supported the plan with financial commitments. However, the situation in Europe became worse as time passed by. There was a serious problem of industrial return associated with these changes. Italy, the second largest contributor to the Columbus program, received industrial contracts for significantly less than that for which it had paid, due to the radical redesign. It began to threaten other ESA Member States that it would not continue to support the Columbus program unless some readjustments of return were made. Thus, the next Ministerial Council that took place in Toulouse in 1995 had to reach painful decisions not only about further redesign (or cancellation) of the manned space programs, but also about how to satisfy Italy so that it would maintain its level of contribution to Columbus.

Table 5.1   Overall Return Coefficients as of 30/9/1995

	Contrib. (%)	Ideal Amount (KAU)*	Contract Value (KAU)	Return Coefficient	Surplus/ Deficit (KAU)
Austria	0.77%	144,108	148,899	1.03	4,791
Belgium	5.10%	959,443	992,079	1.03	32,636
Denmark	0.99%	186,172	206,240	1.11	20,068
Finland	0.24%	45,432	30,075	0.66	-15,357
France	33.18%	6,237,005	6,459,136	1.04	222,131
Germany	23.52%	4,420,291	4,344,349	0.98	-75,942
Ireland	0.16%	31,099	36,561	1.18	5,462
Italy	15.39%	2,891,831	2,683,454	0.93	-208,377
The Netherlands	2.76%	519,637	545,676	1.05	26,039
Norway	0.64%	120,581	135,436	1.12	14,855
Spain	3.75%	705,138	715,323	1.01	10,185
Sweden	2.38%	447,080	430,408	0.96	-16,672
Switzerland	2.22%	416,561	403,325	0.97	-13,236
United Kingdom	8.04%	1,511,454	1,559,878	1.03	48,424
Canada (assoc.)	0.86%	162,116	145,880	0.90	-16,236
Grand total		18,797,948	18,836,719		

* AU (Accounting Unit) is almost equal to ECU, but the exchange rate is fixed at the beginning of the year.
Source: ESA/C-WG-WP(97)3.

Table 5.2   Overall Return Coefficients as of 31/12/1996

	Contrib. (%)	Ideal Amount (KAU)	Contract Value (KAU)	Return Coefficient	Surplus/ Deficit (KAU)
Austria	0.79%	171,944	172,446	1.00	502
Belgium	5.22%	1,142,181	1,139,626	1.00	-2,555
Denmark	1.01%	219,806	242,011	1.10	22,205
Finland	0.27%	60,303	44,385	0.74	-15,918
France	32.98%	7,209,497	7,400,865	1.03	191,368
Germany	23.80%	5,203,827	5,157,166	0.99	-46,661
Ireland	0.16%	34,663	41,099	1.19	6,436
Italy	15.12%	3,306,726	3,192,087	0.97	-114,639
The Netherlands	3.03%	661,472	664,411	1.00	2,939
Norway	0.67%	145,932	155,031	1.06	9,099
Spain	3.72%	813,710	814,041	1.00	331
Sweden	2.45%	536,131	493,264	0.92	-42,867
Switzerland	2.28%	498,764	467,324	0.94	-31,440
United Kingdom	7.70%	1,682,421	1,759,984	1.05	77,563
Canada (assoc.)	0.80%	175,316	158,441	0.90	-16,875
Grand total		21,862,693	21,902,181		

Source: ESA/C-WG-WP(97)3.

Perhaps, the most important factor in this process was the French position. Although the French government wanted to protect the concept of European autonomy, its strategy toward the manned space program had changed a great deal. There was a conflict between CNES and the Ministry of Industry over priorities in French space policy. The president of CNES, André Lebeau, claimed that the manned space program was "nothing but luxury", and that European autonomy should be pursued through application programs, whereas the Ministry for Space and its minister, François Fillon, programs, whereas the Ministry for Space and its minister, François Fillon, insisted that manned space programs could not be abandoned because they had too much political importance and international commitment (interview with former CNES president, 18/5/98). Even in France, it became clear that the concept of 'European autonomy' had begun gradually to shift away from the manned space program.

The Ministerial Council, held at Toulouse in October 1995, thus became the final stage for the long-lasting dispute over the manned space program. The ministers agreed to further shrink the Columbus program (it was renamed as the Columbus Orbital Facility: COF) and to effectively cancel the Hermes program. This outcome showed that the 'Spirit of Rome' had disappeared, and the logic of finance had overwhelmed the manned space program. Another problem the ESA had to deal with was the question of *juste retour* in connection with Italy's share in the manned space programs. Although Italy's contribution amounted to about 25% of Columbus and 15% of Hermes, the industrial return was not sufficient to cover the Italian share. The lack of return consisted in a large part of a deficit in return coefficients of over 200 million AU[1] in 1995 (Table 5.1). During the Toulouse meeting, the Italian and French ministers discussed the matter bilaterally and agreed that France would transfer 52 MECU worth of contracts to Italy. Several other Member States also agreed to take measures. As a result, the Italian return coefficient improved to 0.97 (Table 5.2), and the Italian government withdrew its threat to leave from the manned space program. This process signified that France was still committed to the ISS participation programs even after the cancellation of Hermes. Even when the French policy logic of autonomy was no longer the central driving force, the manned space programs took priority over the logic of finance within the French government.

However, the French decision to increase spending and shoulder a part of the Italian industrial return deficit was strongly criticized by the French Parliament. The Parliament had long been considered 'a rubber stamp' for government decisions, but the Parliamentary Space Group, established in 1994, started to campaign for increased attention to the evaluation of national spending on space. This campaign aimed at avoiding what had happened at the 1995 Toulouse Ministerial Council, where the French government agreed to finance manned space programs without the consent of the Assembly (*Space News* 19/1/98).

Cost-effectiveness of ESA Management

Another issue discussed in Toulouse was the Member States' demand for more cost-effective ESA management. Through numerous redesigns, delays, and cost overruns of manned space programs, Member States began to question the efficiency and effectiveness of ESA management. Moreover, the governments put pressure on ESA Executives to come up with the best results for the minimum investment. Among Member States, the British and German governments were the frontliners in demanding close scrutiny of ESA management. Britain, with its "we want more for less" principle (interview with BNSC official, 3/9/99), strongly demanded a reduction of 15–25% in spending on mandatory programs — general budget and science programs — over three years in order to squeeze the management to extract the most out of the limited budget. And, surprisingly, though to the British delegation, the argument was supported by the majority of Member States, which shared the sentiment that something had to be done with ESA management (interview with British MP, 21/4/98). As Montague (1995) argues, some Member States supported the British proposal because they preferred to go 'native' — to use their resources on national programs, instead of ESA. Thus, the Council agreed to freeze spending on science programs for three to five years (see Table 5.3) and to tighten contract management, particularly by introducing fixed-price contracts. In addition, Member States demanded that ESA executives shed 12% of staff by 1998 (Charts 5.1 and 5.2). Of course, the scientists were very disappointed by the decision, but they had few means by which to convince the national delegations to overcome these financial and political pressures. The policy logics of ESA were clearly turning towards commerce and finance at the expense of science, as well as that of autonomy.

Table 5.3   Budget Plan for Mandatory Programs as of 1995 (MAU)*

	1996	1997	1998	1999	2000	Total
Scientific Programs	347.0	347.0	347.0	347.0	347.0	1735
General Budget	166.5	162.5	158.4	158.4	158.4	804.2

*   Prices are current, so the actual spending would be less in the case of inflation.
Source: ESA/C-M/CXXII/Res.1 (final).

Chart 5.1   ESA Staff Distribution by Nationality

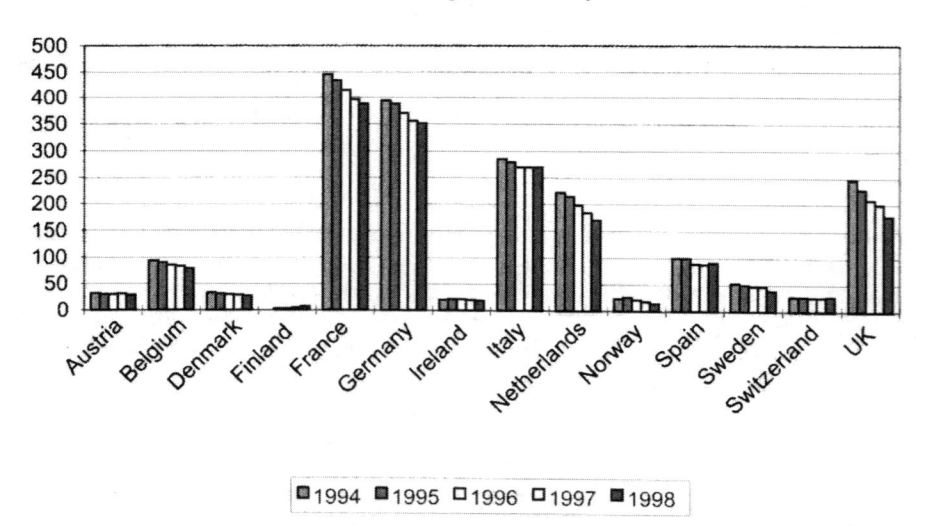

Source: ESA Annual Reports (1994–1998).

Chart 5.2   ESA Staff Changes from 1984 to 1998

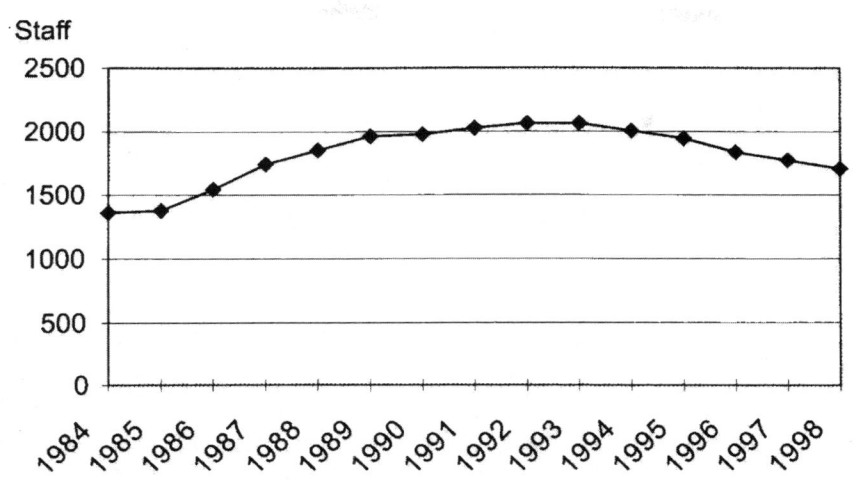

Source: ESA Annual Reports (1994–1998).

Summary

What became explicit in this argument was that the logic of autonomy, which had dominated the process of European space collaboration, was retreating behind other logics, especially finance. The impact of German reunification, as well as financial constraints imposed by Economic and Monetary Union under the Maastricht Treaty, squeezed the budget of manned space programs whose scientific and commercial benefits were not always convincing. It should also be noted that it was not only the logic of finance, but also others, commerce in particular, which emerged through the 1990s. We shall take a closer look at this matter in the next section.

European Responses to the Commercialization of Space

The commercialization of space as such started a long time ago, but the vast majority of space activities were conducted as public programs. The issue of commercialization appeared in the late 1980s, when satellite broadcasting and telecommunications came to be recognized as a big 'money-making' business (see, for example, OECD 1985, Tomsa 1987). It was mainly discussed in the context of how technological developments and their spin-offs might impact on established commercial sectors, such as consumer electronics (see, for example Shachar and Zuscovitch 1991, Giget *et al.* 1996). Aware of the importance of commercial activities, ESA invited national delegations in economic affairs and operators such as Eutelsat to a 'Spacecommerce' meeting on 17–20 June 1987 (Collette 1987).

However, the pattern of space commercialization in the 1990s seemed to have been both qualitatively and quantitatively different from that of the 1980s. First of all, the amount of telecommunications traffic across the world had risen enormously because of technological breakthroughs such as the Internet and an ever-increasing demand for global mobile communication. The existing space telecommunications infrastructure became incapable of coping with such a demand, and, therefore, public and private sectors focused their attention on how to exploit this market. Secondly, a new concept, a 'constellation' of satellites in Low Earth Orbit (LEO), expanded the possibilities of space telecommunications. In the past, huge high-powered telecommunications satellites were placed in Geostationary Orbit (GEO), but because of the scarcity of available orbits and frequencies, it was not possible to inject more than a certain number of satellites into GEO. The emergence of the 'constellation' concept suddenly increased the demand for satellite production and launch services. Thirdly, the prospects for commercial exploitation of earth observation (EO) data added opportunities for further commercialization of space applications. The introduction of 1–meter resolution satellite photos by Space Imaging, a US private enterprise, expanded to new horizons the commercial use of EO data, which had been mostly limited to public use. Furthermore, both American and European military authorities – the National Imagery and Mapping Agency (NIMA) of the US and the Satellite Center of the Western European Union (WEU) at Torrejon, Spain – began to use commercial sources, in addition to traditional military satellite data, in the 1990s (O'Cornell *et al.* 2001). These changes certainly stimulated the EO data distribution market and further drove the commercialization of space.

What would be more important was the adjustment that took place at the industrial level to respond to these changes. Since the beginning of 1990s, dynamic industrial restructuring had been taking place in the United States. American industrial giants, such as Boeing and Lockheed Martin, became more aggressive in their commercial operations, particularly creating launch services companies through joint ventures with former Soviet launchers (Sea Launch and International Launch Service, respectively), to regain their share in the market where the Europeans had advantages.

These changes widely impacted European industry as well as European governments. They became aware that the traditional industrial policy for big projects, namely the 'national champion' strategy, was no longer appropriate in the new market situation and industrial circumstances. The industrialists realized that they should become more independent from government strategy and consolidate across national borders, but they were also aware that industry could not face the competition against US giants without government financial and political support. For their part, governments slowly began to understand the importance of commercial- and user-oriented programs. In other words, the traditional roles of government and industry came under close scrutiny, and the context of the 'policy logic of commerce' began to change during 1990s.

Under such circumstances, the Industrial Working Group under the chairmanship of Armand Carlier, CEO of Matra Marconi Space, submitted a report to ESA Director-General, Jean-Marie Luton, in August 1994. The report (called the Carlier report), a consensus of 20 representatives from major space-related companies, criticized the principle of *juste retour* for being "cumbersome and bureaucratic" and less successful in fulfilling its purpose of improving industrial competitiveness. It also argued critically that the narrow conception of the return coefficient resulted in political micro-management, which meant that Member States turned their attention to an adjustment of fractions of numbers instead of the big picture strategy. This report had particular importance because these ideas were taken seriously by ESA Executives and widely circulated among the Member States. In fact, most of the ideas proposed in the report were adopted on the agendas of the Ministerial Councils of 1997 and 1999.

Redefining ESA's Industrial Policy

The first issue that ESA Member States took up in order to address the changing situation was to rearrange its industrial policy, namely the principle of *juste retour*. As we discussed in chapter 4, the principle of *juste retour* was fundamentally contradictory to developing competitive industry. The concept of 'world-wide competitiveness of European industry' was thus interpreted for a long time as "the creation of an independent European capability in space applications" (Lebeau 1976, p.3) to make sense of the principle of *juste retour*. However, since the capability of European industry had improved beyond just becoming independent, several Member States began to consider that the time had come to reconsider the concept of *juste retour* and to construct a genuine European industrial policy in order to improve international competitiveness in a more commercialized international space market. Thus, the Ministerial Council was convened at Paris in 1997 to seek a new strategy for European industrial policy. Nevertheless, assuming that an institution such as *juste retour* was deeply embedded in European space collaboration, it could easily be expected that the attempt to amend the principle of *juste retour* would face vigorous resistance.

Based on the proposal made in the Carlier report, ESA produced a working paper which focused on three issues: reform of the distribution of contracts for mandatory programs; distinctions in the rules for optional programs between preparatory and development programs; and protection of SMEs. The basis of ESA's proposal was that industrial contracts should be distributed by competitive bidding wherever this could be applied, and Member States' contributions should be adjusted according to the results of contract distribution (the rule of 'fair contribution'), while guaranteeing a minimum return coefficient (ESA/C-WG-WP(97)).[2]

The British and German delegations stood against this proposal on the grounds that there was no justification to maintain a minimum guaranteed return coefficient. They remained consistent in their view that science programs should be managed more efficiently and, therefore, the concept of *juste retour* should be abandoned. However, the majority of smaller Member States rejected their position on the grounds that it would jeopardize their industries, which expected constant industrial contracts from scientific programs. Thus, the meeting concluded with relaxing the rule by setting the coefficient at 0.9 instead of the ideal coefficient of 1, with deficits to be paid back following a review at the end of three years.

The second issue was to separate optional programs into two phases, a preparatory and a development phase, and to apply to each different contracting rule. The idea was to induce competition at the early phases of programs. However, the smaller Member States again opposed the proposal, and at the end of the meeting it was agreed that imbalances occurring in a preparatory program should be restored through an adjustment of the contribution scales for the next period.

The third amendment of the rule sought to find a proper balance between prime and non-prime contractor companies. This issue was introduced because of a strong criticism that non-prime contractors had difficulty competing against the big prime contractors for components and parts contracts (see chapter 4). Although the issue was equally important to the big Member States, it was more vital to the smaller ones, which did not have prime contractor capability for major programs. Among them, the Netherlands was the most enthusiastic for fundamental revisions in the process of decision-making about industrial contracts. Having received support from big Member States, this issue was well accepted in the meeting. Furthermore, a new dialog with the European Commission (DGXXIII) was launched immediately after the Ministerial Council to support SMEs (interview with ESA official, 12/5/98).

Though these rules were introduced in response to strong demands for ESA reform, the new rules were not an easy pill for the smaller Member States to swallow. Thus, the new measures agreed on in the Ministerial Council in Paris were introduced on a trial basis for three years, and were eventually extended to mid-2001. It is also important to note that the new rules were not designed to abandon the principle of *juste retour*. The essence of this reform was to clear up the past imbalances in industrial returns, and to introduce flexibility in their calculation. Thus, the ministers agreed that "improved performance-to-cost ratios should be sought through competitive bidding", but also "providing at the same time the flexibility required for organizing industrial competitions and the means of aiming for the ideal overall geographical return coefficient of 1" (ESA/C-M/CXXIX/Res.1 (final)). This outcome suggests that some Member States, particularly the smaller ones, were not ready to accept the shift of policy logic from (national) autonomy and technology to the logic of commerce. Without national agencies of their own, ESA had been the smaller countries' *own* space agency, and they were very reluctant to give up their control over the industrial arrangements made through ESA programs (interview with ESA official, 12/5/98). Thus, a reform of the rules of *juste retour* was the last thing that they wanted to achieve in this meeting, even though they understood the importance of improving the competitiveness of European industry. In fact, there was one Member State — Spain — which voiced its complete dissatisfaction with this arrangement all the way from the beginning to the end of the meeting.

Throughout the history of European space collaboration, Spain had always been the beneficiary of the principle of *juste retour*. Spanish industry was quite immature at the beginning of European space history, but it gradually developed thanks to the *juste retour* distribution of contracts. Currently, Spanish industry is the sixth largest in Europe after Belgium with a global turnover of 201.5 million euros (Table 5.5), of which a majority of contracts goes to *Construcciones Aeronauticas SA* (CASA).[3] Given the relatively small size and weak competitiveness of its industry, Spain would be the most vulnerable among the Member States if the new rules were implemented.

At the Ministerial Council in Paris, the Spanish delegates claimed that the success of ESA depended on its role in building up European industrial capability, and the principle of *juste retour* had been "a key factor in the development of a competitive space industry". This industrial policy "remained a cornerstone of solidarity" for ESA, because it guaranteed access to all the Agency's programs for the companies of smaller countries, which delegated their sovereignty to ESA. The Spanish delegates argued that the ESA proposal to reform the rules of *juste retour* "tended to sanction the surrender of some of the Executive's power to prime contractors, while the guarantee of smaller Member States access to industrial development work was given only a vague mention" (ESA/C-M/MIN/129).

Table 5.4   Employment and Turnover Distribution by Country, 1998 (in Million Euro)

Country	Employment	Consolidated Turnover*	Total Turnover**
Austria	210	18.7	19.1
Belgium	1605	192.3	220.5
Denmark	347	45.6	47.2
Finland	237	18.4	19.9
France	13252	2062.8	4261.8
Germany	5963	1026.7	1589.9
Ireland	71	5.7	5.7
Italy	5741	931.8	1128.9
The Netherlands	671	106.4	114.6
Norway	399	40.1	42.1
Spain	1495	158.7	201.5
Sweden	801	101.8	175.1
Switzerland	513	119.4	169.5
United Kingdom	3577	490.0	577.5
Total	34883	5318.5	8573.5

* Consolidated turnover: the consolidated amount for space contracts actually done in house, which reflects the true level of space industrial activities.
** Total turnover: nominal space contracts accounts. The difference between total and consolidated turnover indicates the activeness of 'space business'.
Source: Eurospace.

In desperation, the Spanish delegates threatened to use their veto, but the Chairman, Yvan Ylieff, Belgian Minister for Scientific Policy, stood firm on making a decision at this meeting even if a consensus could not be reached, in order to demonstrate the European position to the outside world. Thus, the Ministerial Council in Paris made decisions, for the first time in the history of European space collaboration, by majority vote, with one vote against (Spain) and one vote cast *ad referendum* (UK).

The entire process of redefining ESA's industrial policy was, retrospectively, a small step toward reforming the principle of *juste retour*. As evidenced by the Spanish case, resentment and resistance against reform were still strong, and even some pro-reform officials from Member States thought that it would be impossible to change the rules (interview with CNES official, 17/11/97; with DLR official, 12/6/98). The concept of *juste retour* was deeply embedded in the institutions of European space collaboration, and the logics of commerce and finance alone would not be able to change this fundamental 'cornerstone of European solidarity'. The fact that ESA Member States were unable to establish a new rule by the end of 1999 and had decided to extend the transitional period until mid-2001 shows the lack of consensus and the determination among Member States to change the principle of *juste retour* (ESA/C-M/CXLI/Res.2 (final)). However, as we will discuss below, two movements, European industrial consolidation and a strengthening of the relationship between ESA and the EU, have significant potential to alter the principle of *juste retour* and the institutions of European space collaboration.

Industrial Consolidation

While the European governments were struggling to reach a consensus on how to improve the competitiveness of European industry, industry itself moved far ahead. For major European prime companies, it was a "merger or die" situation (Williamson 1997), since the American mega-mergers —particularly between Lockheed and Martin Marietta and between Boeing and McDonnell Douglas — were proceeding very quickly, while European manufacturers were fragmented into small national markets under a 'national champion' strategy. By the end of the 1990s, mergers and acquisitions had become the name of the game in the space industry, and what became important was not if, but when and with whom the companies were going to merge.

Unlike the American case, European industrial consolidation had a number of high hurdles to overcome in order to merge companies across borders. First of all, most of the European space industry was affiliated to the big aerospace-defense companies. Although they had been building an intensive network of collaboration through civilian and military collaborative programs, the question of technological confidentiality was always raised when they negotiated a merger (Hartley 1983; Gummett and Walker 1993; Kapstein 1992; Moravcsik 1990; Walker and Willett 1993). National strategic concern for maintaining technological and industrial competence was extremely significant (for example, see the French government's hesitation to privatize Aérospatiale). Secondly, laws and regulations within Europe were yet fragmented, and there were invisible barriers to intra-European mergers. Thirdly, and perhaps most important, there was a fear of high-tech unemployment.

As seen in Table 5.4 above, the countries with big prime companies employed around 30,000 in a space sector heavily dependent on the performance of prime contractors. European consolidation might generate pressures to rationalize the workforce and production sites, which would seriously hurt the high-tech labor market in those countries (interview with French government official, 8/7/99).

However, there has been one company that operated as a 'European' company. Matra Marconi Space (MMS) was a joint venture between French Matra (Lagardère group) and the British Marconi Electronics Systems. The two companies merged their space divisions in 1990 to strengthen their competitiveness in producing satellite platforms, and also to expand their market in both France and Britain. Although the MMS was by definition a European company, its strategy was to have a right balance between its image as a European company and a national company at the same time (interview with former Chairman of MMS, 27/3/97). On the one hand, the MMS tried to win ESA contracts allocated to both Britain and France, but on the other hand, the MMS kept their 'national' characteristics so as to have access to the defense programs in both countries. The experience of MMS demonstrates that, on the one hand, a cross-border merger is generally more cost-efficient and helps to give customers the confidence that the company has the resources required for a large project. On the other hand, there are other areas, particularly in company law and employment practice, where it is advantageous to retain a degree of disparity between the national contingents of the company.

Whatever the disadvantages were, European prime companies were urging themselves to gather forces. It is sometimes understood that a consolidation was taking place because of mergers between parent companies, namely Aérospatiale, Matra, Daimler Chrysler Aerospace, and CASA, for the Airbus production. Of course, the merger of these companies into the European Aeronautic, Defense and Space Company (EADS) eased the process of consolidation in the space segment, but given the relatively low commercial and military importance, space consolidation was taking place in a very different context. One example of this might be the fate of Aérospatiale (see Table 5.6 and Figure 5.1). As the most prestigious French — and European — space company, Aérospatiale had been located at the heart of French space strategy, and the French government enjoyed control through a 100% share of the company. However, under huge pressure from outside, the French government gave up its exclusive ownership and partially privatized Aérospatiale, while maintaining its 'golden share'.[4] In this process, Aérospatiale sold its satellite manufacturing capacity to Alcatel Espace in 1998. Furthermore, the French government decided to merge the entire Aérospatiale with Matra Haute Technologies (MHT) to form Aérospatiale-Matra in July 1999. This was, for the space industry, ironic because Aérospatiale regained satellite-manufacturing capacity by acquiring MMS via MHT. The process of European space consolidation was, therefore, strongly influenced by the process of consolidation of parent companies, but it had its own dynamics.

Would this new structure be good for Europe? Perhaps the upside is the expectation of economies of scale and increasing efficiency. Astrium, with its large resources, would be able to operate bigger projects and produce commercially competitive products. But the downside would be the fear of monopoly and abuse of market power. European space industry was somehow protected from this by the principle of *juste retour*, and there was a sort of competition in the European market, but what would happen when there was only one prime company capable of receiving a contract? Even the industrialists were concerned with the consequences of the monopoly of Astrium (interview with Secretary-General of Eurospace, 7/3/00). The other question to be raised is whether Astrium has genuine 'European' characteristics. As we have seen in the case of the MMS, it would be possible for the 'national' structure to remain, and national governments would treat them as if they were national companies. In fact, Astrium itself is a holding company registered in the Netherlands as Astrium N.V., but there are 'national' subsidiaries. Gerald Brachet, the Director-General of CNES commented that "a strong European industry is a primary requirement and is not incompatible with national goals" (*AWST* 1/3/99), and affirmed that the behavior of national governments, including the practice of the principle of *juste retour*, would not change significantly in the near future (interview, 10/3/00).

Table 5.5   Process of European Aerospace Consolidation in the Late 1990s

	Merging Parties		Merged Company
May 1998	British Aerospace	SAAB	British Aerospace[1]
June 1998	Alcatel	Aérospatiale (Satellite) Thomson-CSF	Alcatel Espace
Dec. 1998	GEC Marconi	Alenia	Alenia Marconi Systems
Jan. 1999	British Aerospace	GEC Marconi	BAE Systems
June 1999	DASA	CASA	DASA
July 1999	Aérospatiale	Matra	Aérospatiale-Matra
Oct. 1999	Aérospatiale-Matra	DASA	EADS
Dec. 1999	Matra Marconi Space	DASA	Astrium

1 British Aerospace acquired 35% of SAAB.
Source: *Financial Times, Space News.*

The industrial consolidation in Europe is bound to have a strong impact on the ways in which governments and ESA relate to the industry. The industry will be more independent from public resources and government support, but at the same time, it will take full advantage. Besides, European governments and the ESA, under serious financial constraints, are trying to use the resources of industry with a new concept of 'Public-Private Partnership' (PPP).

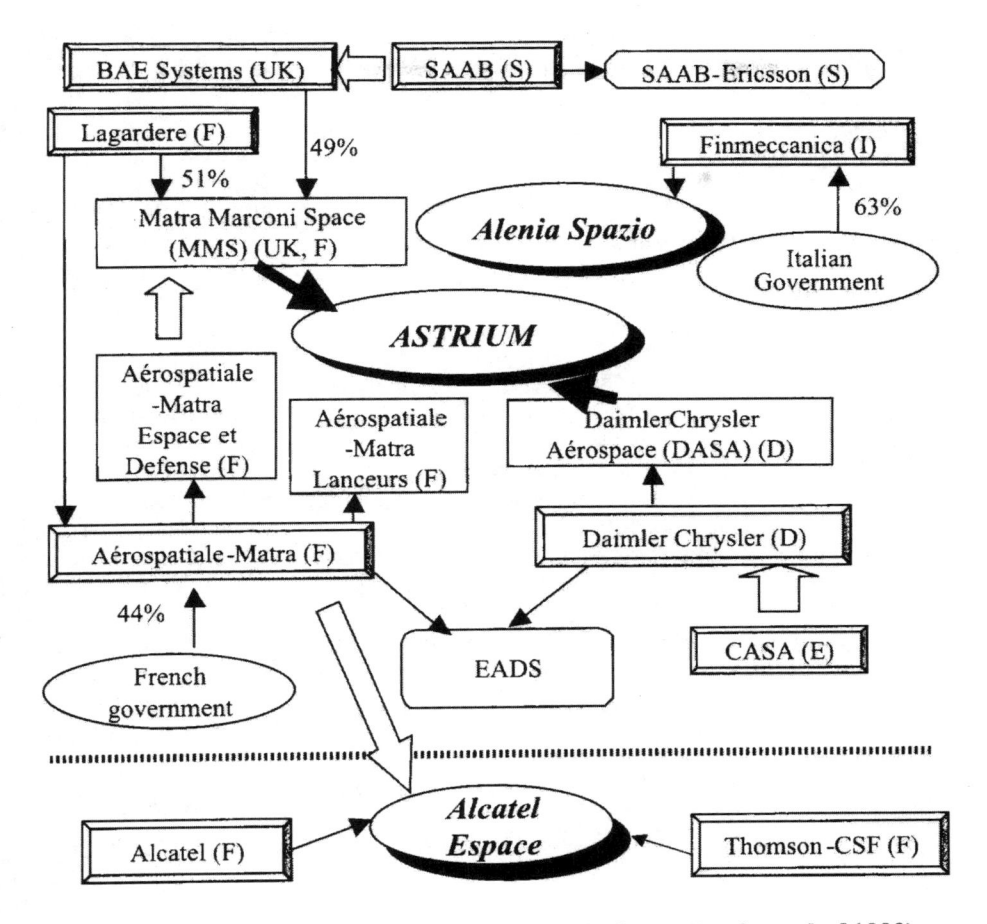

Figure 5.1   Consolidation of European Space Industry (at the end of 1999)

Public-Private Partnership

The concept of Public-Private Partnership (PPP) was developed as a new management method for policy implementation during the 1990s. It was used in many policy areas, such as transport, medical care, waste management and so forth. But in each case the ways in which PPP was used were quite different (for example, see Henk 1998). In other words, the PPP concept was applied flexibly to justify the involvement of private entities in public works, but its definition was not yet firmly established. This is true in the context of European space collaboration.

Indeed, the concept of PPP was attractive to ESA and many Member States as a fashionable way to meet the changing nature of space activities. It is generally considered (1) a joint definition of actions and programs between space agency and industry; (2) sharing financial burdens and risks, particularly for commercially oriented programs; (3) sharing technical expertise between national research centers and industry laboratories. However, the concept is interpreted in various ways according to national strategies and industrial and technological structures.

Among ESA Member States, Britain has the most advanced experience in PPP. Its national agency, BNSC, stands on a partnership with different ministries, and it can be said that BNSC has been exercising a policy of PPP since its creation. Nevertheless, PPP was introduced into some British programs partly because the government could – or would – no longer support big programs and national industry, and also because the City of London became less interested in mega-projects (interview with BNSC official, 9/3/99). The best example of this renewed emphasis on PPP can be found in the case of the Skynet 5 military communications satellite program. Although the British government was involved in negotiations with France and Germany to develop a common military satellite system called Trimilsatcom during the 1990s, it withdrew unilaterally from the project because the British government wanted to develop its own military satellite under a PPP scheme. The British government proposed a so-called Private Finance Initiative (PFI), under which an industrial consortium would finance, develop, build and operate a dual-use fixed/mobile satellite telecommunications system, leasing capacity to the Ministry of Defense under a long-term contract and offering unneeded capacity to private users on a commercial basis (*AWST* 21/9/98). What is even more interesting is that the British government has opened opportunities to establish partnerships not only with British companies, but also with foreign manufacturers and operators. Lockheed Martin and Matra Marconi Space, which lead the two competing teams, informed the Ministry of Defense at the end of 1999 that a public-private partnership (PPP) concept was workable. Lockheed Martin was teamed with British Aerospace, which would be responsible for the ground system, British Telecommunications and TRW. Matra Marconi Space's 'Paradigm' consortium includes TRW, Motorola, the British facilities management services company SERCO, Logica and Cogent (*AWST* 22/11/99).

For France, the concept of PPP was somehow quite unfamiliar because of its tradition of *dirigisme* in high-tech projects (Cohen 1992). CNES has recognized itself as a *donneur d'ordre*, which means that CNES stands superior to French industry and gives the orders (interview with CNES official, 19/11/97). However, faced with such changes in the market and industry, CNES introduced the concept of 'partnership' in the first *Plan Stratégique du CNES* in 1996. The rationale for such a new policy was, according to Clerc (then head of the partnership division of CNES), "to go beyond [CNES'] role of an agency distributing funds to industry for the development of government space programs" (Clerc 1998, p.13). He defined partnership as the "pooling of various resources (financial, technical and human) for the purpose of attaining a particular objective, providing each party with satisfactory returns, which may be of different types depending on the partners involved" (ibid., p.17). Two things should be pointed out. First, as *Plan Stratégique* carefully mentions, the 'partnership' policy was applied only to certain area of activities, closely linked with market activities, and the role of CNES as 'public client' should remain for the large programs such as Ariane and SPOT. Second, the 'partnership policy' also emphasized 'mutuality' and 'satisfactory returns' for all partners involved, including CNES. For example, CNES participates in the Alcatel-led Skybridge program because CNES can also get expertise relating to the constellation of satellites from industry (interview with CNES official, 17/11/97). The government was not only pursuing financial and commercial benefits through PPP programs, but also looking for a return in the form of technical expertise. In other words, PPP was introduced not only on account of the logic of finance and commerce, but also the logic of technology.

In the case of Germany, the concept of PPP had not yet matured, but was regarded as a policy guideline for establishing a new link with industry. In the Federal Strategic Paper, *Space: Prospects for Research and Applications* of 1997, PPP was defined as a "new approach that calls for a change in the thinking of all the partners involved, and a new kind of collaboration between government support, industry and science" (BMBF 1997). Through PPP, government, industry and science expected to find an appropriate joining of forces and agreement on long-term aims. However, the notion was still vague, and some German space agency officials admitted that the concept might be targeted at inviting industry to co-fund commercially viable programs such as navigation or telecommunications (interview with DLR official, 16/6/98). A unique feature of this Federal paper is the emphasis on partnership with scientists, particularly as regards the commercialization of Space Station utilization. In fact, the question of PPP was not mentioned in the second Federal Strategic Paper, issued in 2001, but the partnership with scientists was further emphasized in the second paper (BMBF 2001). It can be seen that the German concept of PPP was driven by the logic of finance as well as the logic of science. Through PPP programs, it was hoped that the participation of scientists in the planning process might be strengthened.

Based on such different attitudes to the concept, it was difficult to define how PPP should be implemented at the level of ESA. Given the emergence of PPP in some Member States, the concept was discussed at the Ministerial Council in Brussels in 1999. The meeting decided to "[e]ncourage industry and the private sector, taking into account the industrial restructuring in Europe, to assume a strategic responsibility in the opening up of new areas of business with full exploitation of the potential for enhanced cost-effectiveness and synergies, on the basis of the concept of private/public partnership including a significant funding by industry" (ESA/C-M/ CXLI/Res.1 (final)). This clause suggested that the concept was defined at the 'lowest-common-denominator' of British, French and German understanding. On the one hand, the ESA Council recognized that PPP would enhance cost-effectiveness and synergies, but on the other, PPP was defined to include significant funding by industry. Given the complex system of financial management (due to the principle of *juste retour*) and institutional constraints for commercial activities, it would be very difficult for ESA to implement programs on a PPP basis where national agencies would have less problem (CNES 1999, p.20). However, the ESA Executive is gradually building up a link with industry, particularly for the Galileo satellite navigation program (see chapter 7). Given the limited funding available for Galileo within the ESA framework, it is crucial to have financial support from industry, or to devise some sort of industrial involvement to generate revenue from Galileo utilization (interview with Director-General of ESA, 7/7/99).

The concept of PPP was thus developed primarily to seek financial engagement on the part of industry for programs oriented toward commercial use. Although the understanding of the concept differs according to each agency, increasing industrial competitiveness and supplementing financial resources are the two important motivations. However, since the industrial structure is becoming less and less 'national', it is questionable if PPP at a national level would provide a suitable framework. Perhaps the British concept of PPP would be a good template for the future of European partnership with an increasingly integrated European industry, if the Member States agreed to let ESA become a more commercially oriented organization.

Union of Centers

As we will discuss in the next chapter, national institutions and the role of national agencies have shaped, and been shaped by, the national policy logics. However, the emergence of the logic of finance and commerce similarly caused the space agencies and their technological centers in particular to have grave concerns for the future of their role in space activities. On the one hand, the shrinking budget immediately meant that the funding for programs and personnel for space agencies was decreasing, and it would be more difficult not only to develop new technology, but also to maintain their current level of technical expertise. On the other hand, as we will see in the case of Britain, ministries of finance and budgets are less likely to be willing to give public funding for commercially oriented programs because they expect the space industry to find the money in the marketplace. At the same time, European governments prefer more collaborative programs at the ESA level to save costs (for example, the Italian government chose to develop its ambitious small launcher program called Vega within the ESA framework instead of the national agency). Under these circumstances, big national space agencies, particularly those of France, Germany and Italy, were the most serious about finding a breakthrough.

The most concerned agency was the French CNES. Since the beginning of the 1990s, frustration and a sense of injustice over the higher salaries for ESA engineers than CNES engineers developed into a sort of hostility against ESA (particularly the European Space Technology Center: ESTEC). At the same time, the transfer of CNES-developed technologies to other countries was considered a difficult sacrifice (*Office Parlementaire d'Evaluation des Choix Scientifiques et Technologiques* 1991, p.246). Even the top managers of the CNES like Jean-Daniel Lévi, then the Director-General, explicitly expressed the difficulties of engaging in European collaboration, saying in 1994 that "[i]t is easier to take decisions alone than with 13 others" (Euroconsult 1994, p.6). From CNES' point of view, European collaboration and the existence of the ESA technical center were obstacles for attracting financial and political attention, and they began to promote 'alternative' ways (i.e., bilateral or unilateral programs).

To some extent, German agencies were in a similar position. The institutional confusion in 1997 (see chapter 6) and increasing pressure from the Ministry of Finance pushed them to protect their own programs. The DLR managers began to question the necessity of dual space agencies at national and European levels, and initiated a plan to reform ESA institutions. Meanwhile, Italy developed a national space strategic plan for the first time (ASI 1997), and argued that the balance between national and European programs should be corrected in favor of its space agency, *Agenzia Spaziale Italiana* (ASI). It recognized that the weakness of ASI was its inadequate organizational structure, and therefore, further development of bilateral collaboration was called for, in order to supplement that weakness. It was also discussed that the debts of ASI be removed immediately by various means, including partnerships with industry and other countries, particularly France (Montluc 1997; Reibaldi 1996).

With this development of a 'go native' feeling among the space agencies in the three major contributing countries to ESA, ASI, CNES and DLR issued a position paper to reform ESA in March 1998. The paper largely reflected the frustration and dissatisfaction of the big countries, pointing out the lack of reflection of the main contributors to program management, inefficiencies of the principle of *juste retour*, injustice in granting the possibility of veto to small countries, and unequal salaries for ESTEC engineers (Cheli and Schrogl 1999, p.65). The most innovative proposal in this paper was the idea of the Union of Centers, brought forward by Germany from its experience in other sectors. The DLR has already been involved in a bilateral 'union' with the French R&D agency, *Office National d'Études et de Recherches Aérospatiales* (ONERA), in helicopter development.[5] The DLR-ONERA union aimed at keeping pace with the process of industrial integration, which was increasingly concentrated in the Eurocopter, a joint subsidiary of Aérospatiale-Matra and DASA (both companies were merged into EADS).

The principal concept of the 'Union of Centers' was to redefine current national policies on subsidies and research infrastructure to meet European requirements, especially to meet the needs of industry. The big national research establishments would each be specialized in a particular technology – for example, the CNES Toulouse Center in optical Earth observation sensors and system integration and the DLR Oberpfaffenhofen Center in radar sensors – in order to avoid duplication of technology and engineers, and they would form a partnership for joint programs under standardized technical and management procedures (DLR 1997). The most interesting feature of this proposal was that all existing centers would be granted status as 'European' centers on an equal footing with frequent access to all partner states and institutions (Cheli and Schrogl 1999). It was, on the one hand, predetermined in the ESA Convention in which the ESA would promote cooperation among Member States "by coordinating the European space program and national programs, and by integrating the latter progressively and as completely as possible into the European space program" (ESA Convention Article II-c). Promoting national space centers to 'European' centers can be regarded as a successful achievement of European space collaboration. However, some people in ESA, particularly those who came from smaller Member States, were concerned that such 'centers of excellence' would undermine the status of ESA centers, particularly ESTEC and ESOC (European Space Operations Center). Peter Creola, an outspoken Swiss Minister for Space, contested that although smaller countries are in favor of ESA reform, they "will not participate in the slow erosion and ultimate destruction of what we have helped to build and are today proud of" (Creola 1999, p.43). To raise the status of national centers to 'European' ones would mean facing again the conflict between larger and smaller countries.

Nevertheless, the concept of a 'Union of Centers' was adopted as an agenda item for the Ministerial Council in Brussels in 1999. The ministers came to conclude that the Director-General of ESA would establish a plan of action in a spirit of transparency, complementarity and reciprocity, showing the potential savings for all Member States, and those national centers "shall make their services available to all Member States on an equal basis, at the cost of the requesting State, without discrimination among requests" (ESA/C-M/CXLI/Res.2 (final)). The decision suggested that the smaller Member States had no choice but to accept the concept, but at the same time, it ensured that they could maintain their access to the high level technology and programs. Perhaps the remaining problem is how to guarantee that engineers from smaller countries join the network of 'European' centers.

The concept of a 'Union of Centers', though developed to satisfy 'national' centers, seems to pioneer a new frontier for European space activities, and it would certainly constitute a new institution of European space collaboration. Whether this new concept would change the institutions at the national level is a question waiting to be answered, but given the dynamic changes in the policy logics and institutions at the European level, the move toward a 'Union of Centers' could be one of the ways in which the changes influence national space policy-making process.

Conclusion

There is no doubt that the changes in international structure after the end of the Cold War induced a series of changes in the sphere of European space collaboration and the policy logics of European governments. On the one hand, the emergence of the logic of finance, i.e. putting the priority on balancing the budget and minimum public investment for maximum output promoted by the ministries of finance, became a very influential policy logic. What is more interesting is that the logic of finance appeared in almost all of the Member States of ESA at a similar point in time. The convergence of policy logic to the logic of finance made it possible to reflect on the institutional arrangement of European space collaboration. Introducing the concept of Public-Private Partnership is one of the examples of such an institutional change.

On the other hand, the logic of commerce had a particularly strong influence on the big Member States. Improving international competitiveness, user-oriented programs, and a pragmatic approach *vis-à-vis* industry became the normative concepts for space agencies and relevant ministries in the governments. The question of the reform of *juste retour* was a typical example of the emergence of the logic of commerce. However, this logic did not spread to the smaller countries, whose industry was more or less detached from competition at the international level, and they jealously protected the rules in order to maintain their own logic of (national) autonomy and technology. In fact, the national governments and space agencies in the bigger countries were frustrated by the resistance of the small countries, as seen in the movement of the ASI-CNES-DLR proposal for the 'Union of Centers', but it is important to stress that ESA's institutional structure was flexible enough to absorb such conflicts, and provided a platform for further integration of national capability into the European level.

Notes

1 AU (Accounting Units) are practically the same value as ECU, with the difference that the AU is fixed at a stable level for the year.
2 Minimum coefficient meant that Member States would be guaranteed to receive a certain amount of industrial return much lower than 100% (coefficient of 1). The minimum coefficient was subject to negotiation.
3 CASA was merged with DaimlerChrysler Aerospace (DASA) of Germany in 1999 in the process of European industrial consolidation and further integrated to Astrium as a result of the merger of DASA and Matra Marconi, but the industrial structure in Spain would not change in the foreseeable future.
4 Golden share is a right to veto management decisions no matter how small the share is.
5 Unlike the CNES, the 'institution section' of the DLR is involved in aeronautic research as well as space.

Chapter 6

National Space Policy-making Institutions

The dynamic changes in European space collaboration during the 1990s have had a significant influence on space agencies. For a long time, European and national space agencies had played a central role in defining space policies and implementing them with considerably large budgets and relative autonomy with some variations, depending on the institutional structures. However, the emergence of the logics of finance and commerce has changed the role and the importance of European space agencies for two reasons. Firstly, the demand for space programs increasingly became user- and commercial-oriented and industry expected to receive contracts which contained more pro-competitive — instead of pre-competitive — technologies. The conventional government-oriented space programs were driven more by the logic of technology and autonomy (i.e. increasing technological competence and ensuring access to and capabilities in space). Although the importance of such technological programs remains unchanged, the commercialization of the space market began to demand more flexible and closer-to-market approaches for which space agencies were not fully equipped and well-experienced. Space agencies can no longer act as the 'contract provider' and 'client for industry' but as a 'partner of industry' to co-define space programs and technological requirements.

Secondly, the increasing budget constraints for space programs reduced the political influence and capabilities of the space agencies. The best and brightest engineers were attracted to the space agencies where the most advanced technological programs were being undertaken, but given the limited financial resources, the space agencies could no longer guarantee the best programs and highest salaries. At the same time, the space agencies were involving themselves in collaborative programs in order to reduce program costs, and, consequently, the justification to conduct 'national' programs was being undermined.

Concerned for their survival, space agencies began searching for new roles. However, the space agencies have different roles and political influences in their national institutional contexts. It is therefore impossible to fully understand the changing role of national agencies without scrutinizing the national institutions and the policy-making processes. Hence, before elaborating on the changes that have occurred at national agency level, we shall first discuss how those national agencies, the French, German and British agencies in particular, developed their competence and influence in policy-making processes and how powerful they were vis-à-vis national governments. Particular attention shall be paid to budgetary and financial issues so as to gauge the influence of the logic of finance. For ease of analysis, this chapter is broken down into the following major themes; (1) national characteristics of space policy; (2) space agency's role, missions and historical development in the context of national space policy-making; (3) government supervision including budgetary control; (4) relationship with industry.

France

Among all European countries, France is the largest state in terms of the size of national space program and contribution to ESA. French commitment to space has begun to meet the needs for strategic capability, particularly ballistic missile development that is clearly linked to De Gaulle's *'une certaine idée de la France'*.[1] His idea, in short, was to secure independence in decision-making and to resist domination by the United States in the domain of military and technology.

To this end, the powerful politicians — not only Gaullists, but also Socialists — relentlessly support space policy. They protect space programs which sometimes seem to be contradictory to government macroeconomic policies. For example, the dramatic increase in space spending during the 1980s was made possible by the strong support from the government, even though Socialist governments took *rigueur* policy to tighten government spending (Chart 6.1).

Chart 6.1 French Civil Space Spending (MAU)

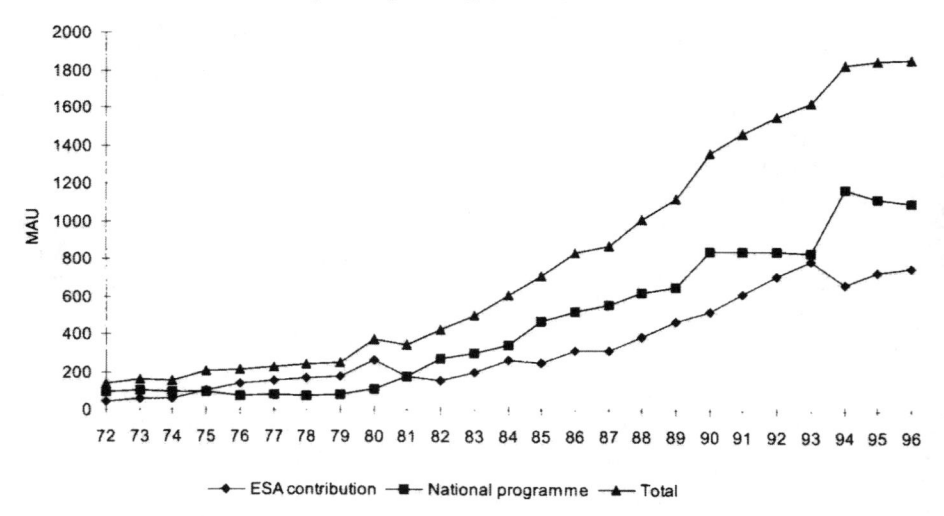

Source: European Space Directory.

Since the creation of ESA, French contributions to ESA have exceeded spending on the national program due to the huge development cost for Ariane launchers. However, programs such as Télécom 1 and SPOT pushed up the proportion of national programs throughout the 1980s (see chapter 4). After *de facto* cancellation of the Hermès program and the reduction of the Columbus program in the ESA Ministerial Council at Granada in 1992, the French ESA contribution was reduced significantly. As we will discuss below, sharp criticism towards space spending, rigid budgetary discipline, and the departure of strong guardian politicians during 1993 constrained the constant increase in space spending.

Centre National d'Études Spatiales (CNES)

The most important organization for French space policy-making, and possibly the most influential in European space policy-making is the *Centre National d'Études Spatiales* (CNES). Created in 1962, CNES was conceived as an *Établissement public à caractère industriel et commercial* (EPIC), guaranteeing it civil status and relative independence despite the fact that it is placed under the ultimate authority and control of the Prime Minister. The status of EPIC gives ambivalent position to CNES. Although it is fundamentally a public company under a supervision of government, its responsibility to prepare and implement space policy and the sheer size of its budget generate a certain feeling that CNES is the center of space policy-making with a potential for causing tension between CNES and government.

Proposition and implementation of space programs The most important responsibility and activity of CNES are to prepare and implement space programs. CNES has principal, if not exclusive, rights to initiate space programs of international cooperation which should be introduced to and approved by the *Conseil d'Administration*. The capacity to propose space programs puts the CNES in an authoritative position to shape the space policy of France.

One particular role of CNES is that it delegates the development of the Ariane launcher on behalf of ESA. When French L-IIIS program was proposed to be 'Europeanized' under ESA framework in mid-1970s, ESA granted CNES a role to implement the Ariane program. CNES was responsible for designing, providing technological requirements and supervising the overall production program.

CNES has also been involved in military space programs. Although political *tutelle* by the Ministry of Defense officially began in 1993, CNES is given responsibility to help the development of military telecommunications satellite payload SYRACUSE series which is on board civilian telecommunications satellite, Télécom 1 and 2, and military reconnaissance satellite Hélios which would eventually use technologies developed in the civilian Earth observation satellite, SPOT.

Research and technology development Being a center of excellence, research and technology are fundamental and basic activities for CNES. Usually, CNES presents a three-year strategic plan for research and technology, *Le plan de recherche et technologie amont* (RTA). According to Clerc (1997), the three objectives of research and technology developments are; (1) preparation for future programs (thematic R&D, basic study); (2) creation and maintenance of competencies and basic technology (generic R&D, fundamental research); (3) promotion and improvement of competitiveness of national industry.

Industrial policy   Since its creation, the *raison d'être* of CNES was to promote and increase industrial capacity and international competitiveness. In this sense, industrial policy is at the heart of CNES' activities. Because space is a typical sector for the French philosophy of *dirigisme* where the government justifies its intervention in the 'market failure' sectors, CNES enjoys its commanding position *vis-à-vis* industry as a government agency. In addition, space is strategically important for developing both military and high technology capability in order to fill the 'technological gap' between France and the United States. These concerns brought CNES a central role for conducting industrial policy for French space industry.

Industrial policy of CNES is usually channeled through awarding contracts. While awarding contracts to industry, several aspects are taken into consideration; (1) regional development: particularly the region of Midi-Pyrénées or region which has more than 6,000 employees in space sector; (2) opportunities for R&D; (3) industrial concentration and restructure. CNES also plays an important role in the development of user industries.

As EPIC, CNES cannot operate profit-making activities, but has the authority to create subsidiaries to transfer its programs for commercial use. There are 18 subsidiaries including pioneering commercial space marketing companies such as Arianespace, SPOT image (see below). Those subsidiaries helped to stimulate and develop marketing expertise in the space market in Europe where space market was generally regarded as risky and non-profitable. The profits from these subsidiaries are considered as *ressources propres*, independent financial resources for CNES.

In spite of such a long tradition of *dirigisme*, industrial policy of CNES is in an initial phase of change. The first *plan stratégique du CNES* published in 1996 set up the concept of 'Public-Private Partnership (PPP)' in the center of space policy planning. For CNES, PPP is intended to review and restructure its relationship with industry and to maximize the efficiency of research and development, including saving program costs to meet tight budget lines. For industry, the concept of PPP means a reduction of government intervention and industry's participation in the decision-making process as equal partners to CNES. In short, the concept of PPP represents a changing relationship between industry and CNES, and its industrial policy.

Defense activities   Defense is a relatively new sphere of activities for CNES. The mission of CNES was originally restricted to civilian activities when the law of establishment was drafted in 1961. However, there was a slow but steady increase of interest in military space programs at the beginning of the 1980s when the *plan pluriannuel spatiale militaire* (PPSM) was introduced. CNES was asked to participate in SYRACUSE 1 military telecom satellite as technological advisory agency, because SYRACUSE was not an independent satellite system but a payload that shared the satellite platform with Télécom 1 civilian telecom satellite as CNES was responsible for its development. In the same manner, CNES participated in the development program of Hélios 1, a military optical reconnaissance satellite, that used the same platform technology of SPOT 4.

However, the experience of the Gulf War in 1991 shifted political and military attention to the use of space for military purposes. During the war, France experienced difficulties in getting satellite imagery data, which clearly reflected the lack of reconnaissance capability of France. After the Gulf War, Hubert Curien, Minister of Research and Pierre Joxe, Minister of Defense discussed placing CNES under *tutelle* of Ministry of Defense. By the décree of March 1993, CNES was put under triple *tutelle* of the Ministries of Research, Industry, and Defense. The new supervisory system was expected to provide further close links between CNES and the Ministry of Defense. One of the important consequences is that MoD staff came to occupy the post of the Director of Programs in CNES, one of the very important positions in CNES (interview with French space analyst, 11/5/98). However, cooperation between CNES and the Ministry of Defense has not reached the expected level. As shown in Table 6.1, most of the programs are follow-on programs to replace or upgrade existing systems, and MoD spared a little share of its budget to space-related activities.

Table 6.1 French Military Satellites

Spacecraft	Launch date	Mission	Development cost (MF)	Prime contractor
Syracuse 1	1984	Communications	2,000	Alcatel
Syracuse 2	1994	Communications	9,230	Alcatel
Helios 1A/1B	1995–98	Optical surveillance	8,000	Matra
Cerise	1995	ELINT	87	Alcatel
Clementine	1995	ELINT	90	Alcatel
Helios 2A/2B	2002–05	Optical/Infra-red surveillance	10,000	Matra
Syracuse 3	2002–05	Communications	N/A	N/A

Source: Chanard (1994).

Internal structure of CNES As a research and development center, CNES consists of three technological centers in Toulouse (CST: space science and application technology), Evry (CSE: launcher and propulsion), and Kourou (CSG: spaceport). About 70% of the entire employees of CNES work in the Toulouse center which is the largest and most influential center of the three. As discussed in chapter 4, CST personnel went on strike in protest of the government's decision to integrate European space effort at the European Space Agency and this resulted in the resignation of Director General Michel Bignier and the authorization of the SPOT program which Toulouse engineers demanded to secure their workload. CST was also active when the International Space Station program was under serious revision in the mid-1990s. CST campaigned to reduce spending for manned space programs and increase application programs in order to increase their work share. CNES President André Lebeau, who also held strong objections to manned space programs, led this campaign and finally he was forced to resign by François Fillon, Minister for Space (interview with former CNES official, 30/6/98).

Government Supervision or 'Tutelle'

The most distinctive feature of the French version of political supervision is the concept of *tutelle*. As EPIC, CNES is supposed to have a certain degree of autonomy from government hierarchic order; therefore, the concept of *tutelle* should be different from *subordination hiérarchique* (Dauncey 1994). Such an ambiguity in the concept of *tutelle* has been the source of conflict between CNES and government over how much CNES should be autonomous. At times the government attempted to control the CNES' activity and power over space policy-making, and at other times the government let CNES take charge. However, it would be misleading to look at the exercise of *tutelle* just as an idea for controlling CNES. The concept of *tutelle* is also a concept to protect the space program (interview with former DGE official, 18/ 5/98). When the CNES faced difficult situations or criticism from other ministries or the general public, it was the tutelle ministries who defended it. In other words, if *tutelle* ministries were only to control CNES programs, it would not have been possible for CNES to have enjoyed a large degree of autonomy over many years and under many governments.

Le Conseil d'Administration   Before we proceed to a more detailed discussion of how tutelle ministries exercise their power and fulfill their role, it is important to introduce *Conseil d'Administration* which is the formal interface between government and CNES. As the governing board of CNES, every proposal for space programs should be approved by *Conseil*. Members of Conseil are chosen in three ways. The first group is the representatives of government who are chosen from tutelle ministries (principal *tutelle* ministry provides *Commissaire du gouvernement* as well), budgetary ministry, Ministry of Foreign Affairs and Prime Minister's office. Because these representatives of government come from relatively senior positions in the hierarchy of each ministry who actually engage in the development and utilization of space programs, it is not difficult to imagine that substantive details on CNES proposals are discussed at this level.

The second group is the members chosen according to their competence. They are more or less consultative members who do not have a real stake in the programs but provide technical, regional and industrial aspects which CNES should take into account. The third group is the member elected from CNES. As EPIC, CNES should respect the law of workers' participation in the executive board. They are elected from trade unions within CNES.

Of these members, the most powerful and important are the President of CNES and *Commissaire du gouvernement*. Informally, the *Commissaire* whose role is to verify and to assure the integrity and legality of CNES' activities is thus symbolic rather than political (interview with government official, 20/5/98). Although *Commissaire* has the right to veto the program on a number of key issues in consultation with other members from government, the *Conseil* usually makes its decision by consensus, which means *Commissaire* should listen to those voices from other members notably from CNES representatives (interview with former Commissaire du gouvernement, 18/5/98). However, if there was a situation of conflict between *Commissaire* and representatives from CNES, including those who are elected among the employees, intensive consultation would take place. The ultimate power is, therefore, in the hands of *Commissaire* whose policy logics may be driven by a political one such as the logics of autonomy or finance, but the pressure from CNES representatives whose policy logic is usually dominated by the logic of technology could result in a compromise.

Tutelle ministries The interaction between government and CNES is more complicated than simple 'principle-agent' relationship.[2] First, on the government side, the responsibilities of *tutelle* are divided among ministries. The Ministry of Economy, Finance and Budget hold responsibility for budgetary *tutelle* which is to control and authorize programs proposed by CNES. Ministries in charge of research or industry oversee and verify the technical aspects and costs associated with the technology. In addition, the Ministry of Post and Telecommunication holds a certain *tutelle* capability due to the importance of space telecom networks. Because of such a division of responsibilities among ministries, the government often faces the difficulty of coordination, which eventually weakens its position *vis-à-vis* CNES.

Second, because of the multidisplinary nature of space activities, governments often switch *tutelle* ministries according to their political objectives (Table 6.2). The consequence of such changes undermined the continuity and coherence of government approach to space policy. On the one hand, the government was not able to accumulate technological and managerial expertise to interact with CNES, and on the other, CNES could maintain its influence with knowledge and expertise over *tutelle* ministries. These changes brought important consequences in shaping the policy logic of France. Although CNES' influence was so significant *vis-à-vis* the government, its formal access to decision-makers was channeled through *tutelle* ministries thus making its power to influence the decision-making process contingent upon whether *tutelle* ministries could share and support the policy logics of CNES, namely the logics of technology and autonomy.

As seen in Table 6.2, the changes of *tutelle* ministries almost coincided with the change of government and presidency. However, the frequency of change increased during Mitterrand's presidency, particularly after 1983 when the Socialist government overcame the currency crisis by shifting its policy toward a more technology-oriented and a neoliberalist direction (see Cole 1994; Paolini 1987; Peterson 1993; Sandholz 1992). The intention of the Socialist government to give space policy a high priority was evident from the establishment of the Ministry of Research and Technology headed by powerful Jean-Pierre Chevènement, the leader of Socialist-left faction CERES. During the political turmoil of 1983, Chevènement lost his influence in the government since he was the architect of the Socialist-Communist coalition but the decision to shift towards a more neoliberal policy made his position very difficult.

Table 6.2   CNES *tutelle* Ministries

1962–1969	Prime Minister's Office (*Ministre délégué or Secrétaire d'Etat chargé de la recherche scientifique, des questions atomiques et spatiales*)
Jul. 1969–Apr. 1977	Ministry of Industry and Science
Apr. 1977–May 1978	Prime Minister's Office (*Secrétaire d'Etat chargé de la recherche*)
May 1978–May 1981	Ministry of Industry
May 1981–Jun. 1983	Ministry of Research and Technology
Jul. 1983–Apr. 1984	Ministry of Industry and Research
Apr. 1984–Mar. 1986	Ministry of Research and Technology
Mar. 1986–May 1988	Ministry of Industry and Research
May 1988–May 1991	Ministry of Post, Telecommunications and Space; and Ministry of Research and Technology
May 1991–Apr. 1992	Ministry of Equipment, Housing, Transport and Space; and Ministry of Research and Technology
Apr. 1992–Feb. 1993	Ministry of Research and Space
Mar. 1993–May 1995	Ministry of Industry, Post and Telecommunications; Ministry of Defense; and Ministry of High Education and Research
May 1995–Nov. 1995	Ministry of Industry, Post and Telecommunications; and Ministry of Defense
Nov. 1995–Jan. 1997	Ministry of Industry (*Ministère délégué à la Poste, aux Télécommunication et à l'Espace*); and Ministry of Defense
Jan. 1997–Jul. 1997	Ministry of Industry (*Ministère délégué à la Poste, aux Télécommunication et à l'Espace*); Ministry of National Education, High Education and Research; and Ministry of Defense
Jul. 1997–	Ministry of National Education, Research and Technology; and Ministry of Defense

Source: Dauncey (1994); Clerc (1997); and *Le Monde*.

Then the space portfolio was given to the Ministry of Industry and Research headed by Laurent Fabius who was a strong supporter of neoliberal- and technology-oriented policies and a close friend of President Mitterrand. Such strong patronage by influential politicians certainly helped to ease CNES demand for large

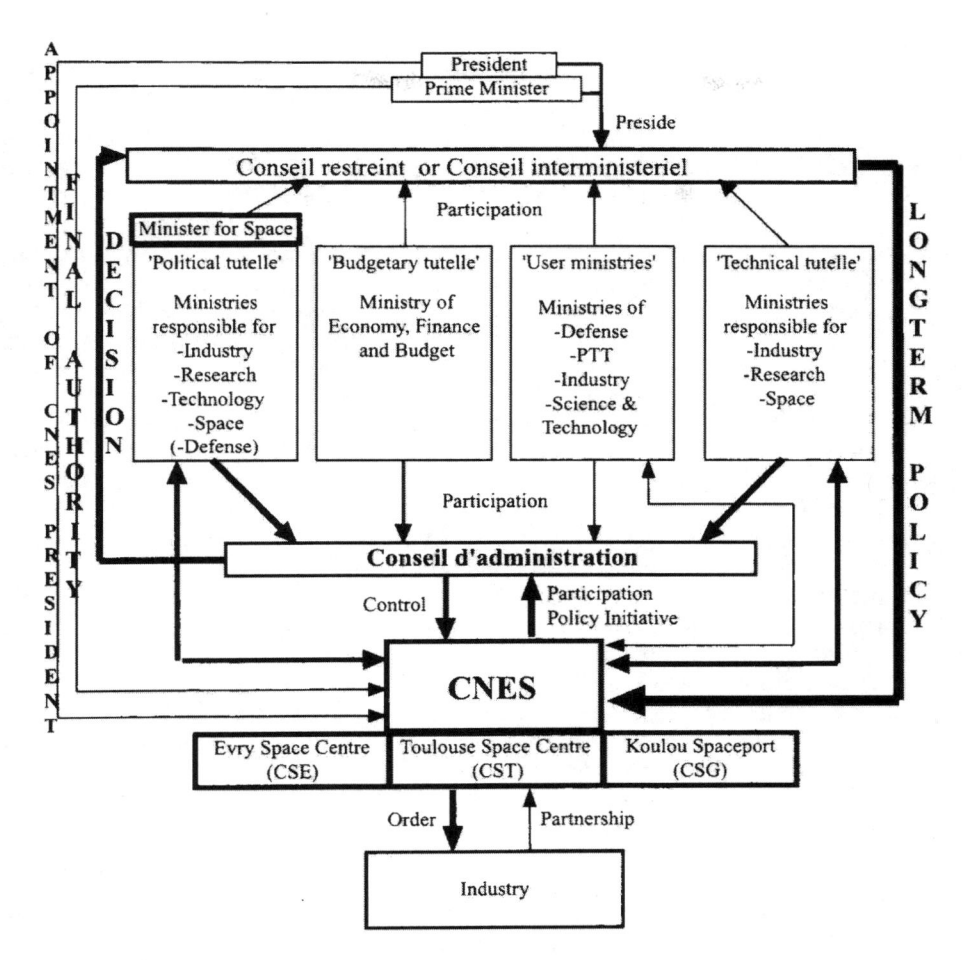

Figure 6.1   French Space Policy-making Process

funding. Even though the Socialists lost power under the *Cohabitation*, the practice of tutelle did not change very much. Again, space was protected by space enthusiastic Prime Minister, Jacques Chirac, and a powerful young politician Alain Madelin was named to take charge of industrial and space affairs. Although Madelin was an outspoken free market protagonist and was not accommodative of the *dirigiste* nature of space policy, he enthusiastically protected space budget and French-led manned space programs.

The second term of Mitterrand's presidency marked three revolutionary changes in space *tutelle* exercise. First, soon after the Socialists regained power, the government named Paul Quilès, a powerful figure in the Socialist Party, as Minister of Space and created *Ministère de la Poste, des Télécommunications, de l'Espace*

(MPTE), which was the first time space appeared as an individual portfolio. Second, *Délégation Générale de l'Espace* (DGE) was created under MPTE and a non-CNES person was appointed as its leader. Third, *Comité de l'Espace* was created, which consisted of high-ranking civil servants (most of them were directors) from tutelle and user ministries. *Comité de l'Espace* has not actually worked as it was expected, but certainly provided a useful forum of discussion for DGE and other ministries (Interview with former DGE official, 18/5/98).

During the second *cohabitation* and subsequent Conservative government until 1997, François Fillon was in charge of space. In this period, the Ministry of Defense was added to two other *tutelle* ministries. Conventional wisdom tells us that the division of *tutelle* among three ministries would undermine the government's power, and enhance the degree of autonomy of CNES. However, the consequence was not what was expected. Because overall spending policy was largely constrained by the monetary policy which was getting tighter to meet Maastricht convergence criteria, CNES needed to have strong support from politicians. The triple *tutelle*, on the one hand, attracted the political attention of the different ministries, but, on the other, it was difficult to unify the voices of the three ministries to push space policy in the face of a difficult financial situation. Consequently, CNES could not enjoy the degree of autonomy it might have during the 1980s.

In 1997, under the third *cohabitation* — this time Socialist and Conservatives took different sides of the table — the Ministry of National Education, Research and Technology (MERT) headed by Claude Allègre became *tutelle* ministry. The Minister for Space in this government was seeking to have a firm grip on CNES activities, so he named Joël Hamelin who held a deputy position in DGE as head of the Department of Space and Aeronautics (DEA). Although it is not privileged as DGE, its missions[3] and mandates were similar to that of DGE. However, at a closer look, DEA is neither capable nor willing to take the place of CNES. Given the small size of the administrative body and the limited technological expertise, DEA's role was rather limited to putting forward proposals of space policy to other ministers, setting priorities and objectives of policy, and coordinating interministerial interests. However, despite the fact that it did not have sufficient administrative resources as DGE, DEA seemed to have a significant influence on the policy-making process, owing to the decisive intervention by Minister for Space who had a preference to the logic of finance instead of the logic of technology.

Interministerial coordination   Since *tutelle* was given to several ministries, interministerial coordination was in need of a coherent space policy. The main forum of interministerial coordination is the *Conseil interministeriel*. It is attended by ministers of space related ministries including user ministries, budgetary ministry and foreign affairs, and is chaired by either the President or the Prime Minister, and consequently its decisions are ultimately binding in regard to the activities of CNES. Interministerial meetings are called when a high level decision-making is necessary, particularly in the case of launching large programs like SPOT. Because of the infrequency of meetings, interministerial council is not the forum to discuss and coordinate space policies on a daily basis, but it is rather to define broad policy direction or to authorize programs.

During the second term of Mitterrand's presidency, another kind of interministerial coordination, *Comité de l'Espace*, was created. It was created in the structure of MPTE under the chairmanship of Minister of Space to advise the Prime Minister with the objective of fostering synergy between civilian and military space programs and generating constructive discussions among ministries by meeting regularly, twice a year. Its members come from high level civil servants in different ministries, armed forces and CNES, including *Délégué Général pour l'Armement*, the Director Generals of Industry, Telecommunications, and Research and Technology, *Chef d'Etat-major des Armées*, the President and Director General of CNES and *Délégué Général à l'Espace* (Dauncey 1994). Although *Comité de l'Espace* was not a forum to make decisions, it helped to create a high level of understanding among the participants and produced valuable advice to the Prime Minister. However, the influence of *Comité de l'Espace* was limited because it was only an advisory body and the major decisions were taken in another interministerial framework (Clerc 1997). As soon as Hubert Curien came in as *tutelle* minister, *Comité de l'Espace* was no longer held. In 1994, the Prime Minister took the initiative to preside over the *'réunion des ministres'* which is a renewed version of *Conseil interministeriel*.

Reform of Space Administration: DGE and Minister of Space

This section deals with the experiment that took place during 1988–92. In retrospect, the emergence and disappearance of strong space administrative machineries raise interesting questions on government-agency relationship, and on locus of power in space policy-making.

The Socialist government formed under Michel Rocard was not the same government as in 1981. Through the experience of policy U-turn in 1983 and *cohabitation*, the Socialists realized that *dirigisme* was not the remedy to cure the economic downturn. It was at this time that *Corbertisme <high-tech>* was called into question (Cohen 1992).

It was also the time when the ESA Ministerial Council at the Hague in 1987 decided to participate in an International Space Station and to launch Ariane 5, Hermès and Columbus programs for European autonomous manned space capability. France became leading contributor to Ariane 5 and Hermès programs by 45% and third contributor to Columbus program by 14% (see chapter 4), which promised a sharp increase in ESA contribution in the long term. For space administration in France, the changing context of European collaboration had two-sided implications. First, given the enormous amount of development cost, the French government had to secure the contribution as long as the French commitment continued. In other words, French space administration had to defend the space budget from critics by other ministries and the general public. However, in order to secure the space budget within limited resources, the government had to control the activities of CNES. It could no longer accept all the proposals from CNES in order to maintain long-term commitment to the manned space programs.

In response to the changing and changed circumstances, the Ministry of Post, Telecommunications and Space was created, with Paul Quilès who was the defense minister as head. It was obvious that the Rocard government wanted to increase links between space and telecommunication activities, and bring in a heavy-weight politician to strengthen the importance of space within the government. However, the distribution of portfolio was to some extent personal rather than institutional. In 1992 when the Cresson government was formed, Quilès was named as Minister for Equipment, Lodgement, Transportation and Space, which was a completely irrelevant ministry to space, except for satellite navigation and some Earth observation activities. This incident tells us that although space appeared on the portfolio, it was not considered as a permanent institutional installation.

The *Délégation Générale de l'Espace* (DGE) was created to provide technical and administrative support and advice to the Minister of Space. Before the creation of DGE, space administration was dominated by the expertise and human resources from CNES. It was a matter of urgency for Paul Quilès to have a robust and competent space administrative body to counterbalance the power and expertise of CNES. Michel Petit who was space scientist in the *Centre National de la Recherche Scientifique* (CNRS) was thus chosen as the *Délégué Général de l'Espace*. Under his leadership, there were some fifteen officials including three *Délégué Général adjoint* and an advisor for strategic affairs. Although its mandate was not clearly defined, two broad objectives were formulated for DGE, coordination and oversight. For the first objective, divisions of civil application, research and observation, and military affairs were created, and for the second, divisions were set up for overseeing international affairs, industrial affairs, and law and budget.

Compared to the conventional practices of *tutelle*, DGE was quite unique in several ways: first, DGE did not act as a 'representative' of CNES. Obviously, DGE had to depend on the expertise of CNES on detail matters, but because members of DGE came from inside the space community and from outside the CNES 'family', they could propose alternative ideas. For example, when the European Radar Satellite (ERS) program was proposed in the ESA council, CNES did not show its interest in radar Earth observation satellite because it had been focusing on optical satellite (SPOT). DGE clearly saw the necessity to develop radar technology and pushed the reluctant CNES to participate in the ERS program (interview with former DGE official, 18/5/98).

Second, DGE was able to delegate some of the power at interministerial meetings. Before the creation of DGE, the long-term policy and program priorities were decided at ministerial level, but in this period, it was DGE which was in charge of defining the French space objectives. Of course, such plans had to be discussed with CNES, approved by the Minister of Space and negotiated at interministerial level, and decided by the Prime Minister. But DGE's initiative was fully respected and its influence was persistent throughout the process. Such initiatives and proposals were valuable in activating the power of government to take the lead in space policy.

Third, there were increasing interactions between the civilian and military personnel through DGE and *Comité de l'Espace*. For the Ministry of Defense, space was not the high priority because of strategic and budgetary reasons. DGE sought to break the ice and try to intensify the dialogue between civil and military. Although DGE was not successful in motivating the French military, the interactions did attract some attention.

Fourth, in addition to the inauguration of civil-military discussions, DGE was responsible for developing civil-military industrial policy. Because of the dual-use nature of space technology, it was obvious that civilian industrial policy for space has an impact on military policy. Yet there were no institutional arrangements for developing 'dual industrial policy'. DGE took an initiative in discussing joint development for new space platform with the military services and *Service pour Coordination des Affaires Industrielles*. DGE also had its own budget to encourage particular programs which would have international competitiveness. Instead of giving grants or subsidies, DGE started programs by 'co-financing' with industry, that is to say, half of the development cost should be funded by industry and government funding should be paid back from the profit that was made through commercialization of programs (note the similarity to the concept of Public-Private Partnership, although different in motivation).

Facing such changes, CNES was forced to respond to such strong governmental supervision. On the one hand, CNES thought that DGE was an obstruction for the promotion of their own programs. Obviously, the more DGE gained control over CNES, the higher the tension as a result of the conflict between CNES and DGE. CNES criticized the staff of the DGE as "the troublemakers" and asserted that the DGE "had no useful purpose" (Dauncey 1994, p.199). On the other hand, CNES believed DGE was not powerful enough to control CNES. One CNES official noted that DGE was an administrative body and not an influential strategist (interview with CNES official, 14/5/98). As long as CNES could enjoy a good relationship with the powerful politicians (for example, Hubert Curien, the Minister for Research), the existence of DGE would not bother the policy initiative of CNES.

The strong governmental supervision over CNES came to an end in 1992–93. When Bérégovoy's government was formed in 1992 the space portfolio was integrated into the Ministry of Research where Hubert Curien was the minister. All this time, Curien was in conflict with Quilès about space policy. Although, Quilès himself was a scientist and understood space policy in general, Curien was 'the space man in France'. He was President of CNES and chairman of ESA, and had strong views that space should be industry- and technology-oriented, thus government should leave CNES to develop its own technology (Curien 1988). Understandably, Curien did not see the necessity to keep DGE. Curien himself also lost his position after the defeat of the Socialists in the general election of 1993. The second *cohabitation* government did not have second thoughts about re-establishing DGE again. CNES was content with having a "favorable relationship that existed between agency and its controlling minister" (Dauncey 1994, p.171).

In other words, the experiment to establish a system for imposing strong political control and for strengthening the link between telecommunications and space was mostly driven by the logic of commerce, and the logic of military to some extent. However, the reintegration of *tutelle* into the Ministry of Research, the dissolution of DGE, and granting the space portfolio to Curien meant that CNES regained the smooth access to the space decision-maker who shared the same logic of technology. The end of the experiment brought CNES 'back in the business as usual'. However, CNES had to face the changing circumstances quite soon.

Budgetary Structure and Ressources Propres

One of the remarkable features of the CNES budget structure is that it has its own disposable income, *ressources propres*, which comes from the profits of its subsidiaries. As EPIC, CNES is allowed to create its own subsidiaries to spin off their technological programs for commercial use. The typical example is the SPOTIMAGE in which CNES holds 38.54% of the share. Although *ressources propres* are not the principal source of income, 20 to 30% of CNES' income comes as ressources propres (Table 6.3). This margin of alternative resource renders a strong foothold for CNES *vis-à-vis* government. Usually CNES would ask for authorization from governments for launching new programs, but because of its alternative sources, CNES is able to start programs under 30 million francs without governmental consent (interview with French government official, 20/5/98).

With strong support from the powerful politicians, CNES has enjoyed its privileged position in its relationship with the Ministry of Budget until the end of the 1980s. As discussed above, *tutelle* ministries, which generally lack scientific and technological knowledge and expertise to verify all technological aspects of the program, have difficulties overriding proposals from CNES.

Table 6.3   CNES Budget Structure (MF)

	Ressources Propres	Subvention of State	% of *Ressources Propres*
1988	1179	5152	18.62%
1989	2158	6164	25.93%
1990	2686	6842	28.19%
1991	2498	7556	24.85%
1992	2335	8288	21.98%
1993	2414	8603	21.91%
1994	2957	9204	24.32%
1995	3517	7954	30.66%
1996	3195	9098	25.99%
1997	3135	9587	24.65%
1998	4104	10169	40.36%
1999	4280	9918	43.25%
2000	3171	9432	33.62%

Source: CNES *Rapport d'activité.*

Civilian space spending is negotiated between representatives from *tutelle* ministry and budgetary ministry in the framework of *budget civil de recherche et de développement* (BCRD). Within BCRD, space spending has to compete with other research and development activities supported by different ministries. In other words, an increase in space spending is only possible at the expense of other research and development activities. From the beginning of French space programs, strong support from powerful politicians was widely accepted, a situation that left little room for maneuver for the budgetary authority such as to reduce or limit ever-increasing space spending. This was particularly evident during the 1980s when François Mitterrand and his ministers supported manned space flight against opposition from budgetary authorities. However, such strong political support was not forthcoming from the beginning of the 1990s. BCRD has been set around 50 billion francs each year (one-fifth of which is devoted for space programs) throughout the 1990s. The ministry responsible for research had been facing the difficult situation to increase BCRD partly because of the downturn of the national economy, Maastricht convergence criteria and rigid government spending reviews. By the nature of space programs, once the government committed to programs the cost of programs accumulated immensely and became inconsistent with the government's financial policy (Creola 1991). Sequential launching of large national and European programs had already accelerated the accumulation of cost. Space spending, which had increased under such circumstances, was heavily criticized by other departments including the Ministry of Budget.

Simultaneously, French parliamentarians developed more interest in national space programs. The Parliament had long been 'a rubber stamp' for government decisions, but French parliamentarians established *Groupe Parlementaire sur l'Espace* (GPE) in 1994 to start a campaign to reevaluate the national spending plan on space. This campaign aimed at avoiding what happened in 1995 Toulouse Ministerial Council where the French government agreed to finance manned space programs without the consent of Parliament (interview with Secretary General of GPE, 9/3/00). The extent to which this parliamentary group could influence French decision-making is yet uncertain, as the move towards 'democratization' of space policy adds to the complexity of long-term policy-making.

Relationship with Industry

As we discussed in chapter 5, European industry was consolidated into a few companies, giving the landscape of French space industry a different picture. Thus in this section, we shall briefly overview the history of industrial development and the relationship between CNES and the industry and discuss the impact of industrial consolidation on CNES.

French industry experienced several industrial concentration processes after World War II. The first one was just after World War II when reconstruction of the aerospace and defense industry was high priority to restore confidence and industrial capability. Most of the aerospace industry was nationalized under the strong influence of economic planning led by Jean Monnet's *Commissariat Général du Plan.*

Table 6.4   Subsidiaries of CNES (1999)

Company and Status	Activities	CNES share	Turnover (MF)
Arianespace Participation (SA)	Holding Company of Arianespace: Production of launcher; marketing of launch service	34.26%	6,560.8
Spot Image (SA)	Marketing and promotion of SPOT data	38.54%	235.3
Intespace (SA)	Marketing test facilities to industry	38.89%	125.0
CLS (SA)	Marketing and collecting of positioning data	54.96%	148.6
Scot Council (SA)	Consulting for remote sensing application	50.99%	31.8
Novespace (SA)	Designing and conducting space technology transfer operation	48.73%	25.6
Telespace Participation (SA)	Acquiring a holding in space-related companies	99.00%	-
Simko (SA)	Kourou real estate	40.00%	148.6
Semeccel (SA)	Museum management in Toulouse	6.17%	29.6
DERSI (SARL)	Development of Franco-Russian industrial relations	99.00%	4.7
Cerfacs (GIP)	R&D for computer technology	26.00%	30.5
GDTA (GIE)	Development of aerospace remote sensing	25.00%	14.6
MEDES-IMPS (GIE)	Medical activities related to manned flights	42.86%	11.1
Satel Conseil (GIE)	Consulting and monitoring world telecom market	50.00%	13.3
Prospace (GIE)	Promoting, and marketing space industry activities	1.61%	6.6
Medias France (GIP)	Environmental research	30.00%	4.4
Renater (GIP)	Data Transfer network development	3.10%	155.0
IFRTP (GIP)	Polar research and technology	0.50%	127.7
OST (GIP)	Publishing science and technology indicator	6.00%	8.5

(SA) = Société anonyme; (SARL) = Société anonyme à responsabilité limitée;
(GIE) = Groupement d'intérêt économique; (GIP) = Groupement d'intérêt publique.
Source: CNES Rapport d'activité; Carlier and Gilli (1994).

In the late-1950s, the idea of 'national champions' became predominant in order to compete at an international level, and further concentration took place leading to the formation of the Nord and Sud Aviation. In the same manner, Nord Aviation and Sud Aviation merged to form *Société nationale industrielle aérospatiale* (SNIAS), better known as Aérospatiale in 1970. The concept of 'national champion' suited Aérospatiale comfortably. Aérospatiale has now become a part of EADS and its launcher division is integrated with EADS Launch Vehicle (LV). Its satellite division has already merged with Alcatel (see chapter 5). Contrary to Aérospatiale, Alcatel Espace, subsidiary of Alcatel Télécom remained a 'French' company. Its business depends very little on government funding. Although it is less dependent on French government funding, its subsidiaries in other European countries benefited from ESA contracts. Its subsidiaries are the first and second largest contractors to ESA in Belgium (ETCA and Alcatel Bell Telephone); the second largest in Denmark (Alcatel Kirk) and in Norway (AME Space); and the fourth largest in Spain (Alcatel Espacio) (*European Space Directory* 1999).

CNES and industry   As we have seen above, the industrial policy of CNES was aimed at developing and improving international competitiveness of French industry. We shall see the two ways of interaction between CNES and industry; *donneur d'ordre* (order provider) and creating subsidiaries.

The *dirigiste* legacy of CNES is well-represented in the expression of *donneur d'ordre*. Until recently industry had neither the surplus capital which would allow self-sufficient R&D activities nor the capacity to raise funding from private capital market. Space was a typical infant industry and it was believed that public procurement and support for R&D by CNES were indispensable. Thus CNES' role as a *donneur d'ordre* was a rational approach to develop the space industry in the early period of space development. However, because the practice of *donneur d'ordre* has continued for such a long period of time, it became a very solid institution, and the relationship between CNES and industry became inflexible in the face of dynamic industrial change, namely the commercialization of the space market. By the same token, industry was linked to a market which was protected by CNES thus rendering it not competitive largely due to the practice of the principle of *juste retour* (notably in case of Aérospatiale).

The second approach of CNES to industry is to create subsidiaries (Table 6.4). CNES is responsible for developing space technology using government funding, but when the technology is proven and experimental programs became operational, CNES cannot commit to the operation as this would have implications for commercialization. In the case of the United States (NASA) or other European states, it is the private companies which enjoy the fruits of technological development, and they are the main agent in the application of these technologies to commercial activities. However, in the case of France, these technologies are mainly developed by CNES technological centers, so CNES needs to create its own subsidiaries for transferring commercially applicable technologies. In other words, even though CNES' mandate is to develop new technologies for improving the competitiveness of the French space industry, it is the CNES itself which receives significant benefit from its activities. Two of the largest subsidiaries, Arianespace and Spot Image, are good examples of this kind of operation. Dauncey (1994) explains that the rationale of the creation of the subsidiaries is "both a justification of CNES action in undertaking responsibilities additional to its traditional role of managing the development of industry and a reflection of the belief that the agency should act to stimulate the continuing development of the sector" (pp.136–137). Not only did CNES spin out experimental programs for commercial use, but it also created consulting and marketing firms in the late 1980s (Table 6.4). In reflection of the intensifying international competition, CNES began to get involved in the consulting activities of promoting French industrial capacity to compete in the international market.

However, the commanding position and role of CNES are gradually changing due to the consolidation of the European industry. As we discussed in chapter 5, the concept of *partenariat* (Public-Private Partnership) became the central strategy for redefining the relationship with industry. Although CNES may still hold its strength in research and development, its position as *donneur d'ordre* may no longer be appropriate. This is why CNES took the leadership in developing the concept of the 'Union of Centers'. The process of significant institutional change is now taking place even in the most influential space agency in Europe.

Germany

Although Germany is the second largest country after France in terms of contributions to the ESA and spending on national programs, the characteristic of its space policy is quite different to that of France. After the defeat in World War II, there were laws and regulations prohibiting Germany from having an aerospace industry until 1955. In 1958, a decision was taken to loosen the regulations and Germany began to develop its own aerospace industry. This followed the decision of the allies to strengthen the German industrial base in order to use German soil and technical expertise to build American aircraft. Such historical conditions shaped the path of the development of German space policy and industry.

The characteristic feature of German space policy can be categorized in three parts: first, international collaboration "was used in Germany as a means of regaining both the technical competence and political respectability of the aerospace sector" (Thornton 1995, p.64). In other words, unlike France, national programs were not chosen as a means to develop and enhance its technological competence (see Chart 6.2). It does not mean that Germany has been always in the subordinate position to other countries. For developing technologies which it targeted as its core competence such as radar sensor for Earth observation, Germany lead in both the existing collaboration scheme such as ESA and *ad hoc* bi- and multi-lateral collaboration.

Second, because of the small scale of its national programs and openness for international collaboration, German space policy exhibited a sensitivity to strategic and diplomatic relationship with other countries. Both European collaboration, namely Franco-German axis, and Transatlantic relationship was reflected upon the formulation of German space policy. On the one hand, European collaboration was a vehicle for promoting German interest, particularly commercial interest, but, on the other hand, Germany accepted the position of a junior partner in collaboration with the US to a certain extent (interview with DLR official, 12/6/98). German involvement in collaborative activities with the US was motivated both by foreign policy consideration and compatriotic ties.

Chart 6.2 German Civil Space Spending (MAU)

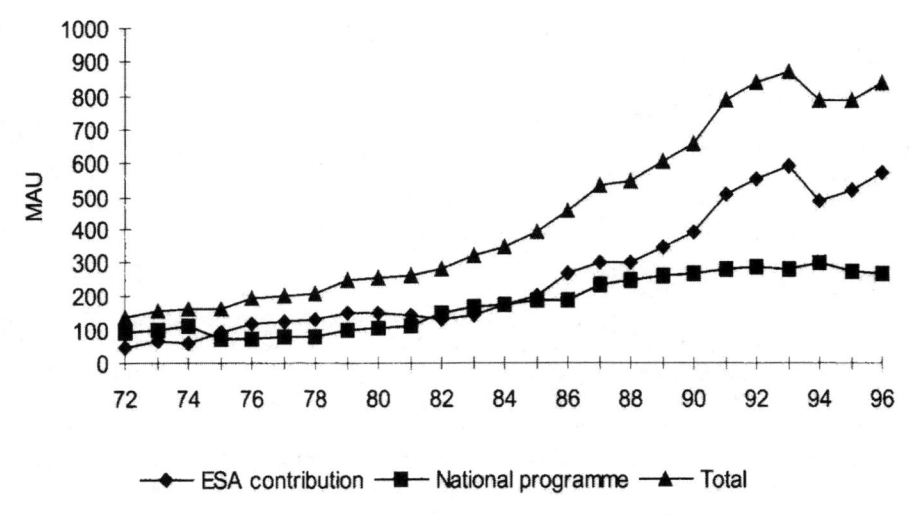

Source: European *Space Directory.*

There were considerable numbers of German exiles working in important positions in NASA at the time of the 1970s and 1980s.[4] However, the experience of *Symphonie* and Spacelab in particular made the German position more 'Europeanist' than 'Atlantist' (see chapter 4). Third, compared to France and the UK, Germany had a different security environment. Because dependence on NATO alliance and constitutional constraints on military activities discouraged Germans from developing a military capability in space, German space policy was not driven by its military strategic needs. Therefore, unlike France and the UK, the development of space capacity in the first place was not motivated by the logic of military, but the logics of science and technology. However, after the end of the Cold War, there emerged an increasing need to have a sort of defense space system in order to meet growing German participation in the UN Peacekeeping Forces, although the German government clearly recognized that the system should be constructed as a European, not a national, system.

The reunification of Germany, following the end of the Cold War, brought a huge impact on the allocation of budgets for space activities. The overall budgetary priority shifted to reconstruction of the Eastern part of Germany at the expense of other spending areas including space. Since many German space programs are conducted with international partners, space expenditure has to be secured until the end of each program. However, the pressure of the logic of finance has been increasing so much that it is expected that Germany would neither launch new programs nor take part in large international or European programs.

German Space Agencies: Historical Development

Unlike the case of France, German space policy as such has never been the central issue of national politics. Neither was it strongly protected by powerful politicians. It was rather subordinated to other policy objectives, particularly technology and foreign policy. Consequently, the German space agency was unable to act in the same way as the CNES did in France. Neither was the German space agency willing to assume such a role. In fact, as we will see below, there was no coherent institutional arrangement for space policy-making at agency level. Although *Deutsche Forschungsanstalt für Luft- und Raumfahrt* (DLR)[5] had been acting as the technological center, its role and responsibility was not focused on policy-making.

GfW period The beginning of German space activities was initiated by the logic of science. International Geophysical Year (IGY) ignited scientific research in space Europe-wide which led to the creation of European Space Research Organization (ESRO) in 1964 as well as in Germany. *Deutsche Forschungs-gemeinschaft* (DFG), one of the major participants in IGY lobbied government to take part in European space activities and promote space research at national level. The government quickly recognized these movements and granted responsibility for space policy to the Federal Ministry of Research and Technology (BMBT) in 1962. At the same time, *Gesellschaft für Weltraumforschung* (GfW) was created as the managing agency for the implementation of space policy, and three existing research institutions for aeronautics and space research, which have been established under local *länders*, were integrated as the federal research institution, DLR.[6]

However, in 1968, the government decided to integrate GfW with DLR. The rationale behind this decision was to rationalize the implementation process and to maximize the efficiency of space programs. It was also because the government realized that most of space programs were to be based on collaboration with European and transatlantic partners, and there were very few significant national programs which ruled out any urgent necessity for keeping a national agency.

Merger of GfW and DLR At the time the government decided to transfer GfW's brief, DLR created an independent 'management department'. Although the transfer was well justified by the federal government, this action was heavily criticized by industry. At that time, DLR as a research institution was competing with industry to get federal contracts. The merger, according to industry, would create an unfair environment for industry since the newly merged 'management department' of DLR would prefer to invest in science and technology programs rather than industrial programs and to provide contracts to the in-house programs of DLR.

Despite the criticism from industry, the 'management department' and research institutions have not yet been integrated. The 'management department' maintained a close relationship with the Ministry of Research and Technology and acted as the agency of the Ministry, whereas DLR as a research institution maintained certain independence from government intervention since it was established as an association (*eingetragener Verein:* e.V.). Such antipathy between the two sections of DLR was welcomed by industry, but it did not create the anticipated effect of a merger (interview with DLR official, 4/6/98).

Space Station programs and creation of DARA In April 1989, the Cabinet made a decision to restructure the management of space activity and to create a central organization, *Deutsche Agentur für Raumfahrt-Angelegenheiten* (DARA). DARA was set up as a private law company with limited liability (GmbH) in order to give DARA flexibility in its activities, promote mobility of personnel between DARA and industry, industry like management, and contacts with industry.

The creation of a space policy agency again was motivated by three objectives. The most immediate one was the decision of Germany to participate in the ESA manned space programs of which it took a leading role in Columbus Space Station program. Primarily, DARA was mandated to manage large-scale programs like Columbus and prepare and enforce decisions of ESA and government. At the same time, the government found that it was necessary to change the management structure in order to establish strong German leadership and influence in ESA. The second objective was to create NASA or CNES-like space center in space policy-making. Similar to the UK (see below), ministerial competence for space policy was segmented among the ministries concerned, and there was no efficient and effective interministerial machinery for space policy-making. Therefore DARA was created to concentrate on space policy competence by transferring them from different ministries, draft space policy and programs. The third objective was to organize a better coordination between government and industry. Germany did not have sufficient institutional arrangements to involve industry in a space policy-making process. DARA was expected to generate much closer coordination with industry to meet the increasing importance of space applications, notably in the telecommunications sector.

In order to meet the three objectives, DARA was given wide responsibilities in relation to space activities. The first and most important one was to propose German space policy. Before the creation of DARA, it was the government (more precisely Ministry of Research and Technology) which drafted the previous four overall space policies. Thus the mission of drafting space policy was supposed to give strong political capability for DARA. In June 1990, the Cabinet proposed a guideline to DARA for drafting the fifth German space policy. However, DARA has not had a chance to draft and submit it because of the sudden change in the international environment, particularly the fall of Berlin Wall. Unfortunately for DARA, the opportunity for establishing a politically strong and competent agency was ruined by unfortunate timing. Ironically, the first time when DARA's draft space policy paper, *Space: Prospects for research and application* was approved by the government, it was after the decision to merge DARA and DLR in 1997 (see below). It should be noted here that the new competence for DARA to formulate German space policy was restricted to the drafting of a strategic plan rather than individual programs which involve budgetary implications. Those decisions were left to the ministerial level.

Secondly, DARA was given a responsibility for the implementation of German space policy. DARA took over the responsibility of the 'management department' of DLR to award industrial contracts and to allocate government funding. Five specific tasks were mentioned as DARA's implementation competence; (1) consultation and support for the federal ministries and public institutions, and coordination with industry and scientific bodies; (2) promotion, control and supervision of projects, and evaluation of results; (3) planning and coordinating operations; (4) taking initiatives to encourage commercialization; (5) allocation of funds from the space budget (Spude 1997). Facing increasing need for military space programs, DARA was also granted a responsibility to manage defense as well as civilian programs. Although political control remained at the level of the Ministry of Defense, there were certain activities that DARA might be responsible for, especially the management of German participation in military programs.

Finally, DARA was given exclusive rights to represent German interest in international fora. DARA was the only representative body in the ESA Council and was authorized to sign MoU (Memorandum of Understanding) with other space agencies. However, a decision to participate or allocate funds in ESA or any type of international program, or any political decision, which might have budgetary implications remained with the supervising ministry.

In order to fulfill those missions, the political competence that has been segmented among ministries has to be transferred to DARA. At the same time that the Cabinet decided to create DARA, the draft law of *Raumfahrtaufgaben-übertragungsgesetz* (RAÜeG) was brought to *Bundestag*, and entered into force in June 1990. The RAÜeG obliged all federal ministries to transfer their competence concerning space activities to DARA by concluding a bilateral agreement between each ministry and DARA, particularly for those whose competence directly relates to DARA missions. However, though RAÜeG was binding to all ministries concerning space, so far the only ministry that has completed a bilateral agreement is the Ministry of Research and Technology which was the supervisory ministry of DARA. Since the political environment has turned around after the fall of the Berlin Wall, the issue of transfer of competence was left out from the political agenda.

Back to DLR   The decision to merge DARA and DLR by the Cabinet in July 1997 surprised the entire space community in Europe. It was firmly believed that the creation of DARA was a reflection of the intention of the government to concentrate and reinforce German space policy. Given the dramatic change of circumstances, however, the German government was not able to keep the flag flying. The law of *Raumfahrtaufgaben-übertragungsgesetz* (RAÜeG) was passed in the *Bundestag* and DARA was integrated with DLR on 1 October 1997.

The primary reason for the re-merger was to reduce significant numbers of personnel in both organizations and eliminate conflicts and duplication in management and R&D. Since most of the German program was managed through ESA (the same reason as GfW/DLR merger), the government realized that it was not a necessity to maintain a management capability in DARA. The Ministry of Education, Science, Research and Technology (BMBF) announced that the merger would improve cooperation between ministries, implementation of policies, managerial functions and finance, and use of means with maximum results for international activities (*DLR Comprehensive Information* no. 3e/97 – Za, 1997).

The renewed and integrated DLR has the following objectives; promoting Germany's role as an internationally leading partner in space; furthering excellence in the field of science, research, and development; realizing technological developments through industrial applications; cutting costs, while maintaining high quality standards. Even though these objectives seem similar to those of DARA, it was clear that the merger with DLR would reemphasize the logic of technology.

Although the merger seemed to make sense under the economic and political situation in Germany, there remained some organizational confusion which would be solved sooner or later. First of all, the transfer of ministerial competence to DARA has remained incomplete, and whether the integrated DLR would have legal authority to receive that competence was not specifically mentioned in RAÜeG. It stated that ministries concerned will continue to supervise DLR, but it did not deny the possibility of transfer of competence as well. Nevertheless, more than eight years of disregarding RAÜeG has shown that neither individual ministries nor the Cabinet were interested in transferring their competence. Secondly, the organizational structure of integrated DLR is not yet very clear. Administratively, the old DARA part maintained its managing function in the office in Bonn whereas research institutions were situated in Köln-Porz. Last but not least, the question of finance of DLR should be answered. Currently there are two kinds of budget provided from BMBF to DLR. One is called 'agency budget' which goes to the old DARA part of DLR to allocate contracts and subsidies to industry, and the other is called 'institutional budget' which runs programs and expenses of R&D in DLR. Learnt from the experience of GfW and DLR merger, the 'agency budget' is subjected to a condition that it should be used neither for the administrative expense of DLR nor for awarding contracts to research institutions of DLR internally (interview with DLR official, 4/6/98).

Government Supervision

The structure of governmental supervision for German space activities has been relatively stable although the management agency structure has changed over time.

The field of space activities is mainly covered by the Ministry of Research and Technology (BMBT, later renamed as Ministry of Education, Science, Research and Technology, BMBF), but other ministries share some responsibilities for space activities according to their competence.

The Ministry of Economy (BMWi) is responsible for all economic and industrial activities. BMWi was the central actor of promoting efficiency and competitiveness of German aerospace industry, and holds a section called *Arbeitsgruppe des Koordinators für die Deutsche Luft- und Raumfahrt* (working group of coordinators of aerospace) which coordinates at the ministerial level. However, this working group rather concentrates on other areas of aerospace activities (e.g. Airbus, Eurocopter etc.) and space has not been treated as the most important area (interview with BMWi official, 17/6/98).

The Ministry of Post and Telecommunications (BMPT) holds responsibilities for developing and operating space telecommunications systems. Although BMPT sponsored several telecommunications satellite programs (TV-Sat, Copernicus etc.), it was, in fact, not willing to invest in space communication infrastructure until the late-1980s because BMPT put higher priority for cable network (firstly copper, then fiber-optics) and considered that the investment in space was a duplication of capacity. Hence it was BMBF which took the initiative to launch *Symphonie* and TV-Sat programs. This implied that even though the German government promoted commercially potential programs, they were driven by the logic of technology.

The Ministry of Transport (BMV) is responsible for meteorology, navigation, Earth observation and development of user industry. Although space is indispensable in some of these areas such as meteorology, BMV considers space as one of the means of pursuing the objectives, and often considers that spacecrafts and data from space are so expensive that it would prefer to use terrestrial means as much as possible.

Until recently, the Ministry of Defense (BMVg) had limited responsibility for space within the NATO framework, but as mentioned above, the change of international climate and German military role gave BMVg a greater responsibility. However, given the increasing pressure from the logic of finance, its potential contribution to the European and German military space development is quite limited.

Except for BMBF, most ministries responsible for space activities do not put space activities as a high priority for many reasons. For them, space is an expensive alternative which can be a less favorable option for implementing their objectives, or a minor category of broader activities of aerospace. In this sense, it is not difficult to understand why these ministries were not willing to proceed with RAÜeG. Since it may authorize an independent space agency to draw up space programs, it will be difficult for the ministries to control unexpected budget increases.

Ministry of Education, Science, Research and Technology (BMBF) Legally, the supervision of German space agency — be it GfW, DLR 'management department', DARA or DLR 'agency section' — is under the supervision of the whole government since it is established as a private association (e.V.) or company (GmbH) and government holds the majority of shares. However because of such low interest shown by other ministries, the Ministry of Education, Science, Research and Technology (BMBF) is in fact the only major actor and protagonist of space activities.

By narrow definition, the section which deals with space is located under Department 6 with 6–10 staff. With such a small number of administrative staffs, it is not designed to follow all the detail of space technology, but concentrate on administrative coordination of overall space policy. However, space has been a major and cross-sectional policy area for BMBF. Department 1 which deals with strategic planning and international cooperation is involved in space policy-making, and Department 4 on energy and environment to a lesser extent. Space policy is formulated through discussion among those staff in different sections and drawn up under the leadership of Department 6. For example, the Federal Government Strategy Document which was drafted by DARA was submitted to the BMBF and circulated through Departments 1, 4, and 6, before it was approved by the Minister of BMBF (interview with DLR official, 04/6/98).

The strong presence of BMBF in the process of policy-making implies that the research institutes (including 'institution section' of DLR) have better access to the community of scientists for promoting their policy logic. In fact, strong scientific institutions such as the Max Planck Institute were the main architects of the German national program for Microgravity research, D1 and D2 (interview with DLR official, 12/6/98). The strength of the logic of science and technology is thus derived from the powerful position of BMBF and the 'institution section' of DLR.

Supervisory board of DARA/DLR Although some years have passed since DARA has merged to DLR, the new supervisory structure for DLR is still in a state of flux. Currently the dual supervisory structures for the 'agency section' and the 'institution section' of DLR co-exist and future plans for integrating supervising boards are yet to come. Since this chapter focuses on the relationship between the government and the policy management agency, we shall focus on the 'agency section' of DLR.

The supervisory board of 'agency section' consists of 12 members; (1) Government representatives from BMBF, BMWi, BMVg, BMV, BMPT, Ministries of Foreign Affairs, Finance; (2) Chairman of DLR ('institution section'); (3) two representatives from industry; (4) two representatives from academia. The BMBF chairs the Board on behalf of Federal Chancellor. Unlike in the case of *Conseil d'Administration* in CNES, the 'agency section' is not allowed to participate in the supervisory board to represent their interests. Instead, the 'agency section' has the main responsibility of the executive board which concerns itself with the implementation of the decisions made by the supervisory board. The clear distinction between the supervisory and executive board and the role of the 'agency section' is a unique feature of German space policy-making. The agency has very limited influence on policy-shaping process, and therefore, has less access to the decision-makers than its French counterpart.

Interministerial coordination Since the beginning of space development in Germany, there was no institutional framework for interministerial coordination except for a few years from 1963 when interministerial committee for space research was established. However, together with the creation of DARA, the Cabinet decided to create interministerial framework to facilitate the interministerial coordination.

First, two institutions were created at the Cabinet level. Ministers from BMBF, BMWi, BMVg, BMV, BMPT, Ministries of Foreign Affairs, Finance — the same ministries representing government in the supervisory board of the 'agency section' — under the chairmanship of Federal Chancellor formed the Cabinet Committee for Space. This is a forum to consult and coordinate fundamental strategy and policy. It is also the ultimate authority to approve large-scale programs. This Committee has held only one meeting since its creation; for the same reason the transfer of competence has not proceeded. The Cabinet Committee is expected to play a strong role in promoting the transfer of competence and German space policy in general, but it does not seem to be ready yet.

On the other hand, the Under-secretary of State Committee for Space which is formed by the under-secretaries from the same ministries in the Cabinet Committee, prepares documents and guidelines for the decisions in the Cabinet Committee. It also gives political guidelines of German space activities for the supervisory board of the 'agency section' and guidance for concluding international agreements between space agencies. Since the Cabinet Committee is not active, it has become an alternative intergovernmental framework at highest level (interview with BMWi official, 17/6/98).

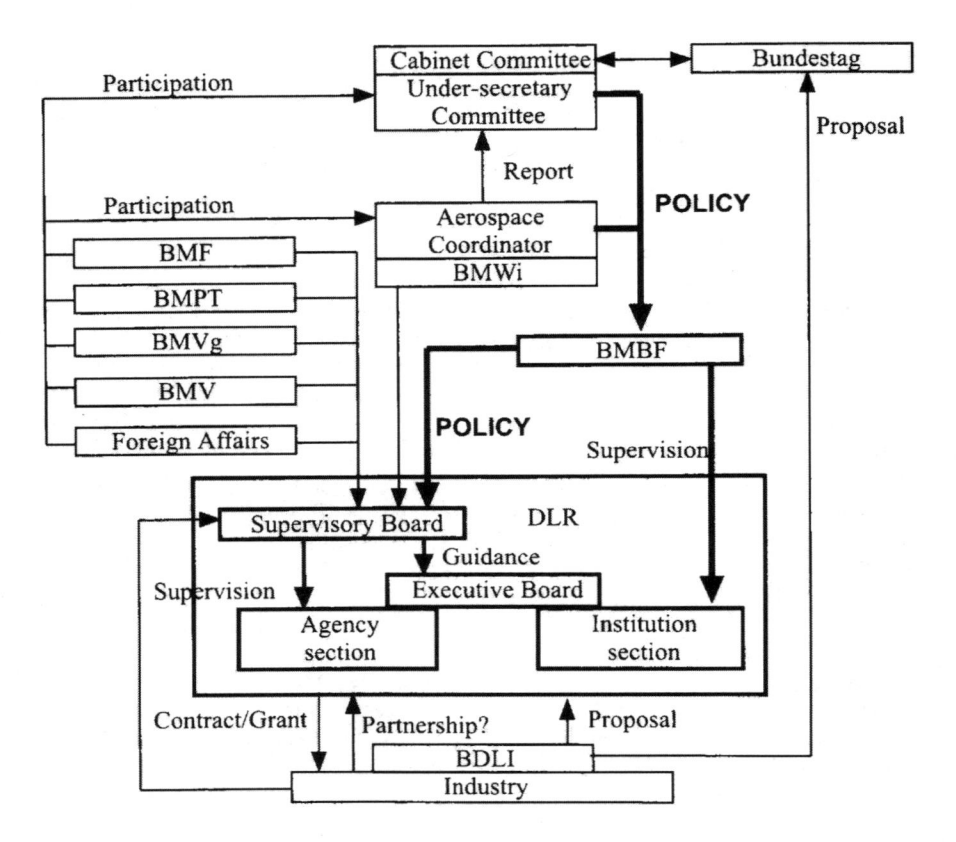

Figure 6.2   German Space Policy-making Process

Budgetary Control by Government

The process of budget allocation is more complicated than in the case of France. Although space agency (DARA, DLR 'agency section' etc.) receives a budget from BMBF, the actual budget is allocated within the budget of respective ministries (Table 6.5). Thus, the space agency should submit proposals for individual programs to ministries according to their competence. The German space agency does not have a right to raise funds other than public funding thus it may not possess its own resources like the French *ressources propres*, although DLR could raise money from local Länders since 10% of its share is held by them.

Once the space budget is allocated to the ministries, the space agency has authority to allocate and dispose of this funding internally. However, given that the space agency is under the strong control of the government, it is often the case that the agency consults with ministries for detailed distribution plans of the resources.

Since budgetary allocation is strictly under the control of ministries concerned, and the space agency does not have the authority on budgetary decisions, it has no direct bilateral relationship with the Ministry of Finance (BMF). However, because of RAÜeG, the space agency can negotiate and conclude bilateral agreements on the administrative cost with BMBF, which binds bilateral negotiations between BMBF and BMF. This may represent a small change but it represents a degree of financial autonomy of the space agency in Germany.

Table 6.5   Funding Allocation by Ministries (DM million)

Ministry	Purpose	DMm
BMBF	ESA Contribution	1070
	National programs	300
	Hypersonic research	20
	Environmental research	14
	DLR institutional budget	180
	DARA administrative cost	54
BMV	Contribution to Eumetsat	69
BMPT (Deutsche Telecom)	Contribution to Intelsat etc.	213
Ministry of Foreign Affairs	-	6
BMWi	-	3
BMVg	-	1
Others	-	1

Source: Spude (1997), p.57.

In the Federal Government Strategic Document, a new principle of 'design to budget' was introduced to improve efficiency of management. This principle aimed to define "what is technically desirable and feasible" first, and only then, to scrutinize if the program "goes beyond what can be afforded" (BMBF 1997, p.13). By this principle, program planning should contain suitable contingency provisions and contracts should be produced on a fixed term basis. The real aim of this principle was to strengthen the control of BMF over the space agency, due to the tight financial constraints and the huge cost overrun of the International Space Station program. The BMF was not at all pleased with the delay and changes of the European module for ISS, the Columbus, to which Germany contributes the largest proportion. Therefore, the introduction of the principle of 'design to budget' was a triumph of the logic of finance to institutionalize the budgetary control over the logic of technology.

Quite unlike the case of France and UK, the German Parliament (*Bundestag*) has specific interest in and exercises influence on space policy-making. Not only has the Bundestag passed several laws concerning management of space programs, but also it sometimes uses its power to modify budgetary requests from BMF. This is particularly evident in recent years. Military space programs, Helios 2 and Horus, were rejected by *Bundestag* (the latest victim was the Airbus 400M). Moreover, *Bundestag* reserves the right to approve all ESA projects with a financial 'envelope' of more than 100 million DM. Since *Bundestag* has a certain influence on budgetary questions, it has close consultation with German Aerospace Industrial Association (BDLI) to seek alternative technological and industrial advice (interview with BDLI official, 15/6/98).

Relationship with Industry

The German industry has experienced two big waves of concentration. The first one was during the 1960s when Germany decided to participate in large programs at European level, namely Airbus and ESRO/ELDO. Since then the German aerospace industry has concentrated on five companies, AEG-Telefunken (electronics), MTU (aero engines), Dornier, MBB and VFW (aircraft and space), and most of them were either nationalized or significantly influenced by government intervention. By the mid-1980s, these companies completed privatization as increasing international competition in the aircraft market needed more efficient management. However, in 1989 the government felt it was necessary to promote the further concentration of German industry under one national champion company, Deutsche Aerospace (DASA). In 1993, DASA acquired troubled Fokker of the Netherlands and became Daimler-Benz Aerospace, but retained the abbreviation DASA.

After the restructuring in 1989, DASA integrated all space facilities into two sections, Space Infrastructure Division based on MBB-ERNO facilities in Bremen and Satellite System Division based on Dornier in Münich. The Space Infrastructure Division is the prime contractor for Spacelab and Columbus Orbital Facility (COF) and provides rocket propulsion systems and subsystems for the Ariane launcher. The Satellite Systems Division has competitive advantages in radar Earth observation satellite primarily due to ERS programs. DASA was not particularly competitive in telecommunication systems partly because Germany did not have comparable military telecom satellite programs, and the government did not sponsor telecom satellite programs after the problematic TV-Sat system (see chapter 4). In other words, DASA's expertise and competitiveness was expanded through government programs.

Britain

Although Britain was one of the first countries to develop space technology in Europe, neither other European partners nor the space community in the UK itself fully appreciated its space policy. Currently the UK is the fourth largest contributor to ESA far below France and Germany. Furthermore, the UK's decision in 1987 not to participate in manned space programs has distinguished the characteristics of the space policy of those two countries.

Table 6.6 British Space Spending in 1999 (£ million)

Area of Activities	National	ESA
Earth Observation	45.28	44.23
Telecommunications	8.67	2.63
Transport/Launcher	0.62	4.53
Technology	4.50	4.83
Science	8.00	(mandatory) 39.08
Navigation	-	5.05
Other National	0.25	-
ESA General Budget	-	(mandatory) 13.25
Total	67.32	113.60

Source: BNSC.

These policies were driven by the strong policy logic of commerce and finance. Ever since the beginning of space development, for example the Carr Report in June 1960, the policy criteria for space activities were shifted from "scientific and technological development to commercial requirements and 'cost effectiveness' criteria" (Vig 1968, p.78). The British decision to 'Europeanize' the Blue Streak missile to a civilian satellite launcher and invite European countries to establish the framework for European space collaboration was made not because the government wanted to develop space capabilities, but because Blue Streak would otherwise be cancelled and significant investment in development would be wasted. By the same token, Kenneth Clarke who represented the UK in The Hague Ministerial Council in 1987 had explained the UK decision not to participate in manned space in terms of the belief that "European projects should be related to financial, economic and scientific returns" (*The Times* 29/10/87).

The characteristic features of the British space policy can also been seen from the breakdown of the space spending (Table 6.6). The majority of national budget is allocated to the Earth observation program for which British government considers that there is a new market opportunity. It may seem strange that the budget on the most profitable activity, telecommunication, is too little to support industry. This is justified, however, on the grounds that space telecommunication has already advanced and the government should leave this area to industry (interview with BNSC official, 4/11/97).

The other important characteristic feature of British space policy is its high commitment to ESA programs. As seen in Chart 6.3, a very high proportion of space budget goes to ESA programs and a very small portion for national or bilateral programs. Although the spending for national programs increased in the late 1980s, its commitment to ESA programs has been continuous throughout its history from the 1970s. It should be noted that because Britain does not participate in manned space programs, its contribution to ESA maintained stability during the late 1980s to mid 1990s.

Chart 6.3   British Civil Space Spending (MAU)

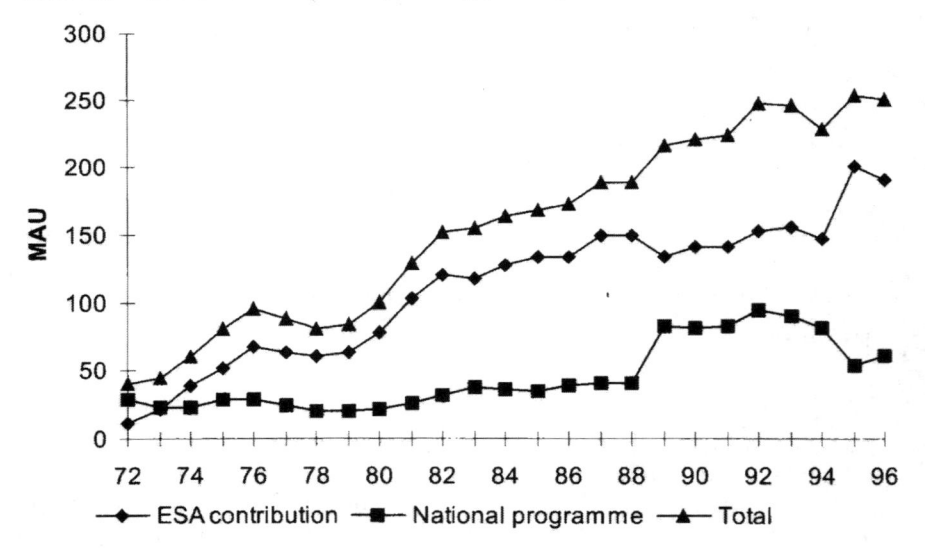

Source: European Space Directory 1989, BNSC.

Contrary to the British commitment to ESA in civilian programs, the UK has acquired its expertise in military space programs through collaboration with the US in the early days of space development. The US was involved in the development of Blue Streak and supplied technical expertise to develop SKYNET 2[7] military telecom satellite. However, as British companies developed their own expertise through ESA programs, the dependency for American technology was reduced even in military programs. The British government launched SKYNET 4 and 5 without collaboration with US firms. Although military and strategic alliance with the US is crucial to the UK defense policy in general, it is not a crucial factor in the UK's military space policy.

British Space Policy Management

When the British scientists, led by Massey, were actively involved in creating ESRO, they also pressed the government to establish a national framework for civilian space research. Scientists had already formed the British Interplanetary Society (BIS) which in fact was the leading organization of British participation in International Geophysical Year (IGY). In 1958, the government and scientists reached an agreement to establish the British National Committee for Space Research (BNCSR) funded by governmental budget. Although BNCSR acted as a management agency for space programs, it did not have authority to represent Britain in international negotiation. It remained a purely domestic organization for allocating funding for space research. The political, financial and diplomatic decisions were made in the Interministerial Steering Committee in the Lord President's Office (Massey and Robins 1986). Thus, neither individual minister nor departments held the responsibility for formulating or implementing space policy, and the Committee was simply mandated to articulate and coordinate inputs from different departments. Thus, in order to create a concrete focus of policy formulation and implementation, BNCSR's responsibility for space science was transferred to the Natural Environment Research Council (NERC) in 1965, an institution largely driven by the logic of science. However, the low profile of NERC in the Cabinet made it difficult to make space policy a high priority.

Under such a loose coordination system at the level of government and lack of political support for a comprehensive space policy, it was up to individual departments in charge of individual programs. The departmentalism in British policy machinery was common in other policy areas, but space in particular was a typical case of "the 'pragmatism' so deeply ingrained in the British process, or the 'disjointed incrementalism' of the policy analyst" (Eberle and Wallace 1987, p.40). Needless to say, the communication with industry, pressure groups and the wider public was channeled through individual departments so that there was no single form of 'space community', but several 'communities' — among them, scientists and industrialists have difficulties in coordinating their action — were formed according to the area of activities.

Before the British National Space Centre (BNSC) was created, there were many attempts to overcome weakness and inconsistency, or to set up strong centers like NASA or CNES in British space policy-making structure. The first attempt was made by a cross-bench group in Parliament called the Space Research Group (SRG) which was active from 1960–62. MPs in SRG were frustrated to see the inconsistency and opportunistic attitude of the government in reaching agreement on issues of the fate of Blue Streak and European collaboration on space research. In March 1961, a Bill was introduced in the Commons to create a Minister of Space to increase coordination among departments involved in space. The Bill did not attract attention from other MPs, and the government refused to create an agency or a board to coordinate space policy (Vig 1968). Another argument was made in the House of Commons Estimates Committee's report on Space Research and Development in

1967, and the fifth report of House of Commons Select Committee on Science and Technology in 1971. Both reports urged the government to create a single independent authority to direct space programs, but again, the report was neglected by the government. A meaningful attempt was made in 1979 when a government think tank (the Central Policy Review Staff) put a proposal to the Prime Minister for a new organization on space matters. This time, Whitehall reacted by setting up a committee chaired by Michael Marshall, junior minister in the Department of Industry, to organize departments including Ministries of Defense, Education and Science, and Agriculture (Marsh 1991). Although the committee could not have the full support of the government, it generated a positive feeling in Whitehall for coordination of space programs and paved the way for the creation of BNSC.

British National Space Centre (BNSC)

In 1985, the government finally made a decision to create a space agency to manage British space programs. Internally, the strong leadership of Geoffrey Pattie, Minister for Information Technology and Sir Robin Nicholson, Chief Scientific Adviser to the government convinced the government of the necessity for a single authority for space policy. More importantly, the decision of the ESA Ministerial Council at Rome in 1985 brought a new environment. Because of the size and impact of the programs, it seemed that the old practice of opportunism and pragmatism were not suitable for the British position. Thus, the British National Space Centre (BNSC) was created to amalgamate British efforts in a single agency and to entrust it with the formation of a coherent strategic position. The selection of Roy Gibson, who was the first Secretary General of ESA, to the position of the Secretary General of BNSC raised a high expectation for space enthusiasts that the future of BNSC was promising.

The urgent mission for BNSC in its creation was to analyze the impact and application of the decision in Rome and to prepare a strategic paper which would reflect the British position in The Hague ministerial council. Immediately after the creation, BNSC set up a Space Station Utilization Study coordinated by representatives of major uses and funding bodies — Department of Trade and Industry (DTI), Met Office, Science and Engineering Research Council (SERC), and NERC — to assess the cost and benefit of participation, and the consequence of non-participation, particularly in Columbus Space Station programs (Harrison 1987).

The report was sent to the Cabinet in 1987, but at that time, the political climate had completely changed from 1985. The strong supporters of BNSC and space activities, Geoffrey Pattie and Michael Heseltine had left or were about to leave the Cabinet, and instead, Michael Shannon and Kenneth Clarke who knew very little about space came in to take over responsibility. Moreover, the Director General had "no firm power base" (Eberle and Wallace 1987, p.53) to persuade or convince ministers. The potential of BNSC and space activities were totally dependent on political support, and it was no longer available in 1987. As a consequence, a surprising decision was made in the ESA Ministerial Council at The Hague in November 1987, and Roy Gibson, Director General of BNSC resigned (see chapter 4). It turned around the fate of BNSC.

After 1987, the missions of BNSC have been revised according to the new stance of the Cabinet. The principal objective of establishing BNSC remained the provision of a better coordination of British space spending, but the mission was reduced to 'advise' and act on behalf of Government, and to provide a focus for UK civil space policies. However, the leadership of BNSC has been changing in the last few years when the policy logics of other European partners came close to that of the British. BNSC under the initiative of Ian Taylor, Minister for Space from 1994–97, published the first strategic document, *UK Space Policy Forward Plan*, which influenced the strategic plans of CNES and the German federal government. The Forward Plan was constantly revised and updated under the Labor government. Although BNSC still remains an advisory organ, its leadership and influence should not be discounted.

Since BNSC was, and still is, separated from the space section of DTI, its administrative status is quite different from its French and German counterpart. Apart from the Director General,[8] its staffs are seconded from 'partner' departments or organizations such as DTI and Met office. Owing to the initiative of Roy Gibson, relatively high rank civil servants from 'partner' departments have come to occupy senior positions in BNSC. Its headquarters is in London with some 40 officials and no affiliating technological centers such as CST of CNES or 'institution section' of DLR, though it collaborates closely with the Defense Evaluation and Research Agency (DERA) and the Central Laboratory of the Research Councils (CLRC). BNSC is thus seen as a center of political coordination rather than independent agency.

Government Supervision

Since the independence of BNSC in terms of human resources, technological expertise, political competence and finance, has been limited compared to CNES and 'agency section' of DLR, the extent of government supervision is much greater. Interestingly, the supervisory framework of BNSC provides an opportunity for interministerial coordination because of the 'departmentalism' in British space policy-making. In other words, the British government does not have a proper interministerial framework for space at ministerial level.

The supervisory board of BNSC, the Resource Board,[9] consists of senior representatives from 'partner' organizations: Department of Trade and Industry (DTI) with the 'partnership' of Office of Science and Technology (OST), Ministry of Defense, Department of Environment, Natural Environment Research Council (NERC), Particle Physics and Astronomy Research Council (PPARC), Meteorological Office, and the Director General of BNSC. From April 1996, representatives from the industrial organization, the UK Industrial Space Committee (UKISC), joined the Resource Board. These representatives meet twice a year under the chairmanship of the DTI's Director General for Industry.[10] Its role is to discuss programs which are to be sponsored by individual departments, and to negotiate possibilities of joint funding. It also has authority to decide management of BNSC and approve annual reports. So far, the Resource Board has been acting as a focus for intergovernmental frameworks, and in British space policy context, it is a significant step forward for having regular interministerial meetings.

Perhaps, the most important institutional innovation in 1985 was the creation of a Minister for Space to take a responsibility to supervise and coordinate all space activities in the UK. The power and influence of the Minister for Space is dependent on the cooperation of the other ministers: however, the creation of the portfolio of space generates a clear and visible responsibility for the individual minister. The Minister for Space was usually a junior minister of DTI, but the current minister, Lord Sainsbury, is the Parliamentary Under-Secretary of State for Science in the Office of Science and Technology. Obviously there was a minister in charge of space in the DTI before the creation of BNSC, but his responsibility was limited within the competence of the DTI and did not have extensive responsibility for interministerial coordination. Although the creation of a Minister for Space crystallized the responsibility of the Cabinet to an individual minister, the influence of the minister depends on the personality of the minister in charge. Ministers are usually not appointed by their competence or interest in space. As seen in the change of political climate from 1985 to 1987, the personality and interest for space involved in the ministerial position has a strong influence on the entire British space program. Furthermore, until the mid 1990s, the Minister for Space has changed

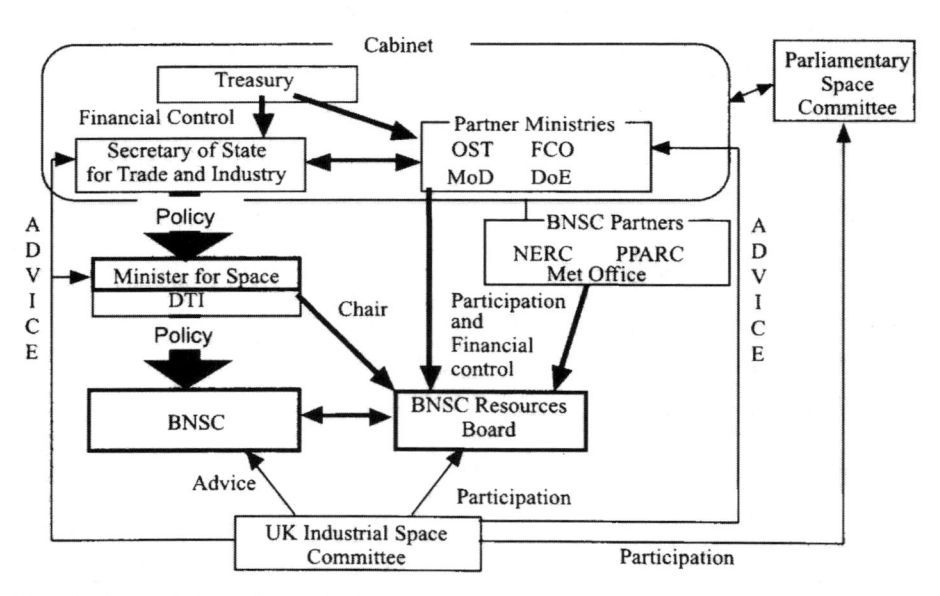

Figure 6.3   British Space Policy-making Process

quite rapidly almost on a yearly basis (Table 6.7). Ministers appointed to space did not have enough time to develop their own ideas and strategies for overall space policy.

Budgetary Control by Government

Even after the creation of BNSC, financial resources came through individual departments to BNSC. Although Geoffrey Pattie gave authority to Roy Gibson to consider arrangements for full budgetary authority to BNSC (*House of Commons Debate*, 26/11/85, c551–552w), the decision of 1987 destroyed the opportunity.

Individual departments maintain their own authorities to decide the amount and objectives of programs for which they grant funds. BNSC itself does not have a budget of its own (funding for programs is decided by partner ministries), and its administrative budget is included in the DTI's budget. Furthermore, BNSC does not have the authority to propose or promote programs. In this sense, its budgetary independence is far less than CNES, and even less than DLR. Since the British overall space spending was kept under rigid control by the Treasury, the increasing cost of space programs, particularly ESA programs, squeeze out the possibility of launching new national programs or participating in new ESA programs. Moreover, because each department holds its own bilateral negotiation with the Treasury, and because each department wants to maintain its principal projects, space is often exposed to the threat of budgetary cuts. The Minister for Space is in the position to convince other departments to hold their budget for space: however, such attempts usually invite severe changes that departments cannot afford to spend on space programs at the expense of other projects (interview with former Minister for Space, 21/4/98).

Table 6.7   British Ministers for Space

Sep. 1985–May 1987	Geoffrey Pattie, John Butcher
May 1987–Jul. 1989	Tony Newton, Kenneth Clarke, John Butcher, Robert Atkins
Jul. 1989–Nov. 1990	Douglas Hogg
Nov. 1990–May 1993	Lord Hesketh (1990–1), Lord Reay (1991–2), Edward Leigh
May 1993–Jul. 1994	Patrick McLoughlin
Jul. 1994–May 1997	Ian Taylor
May 1997–July 1998	John Battle
Jul. 1998	Lord Sainsbury

Source: House of Commons.

Since Britain lost interest in the European civilian launcher development during the 1960s, the space spending has always been vulnerable to pressure from the Treasury. Particularly since the Conservative government took power in 1979, public expenditure became rigorous and increased the pressure to reduce space spending. Space expenditure was an easy target for the Treasury to attack individual department's budgets because the political support for space programs was not too strong to be maintained at the existing level, and space sometimes could become a candidate for spending cuts by each department. The difficulty for BNSC and Minister for Space in its relationship with the Treasury, in addition to the lack of political support from other departments, is "compounded by the continuing debate within government about the relative roles of public and private investors in technology" (Eberle and Wallace 1987, p.55). Unlike France and Germany, the rationale of government space activities in Britain is justified by the commercial and industrial return, hence it is extremely difficult to convince why government should pay for a program in which private investment may come into play in search of commercial return. The role of the Treasury is thus very important in shaping strategy for space policies. In other words, the logics of commerce and finance are institutionally prioritized, and the other logics, particularly the logics of technology and autonomy, have less relevance to the British space policy.

Parliament has not been active in influencing space policy except for the infrequent questions from MPs, reflecting the fact that the government has not been posing serious questions to Parliament. This was partially due to the failure of the Space Research Group (SRG) which was in operation during 1960–62. This was a small group of MPs enthusiastic about aerospace issue, mainly from the Conservative party. The SRG successfully pressed government to convert Blue Streak to the European civilian launcher, but it failed to create a central agency for space activities (see above). It was actively involved in initiating dialogue among industrialists and scientists, and made direct recommendations to the Prime Minister and Minister for Aviation. Nevertheless, when the proposal by SRG to develop national telecommunications systems was rejected by the government in 1962, and Britain joined the American-led global telecom system (later formed as Intelsat), SRG felt its efforts were wasted and dismissed.

However, since the government made a decision not to participate in ESA's manned space programs, the interest in space grew again in both Houses of Parliament. In 1987, the House of Lords Select Committee on Science and Technology (see Williams 1993; Cunningham and Nicholson 1991) appointed a session and published a report on UK space policy. Although the report only binds government to reply in written response, it was able to clarify the agenda and priority for the government space programs. On the other hand, in the House of Commons, the Parliamentary Space Committee (PSC) was formed in 1989. This was established as "a forum of discussion for parliamentarians and industrialists in order to promote a better understanding of space activity in the UK and the economic, technological and scientific benefits it brings" (Williamson 1992, p.159); hence its membership embraces parliamentarians from all party and industrial representatives from UK Industrial Space Committee (UKISC) and British Association of Remote Sensing Companies (BARSC). PSC was created for educational purposes in order to increase political attention and funding for space. Until today, it has not had substantial influence on the UK policy-making partly because PSC still is a group with a very small number of people and they failed to attract the attention of other MPs (interview with former Minister for Space, 21/4/98).

Relationship with Industry

As one of the pioneering countries for aerospace industry, Britain had one of the leading aerospace manufacturing technologies. After World War II, the government supported aerospace as a strategic sector that resulted in "too many individual design centers and companies whose average size was far below those of the more important American firms" (Hayward 1989, p.51). Facing severe international competition, particularly against large US companies, the government encouraged the restructuring of the British industry between 1960 and 1961. The two companies created by the restructuring, Hawker-Siddeley and British Aircraft Corporation, were then merged into one national champion, British Aerospace (BAe). In the case of space, it was a truly national champion company which heavily depended on national and European programs. However, its partial privatization in 1981 and full privatization in 1985 brought about a serious change in the company's culture. BAe ambitiously expanded its business into the car industry (Rover) and telecommunications, but it resulted in disaster. In 1994, BAe decided to sell the unprofitable sectors including its Space Systems. However, BAe has maintained its interest in the military space programs through its Defense Systems Division.

GEC-Marconi was the next largest space company in Britain specializing in building of telecommunications satellites. In 1990 its satellite division merged with Matra of France and formed Matra Marconi space (MMS) to increase its competitiveness in satellite production. MMS was a natural candidate for acquiring BAe Space Systems in order to maintain British industrial capacity, but this time, there was no government intervention in the transaction and it was purely made on commercial considerations.

UK Industrial Space Committee (UKISC) is a trade association of UK space industry. Although UKISC was established in 1975, it appointed its first Secretary General in 1993. Until then, the Society of British Aerospace Companies (SBAC) acted as a secretariat. The appointment of Secretary General and its independence from SBAC gave much freedom and capacity to the activities of UKISC. UKISC actively participates in a number of Advisory Board of BNSC and PSC since 1993. Frequent meeting between the Director General of BNSC and Ministers of 'user departments' inputs updated needs of the industry, and constructs general understanding of both interests of industry and departments (interview with UKISC official, 6/11/97). Compared to French and German counterparts, British industry has a stronger voice in government decision-making and in the shaping of policies. For example, the decision to participate in Ariane 5 production in 1995 was in line with UKISC's anticipation of regaining an access to the launcher program, even though the size of participation was not satisfactory. At the European level, UKISC is the only trade association to be a member of EUROSPACE, the European trade association for space.

Conclusion

In this chapter, we focused on the national institutions of space policy-making and how those institutions shaped national policy logics. The difference national institutions make in space policy is evident. French policy logics of autonomy and technology were clearly shaped by its institutional arrangement: strong presence of a powerful space agency and technological center. German imperatives to develop their space capabilities through international cooperation demonstrate institutional ambivalence to space agencies, causing the technological center ('institution section' of DLR) and research institutes to be constantly present in space policy-making. The German logics of technology and science, which were quite remarkable during the negotiation on Spacelab and Columbus programs, were thus shaped by such institutional arrangements. The British apathetic attitude to space gave no room for its space agency to play a major role in space policy-making and kept old 'departmentalism'. The lack of political resources for a space agency implied the dominance of the logics of commerce and finance. Although these characteristics differ to a large extent, there were some common features shared in the three countries. On the one hand, these countries experienced institutional change in the mid- or late 1980s as a result of the decision of the ESA Ministerial Council in 1985 and 1987. All countries sought the right balance of space program management between government and space agency. On the other hand, the three countries recognized and needed the significant changes in the post cold war period. Increasing global competition, commercialization of space and severe financial constraints to meet Maastricht criteria for single currency made space agencies take the initiative in developing new strategies for national space policy. In the 1996–97, the three countries published long-term strategic reports highlighting some sort of concept of 'partnership' with industry, and the importance of European collaboration.

Notes

1   This phrase is often used to describe the legacy of De Gaulle in French security policy. For further discussion, see Gordon 1993.
2   The principle-agent theory was developed in the field of microeconomics, but there are some studies to apply this theory for policy-making process. See, for example, Kiewiet and McCubbins (1991) and DiIulio (1994).
3   These missions were: first, the DEA proposes and makes use of governmental civilian programs for space and aeronautics. Second, the DEA prepares actions which assures space policies are in coherence with national, European and international contexts. Third, the DEA is in charge of national and international industrial policies, of technological transfer to foreign countries and corresponding actions which work for improvement of competitiveness and the environment of companies. Fourth, the DEA assists the Director of Technology in its exercise of tutelle of CNES. These missions seem ambitious to challenge and control the competence and responsibility of CNES.
4   The best example is Hans Mark who was deputy administrator of NASA during 1981–84, promoting the Shuttle program and the International Space Station program. See Mark (1987).
5   DLR was formerly called DFVLR until 1989.
6   Although DLR came under the control of Federal government, the Länder kept 10% of DLR share.
7   The SKYNET 1 was actually made by an American company, Ford aerospace.

8   Except in a few cases like Roy Gibson, there is a tendency that the Director General should also be recruited from the civil service.
9   The Resource Board was renamed the "UK Space Strategy Council" in December 2002 for strengthening the policy planning function.
10 When Gibson was Director General, he chaired the Board, but when he left, the practice changed.

Chapter 7

Evolution of the Space Activities of the EU

For a long time, the development of space technology and industry has been almost exclusively carried out under the framework of ESA, and the European Union (EU) has been left as a bystander. Security concerns, differences in national strategies, size of investment, budget size (see Chart 7.1), and the principle of *juste retour* were among the reasons why European space collaboration was developed outside of the policy competence of the EU. However, external and internal changes after the mid-1980s — the change in the context of space and extension of policy competence of the EU in other areas such as research and environment[1] — seemed to have brought the EU a larger role in European space activities. Moreover, as Paillon argues, space would contribute as a symbolic feature of European integration in representing itself on the world stage (Paillon 1993). Furthermore, the commercialization of the space market increasingly called on the EU to play an important role in European space collaboration.

Following the previous one, this chapter seeks to explain the impacts and influences of international structural changes on the institutions of European space policy-making with regard to the relationship between ESA and the EU. It will focus on the gradual evolution of the EU's activities in the space domain and the institutional aspects from the 1980s, and then it will pay particular attention to the new developments of the ESA-EU cooperation in the 1990s and the obstacles for it.

EU Involvement in Space in the 1980s and 1990s

The R&D activities of EU (then EC) became more extensive in the 1980s under the leadership of Etienne Davignon, vice-president of the Commission and Commissioner for Science and Research. At the end of Davignon's commissionership, the Single European Act (SEA), which provided an explicit legal base for the Commission in this field, was signed to promote more European-oriented R&D activities. Although it was a major breakthrough for the Commission to extend its policy role to the field of research and technology development (R&TD), it did not have significant impact on European space programs. The French space agency, CNES, published a report immediately after the SEA entered into force, and concluded that "the impact of the Single European Act on the activities of CNES and space industry will probably be limited at least in the first years of 1990s in which the role of ESA will remain predominant" (CNES 1988, p.13).

Chart 7.1   EU R&D Budget and ESA Budget

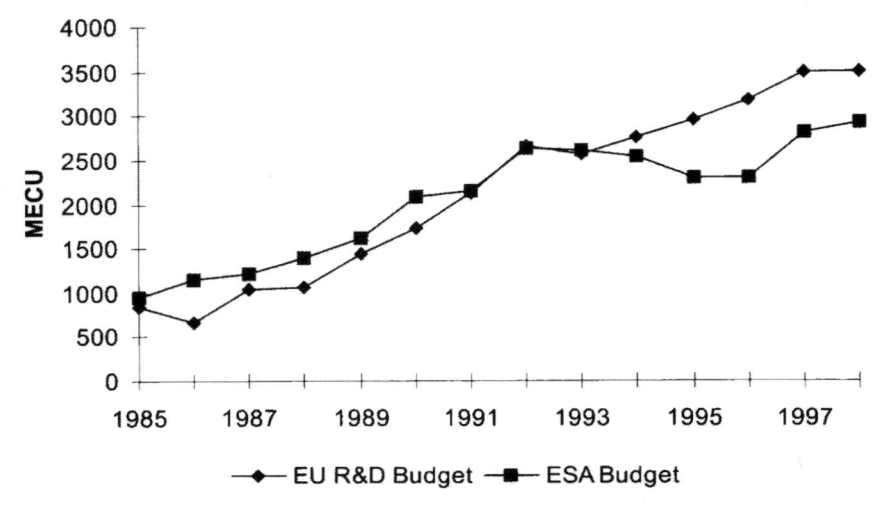

Source: *General Report on Activities of the European Union 1985–1997, European Space Directory 1989–1997* and *ESAS Annual Report.*

In 1988, the first action for improving Commission's involvement in space was taken when Karl-Heinz Narjes — vice-president of the Commission responsible for industrial affairs — called a meeting with representatives from major aerospace companies.[2] This meeting was intended as an aerospace version of the Davignon Roundtable in 1981, which became a springboard for the Commission activities such as ESPRIT and RACE. However, Narjes's meeting did not produce as much as the Davignon Roundtable (Hayward 1994b; Jones 1996), only an ambitious strategic paper (COM(88)417 final). In the paper, the European Commission acknowledged that space "is an area in which the Community now *seems destined* to play a broader and more active role" (emphasis added), because Europe "is still neither active enough nor sufficiently well organized when it comes to exploiting the applications of space technology, for which the ESA does not have the necessary resources at present", and "is still without a cogent overall policy which incorporates technological, industrial, commercial, social and even defense aspects" (*ibid.*).

Although the Narjes report encouraged the Commission to take a more active role in space, the changing environment such as the end of the Cold War and the emergence of commercial opportunities in space application made the Commission consider further elaboration of its strategy. Thus, the Commission asked a panel of experts, headed by former ESA Director General Roy Gibson, to look at various aspects of space in which the Commission should play a role. The panel's report, published in 1991 and known as the Gibson Report, scrutinized institutional and political questions including those related to defense as well as ESA-EC relations.

The report received significant attention from both the ESA and EC councils with strong support from the user community (interview with former ESA DG, 22/5/98). One of the results of this report was that the Commission as well as the European space community began to realize the necessity for developing a coherent Earth observation policy in Europe in order to coordinate the Commission's agriculture and environment policies (interview with Commission official, 26/5/98).

Following the Gibson Report, the Commission issued the second communication on space in 1992 (COM(92)360 final). The message that this document tried to convey was that the Commission was genuinely seeking a way to enter the space sector. It proposed a symbolic program called 'Vegetation', co-funded together with France, Belgium, Sweden and Italy, to put a 1–km-resolution-sensor specialized to monitor land use on the French SPOT 4 satellite. Meanwhile, the EC dedicated about 100MECU to earth observation under several research areas (environment, maritime etc.) in its Fourth R&D framework program. Furthermore, the Commission stepped up the level of cooperation by creating the Space Advisory Group (SAG), which was an *ad hoc* consultative body including representatives from Member States of the EC and the ESA Executive. In contrast to the difficulties that ESA had to face during this period, enthusiasm in the EC rose to its highest point.

The dynamic change in space activities required the EC to act further. Concerning the development of commercialization of space applications and the extent of increasing competition in launching services, the European Parliament (EP) offered an opportunity to gather the representatives from the Commission, ESA, industry and the user community by organizing a 'European Space Forum' in 1995 (EP 1995). This forum marked a very important step in the history of European space collaboration because it provided, almost for the first time, an opportunity to formulate a 'comprehensive' European strategy beyond organizational and agency/ industry boundaries. Although there were business conferences where the representatives from industry and governments met occasionally, this forum offered a formal framework for the European strategy for space. In fact, the issues discussed in this forum were immediately reported to the SAG in order to take appropriate actions. Under the SAG framework, the Commission set up an *ad hoc* group of senior representatives[3] from industry in January 1996. This group, called the High-Level Industry Working Group under the chairmanship of Michel Delaye, head of Aérospatiale Espace et Défense, presented specific recommendations to the Commission. Although the report did not encourage further improvement of the role of the Commission in space, it demonstrated the increasing importance of, and variety of opportunities for, the Commission in the space domain.

Commission's Record

External Relations: Can the EU Be the Political Arm of European Space?

One of the roles that the EU was expected to play was to negotiate with third countries to protect European strategy and commercial interests. Perhaps the case of the negotiations with Russia immediately after the collapse of the Soviet Union suggested the difficulties and weaknesses of the EU in international space negotiations.

The collapse of the Soviet Union posed a great threat to the European space industry, particularly regarding its commercial launch capability. European governments, as well as the US government, were afraid of competing with the former Soviet launcher — extremely cheap and relatively reliable — which was entering the international launch market. The US government put pressure on the Russian government to restrict Russian launchers so as not to disturb the market,[4] and when an agreement between Russia and US was reached, Arianespace sought a similar agreement between Europe and Russia. In the early 1990s, a team comprised of the Commission (represented by DG I), ESA and Arianespace negotiated with Russian counterparts, and achieved an agreement to set a quota for launching European commercial satellites with the former Soviet launcher. However, when the Commission brought the agreement to be authorized by the Council of Ministers, France vetoed it on the basis that the French government was responsible for intergovernmental agreements on matters relating to a French registered company (Arianespace), and the Commission had no authority on this ground (interview with CNES official 17/11/97, Commission official 27/5/98). Interestingly, France initially sought some kind of agreement with Russia when this issue was addressed at the ESA Council. CNES, the largest shareholder in Arianespace, was in favor of the launching quota regardless of who was going to represent Europe. However when the issue was brought up at the EU Council of Ministers, France took a different position to maintain control over space activities at the national level.

So far, the Commission seemed to be the appropriate body to handle external relationships on behalf of European space interests, but when it came to politically and strategically sensitive issues, there seemed to be a lack of political consensus on who was going to be responsible for external matters. However, based on this experience, the Commission as well as the Member States of the EU and ESA learned to take a cautious approach and build up a consensus for external affairs, as was fully demonstrated in the process of the negotiations with the United States on the navigation satellite, Galileo (see below).

Earth Observation

Earth observation was the area of activities in which the Commission was most interested. It was already the largest customer for Earth observation data in Europe to implement its agricultural and environmental policies. The Commission also played a central role as a commercial market developer for Earth observation data, which is largely regarded as a part of the public domain. In order to foster an Earth observation market by demonstrating the uses for the data, the EU created the Institute for Remote Sensing, later named the Space Application Institute (SAI), within the JRC in 1991.

The Commission's activities were substantially limited to software applications demonstrating the use of Earth observation data, as well as organizing users and data providers. But the Commission also had ambitions to develop hardware applications. In 1992, it launched a program called Vegetation, which aimed to develop and construct a satellite sensor on the French SPOT 4 to monitor crop development, "as a test case for supporting the development of new instruments" (COM(92)360 final, p.18). Because the Commission lacked knowledge and expertise in hardware development and management, CNES was given the responsibility of developing the instruments for Vegetation. Although "[i]t would have been more logical if the Commission would have entrusted ESA, as the typical European space entity, with the management of the project" (Cheli and Schrogl, 1999, p.57), the Commission chose to work with CNES because this program was strongly proposed and supported by France, and CNES' SPOT 4 program was available at the time of development. The Commission considered the Vegetation program successful and there was a demand from user industries to continue the Vegetation service, but the Commission decided not to invest in hardware development any longer. Along with the replacement of SPOT 4 to SPOT 5, the follow-on program, Vegetation 2, was proposed for updating the sensor. Unlike Vegetation 1, the proposal and technological definition of sensor for Vegetation 2 were drafted by industry instead of CNES. However, CNES rejected the idea of giving industry a central role in the program and claimed that it should take the leading role (interview with Commission official, 26/7/98), and the program was eventually downgraded to a part of overall program for SPOT 5 without participation of industry or the Commission.

Having said that, confidence and mutual respect between ESA and the European Union in software applications was achieved through various frameworks of institutional cooperation. In 1995, the Earth Observation Program Board (EOPB) of ESA made an initiative to draft a comprehensive European policy for Earth observation from space (ESA/PB-EO(95)7) which was adopted by the Space Advisory Group (SAG/95/11) and reflected in the Commission's paper of 1996. The importance of this document was that both ESA and the EU via the formal decision-making procedure agreed on a coherent European approach for the first time.

Space Advisory Group

Although most of the frameworks for ESA-EU cooperation were conducted on an *ad hoc* basis, various informal practices on cooperation have developed on a variety of occasions. In order to consolidate such practices, an organizational interface, the Space Advisory Group (SAG), has been established as the central institution for coordinating the activities of ESA and the EU since the early 1990s. Furthermore, the development of a joint task force for European Strategy for Space at the end of the 1990s enhanced the institutional cooperation, as we shall discuss later.

The Space Advisory Group (SAG), created in 1992, is an *ad hoc* advisory group (although it usually meets twice a year) which provided opportunities for high-level representatives from ESA,[5] the Commission and relevant ministries of Member States[6] to meet and discuss issues concerned with European matters. Given the importance of national space agencies in the policy-making process at both national and European level, Member States are allowed to bring two delegates to SAG whether to bring two representatives from their governments ('all government team') or one each from their government and space agency ('mixed government-agency team'). The importance of SAG was to provide an effective bridge between the ESA and EU decision-making process, which comprised of representatives from different administrative bodies (government ministries and space agencies). Also, SAG provided a forum to develop a coherent European approach for space activities, which could be introduced in both the ESA Council and the EU Council of Ministers. In fact, the SAG played the role of linchpin between these two organizations.

However, as an advisory group, SAG's activity was limited to identifying the areas where coordination was necessary, and SAG's political influence was subjected to the support from the Commission and Member States. Even though the SAG's proposal for a common European policy for Earth observation in 1995 was successfully introduced and adopted in both the ESA and EU Councils, this success was due to the effort of Jean-Pierre Contzen, the first chairman of SAG in 1992–96, who was enthusiastic about using SAG as an important political framework. But when Herbert Allegeier, Director General of the Joint Research Center (JRC) who held a 'minimalist' view on the Commission's role in space, became chairman, the SAG lost its impetus to influence decisions at the level of the Commission since Allegeier was reluctant to call for SAG meetings (interview with ESA official, 12/5/98, and Commission official, 26/7/98).

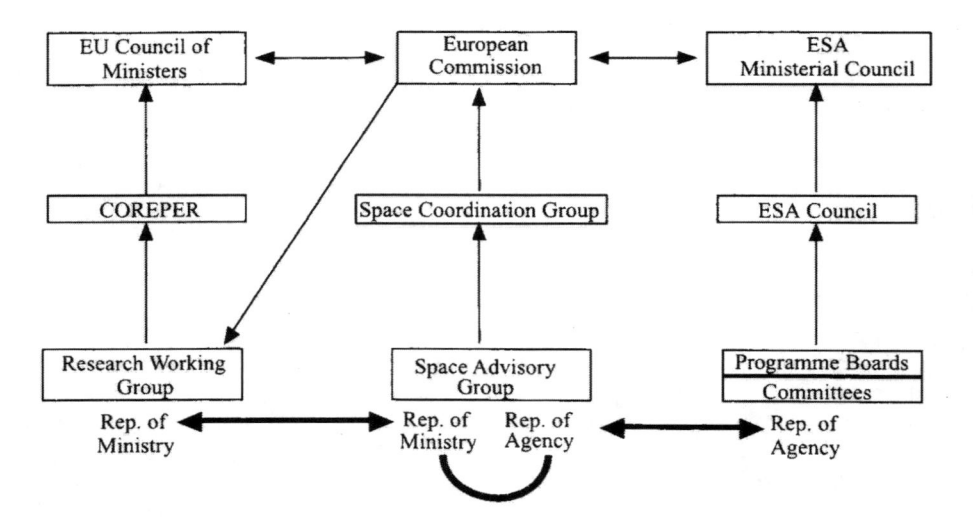

Figure 7.1   The Role of SAG between ESA and the EU

The participants in SAG were by and large frustrated by its limited role *vis-à-vis* the Commission's decision-making. National representatives as well as the ESA officials felt that the SAG could not provide anything more than advice, and it was entirely up to the Commission whether or not to listen to it (interview with ESA official, 12/5/98, DLR official, 16/6/98, and former CNES president, 18/5/98). In other words, participants were fully aware that SAG could become an effective forum for discussions of European space policy if its status was upgraded so as to be able to influence the Commission. If a decision has to be made by both organizations, there should be a close understanding between representatives from governments and agencies in order to secure the same outcome from the different decision-making procedures (Figure 7.1). In this respect, the most important implication of the role of SAG was that it provided a single forum for representatives of national agencies and national government to discuss the space activities of the EU. Moreover, SAG's contribution could go beyond bringing representatives from government and agencies together, to include opening up opportunities to other European entities such as Eumetsat or Eurocontrol. It could become as a base for the European Space Council which the European Parliament repeatedly asked the Commission to consider.

Space Coordination Group

The policy responsibilities for the space sector are divided among different Director-Generals (DGs) of the Commission.[7] Until the late-1980s, these DGs were dealing with space issues independently, using their own budgets. However, in 1992 the Commission appointed Jean-Pierre Contzen, Director General of JRC, as a 'space coordinator' to facilitate inter-DG discussion and to formulate coherent space policy for the Commission. He was responsible for organizing the Space Coordination Group (SCG) where representatives from each DG meet and discuss the Commission's programs relating to space. The SCG was established in order to have a single view of the Commission's policy on space to strengthen its position in negotiations with other entities. Nevertheless, the competence and mandate of the SCG was limited to inter-DG coordination rather than as a single authority over space policy. The *de facto* policy responsibilities were still divided among relevant DGs.

Thus, in view of the increasing importance of space activities three Commissioners – Edith Cresson (Research), Martin Bangemann (Industry), and Neil Kinnock (Transport) – agreed to redefine and strengthen the SCG in 1996. The SCG now has five permanent officials to assure a coherent and synergetic approach to space matters, to monitor Commission activities on space, to assure regular consultation and dialogue with industry, national and international organizations, and to coordinate socio-economic analysis (interview with Commission official, 25/5/98). The regeneration of the SCG has certainly increased the capability of the Commission to deal with space matters, but it is important to note that the SCG does not have the financial means to implement programs, and therefore, SCG officials are well aware that they have to discover the policy logics appropriate for pursuing the different DGs and ministers in order to be able to implement their strategies (interview with Commission official, 23/6/99).

Since the Commission became involved in drafting European Strategy for Space (see below), the SCG was reorganized as the Space Policy Unit in order to strengthen the Commission's policy planning function and communication with industry and ESA. Reflecting the strong interest of Philippe Basquin, Commissioner for Research, the Space Policy Unit increased the number of staff to 11 and extended its role for managing and implementing the Commission's space policy.

Towards New Dimensions of Cooperation

Since the cancellation of Aerosat (see chapter 4), the European airline companies, as well as other users of satellite navigation services, relied heavily on the American Global Positioning System (GPS) which is controlled by the military authority and provides signals with limited accuracy for civilian use. However, when it became clear that GPS was approaching a system renewal, the European governments and industry began to consider developing their own navigation system without American military interference.

At the first instance, the European proposal for a Global Navigation Satellite System (GNSS, later called Galileo) was primarily discussed among the GPS users in the world. Since the navigation program is controlled by American military authority but widely used by civilian users (including non-American users) for air traffic control, intelligence transport system etc., there was a sense of insecurity of the service and fear it might terminate in case of war in which the United States is involved. Thus, European Union, DGVII (transport) in particular, initiated an idea of launching alternative global navigation system by European countries. The intention of this initiative was to put pressure on the US military authority to secure civilian services even in the case of conflict. In order to do so, it was widely recognized that the ESA, as R&D organization, alone would not be appropriate to plan and negotiate the program. At the same time, the EU lacked technical competence in space hardware development, and needed to cooperate with ESA. However, in order to have a successful co-developed program, it was crucial to have a common strategy and institutional linkage between ESA and the EU, something lacking throughout the history of European space collaboration.

The breakthrough was made by the initiative of Lord Sainsbury, British Minister for Space, when Britain held the Presidency of the EU during the first half of 1998. The BNSC under Lord Sainsbury's authority had played a pivotal role in bridging Member States' space agencies (which send representatives to the ESA Council),[8] and ministries in charge of research (to the EU Council of Ministers) by adopting the same text as a common resolution by two Councils. His aim was that the EU should provide the legal and regulatory framework for space and space-related activities in Europe, act as customer or proxy for dispersed customer communities, and represent Europe in international negotiations (Cheli and Schrogl 1999) while ESA act as a center of excellence to provide the necessary technological expertise. However, the common resolution adopted in both Councils made only general remarks without any binding agreement (ESA/C/CXXXVI/Res.1 (final)). Nevertheless, the fact that both councils adopted the same text meant it was politically very important. At least it demonstrated the willingness of the Member States of both organizations to strengthen the institutional relationship.

Galileo

One of the catalysts for the fusion of the ESA and the EU decision-making timetable was the question of European dependence on the US satellite navigation system. The US Global Positioning System (GPS), completed in 1993, was a military system, but it enabled civilian signal receivers to locate themselves, albeit with less accuracy, free of charge. Largely because of this pricing policy, satellite navigation was widely appreciated, sometimes vitally indispensable for all kinds of traffic, particularly for air traffic control. However, since the nature of GPS was a military one, operating via the GPS signal was greatly dependent on the policies of the American military authorities. The US Department of Defense (DoD) retains the option for discontinuing civilian usage if national security is threatened, and in fact, during the Kosovo crisis, the DoD suspended civilian services in the region of the conflict, which greatly disturbed air traffic to and from Greece and Italy. This policy created a situation where the more a civilian application grows, the greater the risk of a shut down of GPS for military purposes. Moreover, the problem was that "no criteria are given on how to determine whether there is a balance between potentially conflicting interest" (Barbance et al. 1996, p.157) in commercial and military use of satellite navigation.

Anticipating such risks, the Toulouse Ministerial Council in 1995 mandated that the Director General of ESA should consult closely with the EU and Eurocontrol[9] on satellite navigation. The Transport Council of Ministers of the EU accepted the idea of tripartite cooperation, and mandated the Commission to formulate a common European strategy. The tripartite group developed a European strategy for a Global Navigation Satellite System (GNSS) with two phases of implementation. First, in addition to the existing GPS, European entities would provide an augmentation service called the European Geostationary Navigation Overlay Service (EGNOS), that sent a supplementary signal to GPS in order to secure civilian use (also called GNSS-1). EGNOS was already being tested using the ARTES 9 satellite and will be operational in 2003 with half-successful ARTEMIS satellite.[10] Second, European entities were preparing to design and implement a fully civilian controlled navigation system (GNSS-2, which is now called Galileo).

The policy objectives of the Galileo program were twofold. First, it was clear that European authorities aimed at securing a navigation signal service without possible US DoD intervention. But at the same time, the Galileo was also used as a diplomatic card to negotiate with the US government. Although European users of the US GPS service enjoyed the cost-free signal, its accuracy was not satisfactory for traffic safety, and European governments as well as the Commission engineered a negotiation strategy to put pressure on the US government to remove so-called Selected Availability (SA), which distinguishes between a very accurate signal for military use and a less precise signal for civilian use. The European strategy was that if Europe decided to 'go it alone' or to cooperate with non-US users such as Japan to develop an alternative satellite navigation system, the US would lose its justification for SA (Hartl and Wlaka 1996). The latter objective was clearly achieved in May 2000 when the Clinton administration decided to remove SA. It was, on the one hand, a success of European strategy, but on the other, a big headache for European governments because the Galileo program was already considered a strategic agenda in the ESA and EU councils, and there were strong voices that even without SA, GPS is still under the control of American military authority.

While the Commission was in negotiations with the US, the Commission passed an initiative to open a forum, so-called GNSS-2 Forum, for leading experts from industry, European institutions and organizations, radio-navigation service providers, user communities and academia over the period from July to December 1998. The forum discussed a wide variety of issues concerning the design, finance, and implementation of the Galileo program, and concluded that the program should be based on a combination of GPS and a European system, instead of 'going it alone'. Concerning the proposal made by the forum, the ESA Ministerial Council in Brussels in May 1999 and the EU Council of Transport Ministers in June 1999 decided to fund the study of Galileo, showing the commitment of European governments to the program. It was expected that cooperation with Russia, which had already developed satellite navigation expertise through its GLONASS program, or with Japan, would reduce the cost of Galileo (COM(99)54 final). The most important feature of the decisions was the strong commitment to avoid the so-called 'zero-option', a conscious decision to use exclusively the US GPS and taking no action on European part. But on the other hand, it was also decided that Galileo should be fully compatible with GPS. Matthias Rüte, Director-General of the European Commission's transport and energy directorate, commented in a news magazine that "[m]ost ministers were convinced that the zero option was the lowest cost solution, but that it would be the costliest over the long-term" (*AWST* 5/7/99). The decisions suggest that the logic of autonomy had regained ground in European space activities, but it was possible in conjunction with the logic of commerce and finance (i.e. the cost calculation) in long term.

While the decisions demonstrated the willingness of European governments to commit themselves to the program, there were still a number of highly controversial issues. First of all, the ways and means to finance the program were not fully designed. The Commission estimated that the source for funding would be the EU's Transport TEN (Trans-European Networks), 5th Framework program, TACIS program (cooperation scheme with Russia), and ESA. The total sum of public funding would be 1.25 billion euros between 2000–06, but the program needed a further 950–1.7 billion euros (COM(99)54 final). The question of the funding was further stressed by the cost estimate reported by a consultancy company to the European Commission. The analysis suggested that Galileo would cost 3.4 billion euros including deployment (PricewaterhouseCoopers 2001), which meant the estimate needed to include a higher contingency under such a high uncertainty.

There were several possible channels to complement the shortage of funding. First, a Public-Private Partnership was sought. The application market for navigation signals, such as tracking and car navigation, was increasing, thanks to the availability of GPS, and the European authorities expected industry to shoulder some of the financial burden. Moreover, given the large number of satellites required, space manufacturers would also be interested in participating in this program. The European Commission would establish a joint undertaking, or Galileo Operating Company, with industry for designing, planning and operating the system jointly. However, there have been few companies that have expressed interest in committing themselves to the program so far, and it is very unlikely that ESA and

European governments would rely on funding from industry (*Space News* 31/7/00). The problem extends further when production contract is concerned. If a company participates in joint undertaking, the company will most certainly receives a contract for development, which may exclude the opportunity for another company to bid in the development of Galileo system under the principle of *juste retour*. Furthermore, there may be a danger of compromising the security and public service function of the system if private industries are involved. For these reasons, the European Parliament issued a report which rejects the idea of joint undertaking and emphasizes the importance of maintaining the public funding for the development of Galileo system (EP 2002).

Secondly, putting a levy on the revenues generated through the Galileo service or putting tax on receivers was considered. For example, a 20–euro levy for navigation on new automobiles would create 140 million euros per year, and a 0.5–euro levy on emergency chips in telephone sets would produce 200 million euros per year (*AWST*, 5/7/99). However, there was a critical problem with putting a levy on the end user because as long as the US GPS remained free of charge without SA, the Galileo service would be less competitive, and it would therefore be impossible to raise revenues through these charges. The third option was a possible contribution from individual Member States. The added-value services (high-precision services), which could be used for safety and security activities, might attract customers among public authorities such as ministries of defense or local governments. However, those authorities were also under very tight budget constraints, and they could not fill the gap between existing funding and the actual cost. For example, the French Ministry of Defense, one of the most 'autonomy-driven' offices, categorically refused to support the Galileo program financially, due to its own financial constraints and the reliability of the US GPS (interview with French MoD official, 1/7/99).[11] The uncertainty of financial sources would greatly influence the progress of the program and the negotiations with the US, but it would also have certain implications for the future of the ESA-EU relationship.

A second problem was the question of security. Since the outbreak of the Kosovo crisis, including Galileo in the construction of a European defense system in space has been widely discussed (*AWST*, 5/7/99). Thus, the Galileo satellites were designed to send three types of signals, mass service, certified service for air traffic, and secured service for safety and security. However, given the lack of decision-making power in military affairs, both the EU and ESA were not able to finalize the question on how to use Galileo in the case of conflict. The report from the Commission briefly explained that the security issue would be discussed in the framework of Common Foreign and Security Policy (CFSP) and Common European Defense and Security Policy (CEDSP) (COM(2000)750 final). Such an undetermined attitude toward security issue increased the frustration of the US authority. It was reported that the deputy US defense secretary Paul Wolfowitz sent letters to Defense Ministers of European countries warning that pursuit of plans for the Galileo global positioning system could conflict with similar NATO military systems (*International Herald Tribune* 19/12/01). Even after the Commission expressed its intention to negotiate with NATO for aligning Galileo with the existing system, the US DoD maintained an offensive position that there is "no compelling need for Galileo" (*Space News* 4/2/02).

Finally, there was the competition for the program leadership, despite the uncertainty of the program's future. Currently, Germany, Italy, France and the UK are competing with each other for the prime contract and operational leadership. Unlike ESA optional programs, Galileo was not led by a single Member State freely undertaking the responsibilities of the total control of programs, such as CNES does for Ariane programs. Two negative consequences might occur as a result of this competition for leadership. First, if one Member State undertook the responsibility for design and development, there would be a less 'European' feature to the program. Galileo was a revolutionary program because it had been proposed and initiated by the European Commission and the ESA Executive. Granting leadership to a particular Member State would undermine the solidarity of Europe. Secondly, under current financial pressures, competition for the leadership of Galileo would further jeopardize the level of funding for other programs. For example, Germany was preparing to take a 30% share in the program even though the budget was, practically speaking, decreasing. The only way for Germany to take the leadership was to cut budgets in other programs, notably the Space Station and science programs (*AWST* 5/6/00). The Galileo program, on the one hand, was a big step toward the integration of European space activities, but on the other, it might endanger the achievement of European space collaboration.

The uncertainty of the Galileo program was further stretched by the decision of the US government to remove the SA and permit commercial users to access the high accuracy signal of GPS in May 2000. The removal of the SA complicated the process of the Galileo development because the justification for Europe's own satellite system came under threat, and given the increasing logic of finance, there might be some Member States which would not be convinced of the necessity of Galileo, such as France. However, as Matthias Rüte, a director-general in the Commission, said in the newspaper, it would have a "marginal effect on Europe's work" because the US government promised to remove SA sometime between 1996 and 2007 (*Space News* 15/5/00), and also Ian Pryke, the ESA representative in Washington DC, claimed that Galileo's main purpose "is to provide Europe with important technology underpinnings in a new area ... [and] also represents autonomy from the US" (*AWST* 5/6/00).

However, the question of commercial prospects, the allocation of financial burden, as well as of the program leadership became big questions in the negotiations at the Transport Council of Ministers during 2000–02. Although the ESA Ministerial Council at Brussels in 2000 approved the budget for Galileo unanimously, Britain, Germany and the Netherlands expressed a concern for the commercial possibilities of Galileo and demanded participation of private industry from the development phase (2001–05) at the Transport Council of the EU (in the original proposal of the Commission, the PPP starts from the deployment phase, 2006–07). They claimed that the program would not be worth investing tax payers' money in if the program was too unattractive for industry. Also those opposing countries were concerned with the possible overrun of the program cost while they were under severe financial constraints. Under such circumstances, the transport ministers agreed to accept funding from industry up to 200 million euros at the meeting in April 2001, but this agreement did not convince those skeptical governments. Added to Sweden, Denmark and Austria, the opposing countries —

Britain, Germany and The Netherlands — further demanded an explanation as to whether Galileo would show financial benefits beyond its cost. After intensive bilateral and multilateral negotiation, the Galileo issue was brought to a higher level of the decision-making process, and it was finally decided to 'go-ahead' at the Barcelona European Council meeting in March 2002.

The Galileo program was undoubtedly a new step for European space collaboration, driven by the logics of commerce and autonomy. Although the logic of finance, which has been a very powerful policy logic in the 1990s, was influential in this process, the Galileo program was finally approved even by the most skeptic Member State, Britain. The concept of "European non-dependence" that emerged during this debate established the foundation for the European position on satellite navigation. The future of Galileo seems to be bright. However, one should note that there are variety of questions for European governments to answer, namely on financial and security issues. Also the countries which finally withdrew their opposition were not fully convinced. The British decision to support Galileo was because there was "no longer a blocking minority", and it would "try to win concessions rather than being the Last of the Mohicans" (*Independent* 10/3/02).

European Strategy for Space

Given the increasing interest in synergy between ESA and the EU, the Ministerial Council in Brussels held in May 1999 paid significant attention to the "European Strategy for Space (ESS)", initiated by Antonio Rodotà, ESA Director-General, and the European Commission. The idea of ESS was largely driven by the experience of the Galileo program. It had the potential to go beyond programmatic issues, and could possibly become the basis of the strategic planning process for European space activities, because the motivation of the Rodotà initiative was more deeply rooted on the weakness of European political commitment in the commercialized space market, particularly when compared to that of the United States.

The Rodotà initiative was motivated by eight concerns and deficiencies in European space policy: (1) low public investments *vis-à-vis* the United States; (2) lack of understanding of space as an instrument and as an integral part of overall political, scientific, economic and military leadership; (3) the US dominance in innovative applications; (4) dependence on the US for satellite navigation; (5) division of strategy and actions at European, multinational and national levels; (6) limited dual-use synergy; (7) lack of ESA commitment to space applications; (8) duplication of facilities and operations in ESA and national operations (ESA/C-WG(99)WP/1, rev.1). In order to overcome these deficiencies and dependences, a new policy principle — "More and Better Europe" — was called for. 'More Europe' meant a more common and coordinated approach among all the actors in Europe, recognizing the legitimacy of national interests and improving their complementary interplay with common (European) interests, whereas 'Better Europe' meant more coordinated policy, joint strategy among ESA, the EU and national authorities, a coherent set of programs, network of public technical centers (*ibid.*). Based on this principle, the ESA Ministerial Council in Brussels asked the ESA Executive to prepare a fully developed strategy together with the European Commission by the end of 2000 (ESA/C-M/CXLI/Res.1 (final)). The Council of Ministers of the EU also put forward a resolution seven months after the ESA Ministerial Council in Brussels, asking the Commission to prepare, as a joint exercise with ESA and using a single and common consultative framework, a comprehensive document on a coherent European Strategy for Space (OJ C 375, 24/12/99).

The decisions at both councils were a big leap not only in terms of the degree in which the Commission became involved in space, but also in terms of the institutional relationship between ESA and the EU. This was practically the first time for both organizations to develop a common comprehensive strategy, and what was more important was that the ESA Executive and the Commission would form a single team which would consult with Member States and industry (interview with Commission official, 23/6/99). This joint exercise would be able not only to structure the relationship between the ESA Executive and the Commission, but also to grant significant importance to the Commission as the central agency for developing European strategy.

During 2000, the joint team consulted with Member States through the newly created Joint Space Strategy Advisory Group (JSSAG),[12] irrespective of whether they were members of ESA or part of the EU, for preparing strategic documents with a focus on four subjects: space-based information and communication services; science, research and space exploration; CFSP-considerations; and access to space. Among these subjects, the CFSP consideration was discussed with the representatives from the Western European Union (WEU) as well as the Member States. The group of representatives discussed issues beyond the narrow scope of space matters, such as a redefinition of security, European objectives and priorities for military affairs, synergies in design, manufacturing, systems and services, and global surveillance capabilities for crisis anticipation. The fact that this consultation process extended to military issues suggested that it would develop a platform for a more integrated forum for a comprehensive European strategy for space, something that has not existed in the history of European space collaboration.

This joint consultation exercise produced a preparatory strategic document, which was adopted both at the EU Council of Ministers and the ESA Ministerial Council in September 2000 (COM(2000)597 final, ESA/C(2000)67, rev.1). One of the unique aspects of this paper, as far as ESA's strategy is concerned, was a strong emphasis on demand-driven use of space for benefiting markets and society. The user-oriented programs had been proposed and discussed since the end of 1990s, but such a strong emphasis on demand-oriented strategy reminded the public and private actors that the practice of European space development had been changing through this joint effort for establishing European strategy. The other interesting aspect in this paper was a clear intention for using space for European security. Since the European Council in Helsinki addressed an issue of establishing the Common European Defense and Security Policy (CEDSP), most of the Member States as well as joint EU-ESA team were well aware of the importance of emphasizing the dual-use potential and consolidating communications and intelligence gathering capabilities in space. Apart from the existing WEU Satellite Center, which was planned to be transferred to the European Union, the strategic document proposed that Europe should exploit space-based infrastructure for enhancing the conflict resolution capability of Europe.

The proposal was called the Global Monitoring for Environment and Security (GMES) initiative which was developed through further consultation with Eumetsat and the European Environmental Agency. The GMES initiative aims to respond to the growing concerns amongst policy makers on sustainable development, global climate change, and conflict resolution (COM(2001)609 final). Its primary concern is to make use of space for environmental affairs, but the GMES also suggests that there is a growing potential in space to strengthen European capability for conflict prevention. In fact, the Commission's communication on "Conflict Prevention" refers specifically to GMES for information gathering and early warning (COM(2001)211 final). It was also considered that GMES would contribute toward implementing the "Petersberg task"[13] which was defined by the Petersberg declaration and also included in the Amsterdam Treaty. However, given the ambivalent position of the EU with regards to security issues, it is notable that the discussion about GMES stresses the environmental issues rather than security alone. Compared to the Commission's hesitation to push security issues forward, the discussion in ESA seems more supportive toward the GMES initiative for security issues. Antonio Rodotà called a group of high level executives — Carl Bildt (former Prime Minister of Sweden), Jean Peyrelevade (President of Crédit Lyonnais) and Lothar Späth (CEO of Jenoptik AG) — in order to provide independent advice for promoting the evolution of the ESA-EU relationship and the necessary institutional change. The report of the group, the so-called "wise men report", recommended ESA and the Commission focus on the dual-use potential of space technology and integrate different national and multinational programs such as Helios into the CEDSP framework (Bildt et al. 2000). The emphasis on further investment in military space was also shared by industry. Armand Carlier, CEO of newly created Astrium, publicly called for more public support in Galileo, GMES and other security programs not only for enhancing European capability and autonomy in military affairs, but also to strengthen the European space industry in order to compete with the American industry which was heavily supported by military R&D funding (Carlier 2001).

In line with the Commission communication in 2000, the Commission and the ESA Executive created the Joint Task Force (JTF) for developing programs defined in the strategic document (Figure 7.2). The JTF consists of two layers of groups: the "designated members" — members who are formally appointed from respective organizations — consisting of Directors of the ESA Executive and the Commission in charge of activities related to ESS; the other layer is the more operational level and is made up of "supporting members" who are assigned by the designated members to carry out tasks decided upon by the Task Force. Primarily the JTF was established for implementing ESS and drafting joint reports on ESA-EU programs such as Galileo and GMES. However, the mandate for JTF was not limited to implementation of two joint programs, but encompassed all areas of common interest between ESA and the EU. Those mandates were (1) to examine horizontal issues related to the implementation of the strategy such as international co-operation, industrial activities, RTD, dual-use, and SMEs; (2) to consult and discuss its findings with the different stakeholders, in particular Member States, and formulate proposals to the ESA Director General and the Commission as appropriate to the relevant decision-making agenda; (3) to propose an EC/ESA framework enabling ESA to act as implementing agency with respect to the EU policy for space. From these mandates it became clear that the ultimate goal of JTF was to provide and create an integrated framework for decision-making in space in which ESA plays the role of "implementing agency". From ESA's point of view, the creation of JTF was a big step forward to put the position of the ESA as an implementing agency in relation to the Commission. As discussed above, the ESA Executive struggled to maintain the leadership in decision-making in space, and was uncomfortable with the cultural differences with the Commission. However, as Rodotà, the ESA Director General, made clear ESA can no longer enjoy its financial and political support by concentrating on technology, and ESA "will become an integral part of the overall political and economic drive to promote the interests of Europe's citizens" (ESA press release, no.12, 2001).

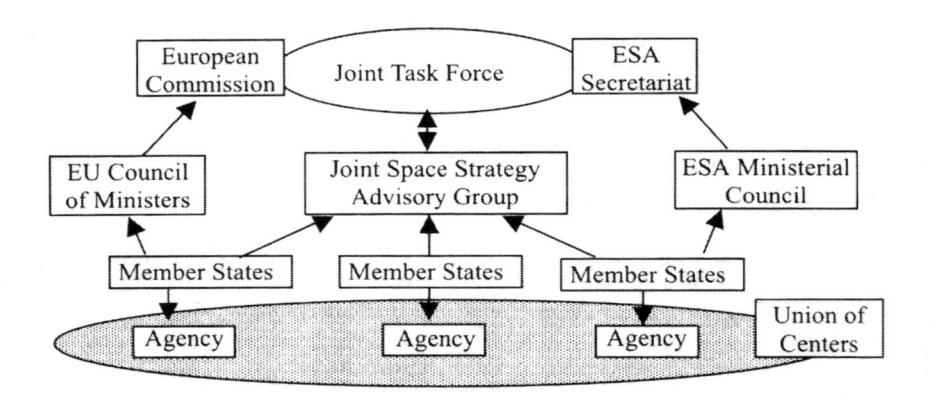

Figure 7.2   The Role of Joint Task Force

The first report of JTF, presented to the Councils of ESA and the EU in December 2001, focused on three subjects: a knowledge-driven economic growth; an independent Europe; and more involvement of citizens in policy-making. Among these three subjects, the question of European autonomy was discussed extensively by using space technology to secure European influence on the world scene. In order to enhance the European capability and autonomy, the report proposed the setting up of a "Space Council" — a joint informal meeting of the EU Council and the ESA Ministerial Council — in order to develop a European Space Policy which would be presented to the European Council where Heads of State and Governments can consider space policy in full, including security and defense aspects (COM(2001)718 final). The report also envisioned possible modifications to the current Treaty of the EU and consequently the ESA Convention. It seems as if the JTF report called for further integration between ESA and the EU and insisted on ESA becoming the "implementing agency" without any decision-making capability.

However, it was unlikely that ESA would give up the degree of autonomy they enjoyed and the institutional framework — notably the optional participation and the principle of *juste retour*. The ESA staff in JTF firmly demanded to insert some paragraphs ensure that the evolution of European Strategy for Space would not jeopardize the current institutional framework of ESA. Thus, the report clearly stated that the "flexibility of [ESA's] programs must be maintained, making it possible for different programs to be initiated by different national or other configurations ("variable geometry")" (*ibid.*, p.22). Although the ESA-EU relationship has progressed to a greater extent, it would take a much longer time to formulate a coherent and integrated institutional framework with regard to the problem of the principle of *juste retour*.

The process of ESS, from the perspective of policy logic analysis, is quite significant. First of all, this process was driven by the concept of a 'European strategy for non-dependence'. The concept was proposed by Eurospace, the European space industrial association (Eurospace 1998), emphasizing the need to develop, at least, a minimum capability in order to avoid commercial, technological, and political dependence on other countries, particularly the United States, in space applications and access to space. The ESS, motivated by industry, can therefore be seen as policy driven by a renovated logic of autonomy. Unlike the previous version, this logic of European autonomy appears to be more sophisticated, pragmatic, and less provocative, but it is certainly shared by the Member States of both ESA and the EU. Secondly, although the ESS touched upon almost all areas of space activities, its objective was to strengthen the competitiveness of European industry to meet the requirements of the space market. In other words, the ESS process is designed to redefine space activities to fit into the logic of commerce. Thirdly, the emphasis on security issues was certainly a big step in the history of European space collaboration. Although the effect of WEU participation has yet to be known, it suggests that a military logic is finally emerging in the forum of European space collaboration.

Conclusion

The space activities in Europe have been divided into the framework of the "two Europes" (Madders and Thiebaut 1992) for a long time. However, the strengthening of the logics of commerce and finance in the 1990s, as seen in the previous chapter, influenced the understanding of the Member States of both ESA and the EU for developing a single political platform for European space activities. In this regard, the evolution of the relationship between ESA and the EU, particularly through the Galileo program and 'European Strategy for Space', seems to have created a new opportunity for 'a better Europe'. It would certainly provide a forum for coordinating not only different national programs but also different policy activities. Space activities are increasingly becoming an instrument in the service of other political, economic and social objectives (Jourdain and Sourbès-Verger 1995), and the institutional development between ESA and the EU has the possibility to put all the pieces together to advance European space to a different stage.

Notes

1   Since the policy competence of the EU extended to the area of environment, the European Commission became the largest user for Earth Observation data from satellite.
2   These companies were: Aeritalia (Italy), Aérospatiale, Dassault (France), British Aerospace (UK), CASA (Spain), Fokker (The Netherlands), Dornier, Messerschmitt-Bolkow-Blohm (Germany) and Société Anonyme Belge de Constructions Aéronautiques (Belgium).
3   These are: Aérospatiale Espace et Défense, Matra Marconi Space, Alcatel, Société Européenne de Propulsion (France), CASA Space Division (Spain), OHB System, DASA (Germany), Fokker Space (The Netherlands), Telespazio, Alenia Spazio (Italy), Smith System Engineering (UK), Volvo Aero Corporation (Sweden).
4   One of the windfalls of this agreement was the joint-venture of an American company (Lockheed Martin) and the Russian launcher company (Khrunichev and RSC Energia) for creating a marketing and sales company under the US law in order to avoid the quota agreement. This joint-venture (International Launch Service) enjoys a significant success competing in the market which the European company (Arianespace) dominated for a long time.
5   The ESA was granted full membership in 1996. Until then, it only had observer status in SAG.
6   The ESA Member States which are not in the EU (Switzerland and Norway) are granted observer status.
7   DG I (External relations), DG III (Industrial policy), DG IV (Competition), DG VI (Agriculture), DG VII (Transport), DG XI (Environment), DG XII (Research), Joint Research Centre (JRC) and DG XIII (Telecommunications) cover a variety of issues concerning space, especially with regard to the user applications and regulations.
8   The Council held in June 1998 was planned for the ministerial level, but because of the German election, the Member States would not be able to arrange any budgetary commitment, and thus the Council was held at agency level.
9   Eurocontrol is an intergovernmental organization for civil aviation control with 29 Member States including Central and Eastern European countries.
10 ARTEMIS was launched in July 2001 by Ariane 5, but injected in the orbit lower than expected. In order to recover from this malfunction, ARTEMIS satellite had to use a lot of fuel to place itself in proper orbit (though it was less damaging thanks to the new invention of ion propulsion). As a result the lifetime of ARTEMIS became much shorter than planned.
11 Though the position of French MoD has changed a little in favor of supporting Galileo if military authorities of other European countries (at least three countries) support it (Space News 18/2/02).
12 JSSAG was initially considered as an enhanced version of SAG from Member States' governments, though they found that it was quite different since the Commission and ESA Executive sit on the same table whereas delegations from Member States sit on the other side (interview with the Commission official 9/3/00).
13 The Petersberg task consists of humanitarian and rescue tasks, peacekeeping tasks and tasks of combat forces in crisis management, including peacemaking.

Chapter 8

Conclusion: Assessing European Space Collaboration

This study has traced the evolution of European space collaboration from the early 1960s to current institutional arrangements and policies. In doing so, it has employed an analytical framework using the concepts of policy logics and historical interaction between policy logics and institutional changes. This final chapter will bring the findings of the study together, evaluate the potential and feasibility of the analytical framework, and draw a general conclusion, which might contribute to the study of wider social scientific research, particularly with regard to the study of European integration.

One of the most important aspects of this research lies in the concept of policy logics. The concept allows us to analyze not only the changes in policy objectives, long-term strategies, and policy discourse within national governments, but also the dynamic evolution of decision-making at the European level. It defies the notion of monolithic state actor and 'national interest', but instead, it regards national policy logics as defined by the competition and cooperation among coalitions of actors who share similar objectives and policy norms, which I call 'logic coalitions'. The members of logic coalitions are assumed to aim at not only material benefits but also achieving their long-term objectives and fulfilling their professional values. They seek to influence the principal decision-makers who have the authority to decide the policies on space programs. The principal decision makers are assumed to have their own preferences among policy logics, but are also constrained by external circumstances. The policy logics of national governments are, therefore, shaped by the interaction between principal decision-makers and logic coalitions. What is more important in utilizing the concept of policy logic is that it explains the outcome of the negotiations at the European level. The principal decision-makers eventually become the negotiators in the European decision-making process, and they promote their national policy logics. The policy logics of governments are often diverse and conflicting, but they seek to find a resolution which satisfies their policy logics within a set of institutional constraints. At the same time, the leaders of European organizations (Director-General of ESA, for example) try to provide initiatives and proposals to articulate different policy logics in order to garner maximum support from the Member States. Hence, the articulation of national policy logics defines the outcome of negotiations at European level.

The other importance of this research is the focus on institutions. It follows the claims of historical institutionalists that institutions shape and structure behavior and strategies. Its findings suggest that European space collaboration provides a very good example for studies of institutions by comparing the different institutional settings of ESRO/ELDO and ESA. However, this study does not share the assumption common to most institutionalist arguments that institutions are robust and stable throughout history. Instead, it argues that institutions become a subject of change when the policy logics become imbalanced within the existing institutions. At first sight, this approach seems to share assumptions with the rational choice institutionalists, but the interesting contribution of this study is that, although it assumes the rationality of the actors, it does not assume that they act only on the basis of 'interests'. This study, on the other hand, argues that institutions are relatively stable until the point where the members participating in the institutions recognize that the institutions are inappropriate to harmonize the differences among policy logics and to adjust to changes in external circumstances. The institutional changes took place because the changes in external environment induced the shift of policy logics in each Member State's government. Eventually the institutions were unable to accommodate the new balance of policy logics.

It is not the intention of this chapter to claim that the two important contributions of this study are full-fledged. These concepts have to be assessed, reviewed and evaluated in order to become better social scientific tools. They also need to be tested in other policy domains in different levels of international cooperation. However, the findings of this study suggest that the framework it proposes can explain the dynamics of European space collaboration and the character of the interactions between institutions and policy logics. This chapter attempts to summarize the findings of this study and proposes an amendment to the framework of policy logic analysis in order to understand the dynamics of European space collaboration. Then it highlights some aspects of European space collaboration that have implications for the study of European integration.

Reviewing the Analytical Framework

Policy Logic Analysis

The framework provided in chapter 2 focused on the interaction between logic coalitions and principal decision makers at a certain point in time within national decision making procedures. However, the study of European space collaboration from the end of the 1950s suggests that policy logic analysis can be used to explain the dynamics of the process of collaboration, if we add two important aspects to this analytical framework.

The first aspect is time. By definition, the concept of dynamics includes the concept of time because it looks at the changes across a certain length of time. In this study, we have discussed the policy logics of European governments since the end of the 1950s, but our analysis remained 'snapshots', i.e. analyzing the policy logics at certain points in time. The analysis of the dynamics of collaboration needs to include the concept of time and to consider the flow of changes from the 1950s to the present.

The second aspect is the relationship between the policy logics of individual governments and the outcome of European negotiations. In chapter 2, we argued that international negotiations are often influenced by national policy logics, and the negotiators/principal decision-makers have to deal not only with their counterparts but also with domestic logic coalitions, using an analogy from the two-level games approach (Putnam 1988). Nevertheless, the linkage between national policy logics and the outcome of European negotiations goes beyond the 'two-level games' concept. This study repeatedly pointed out that the balance of policy logics of each government influenced the outcome of the negotiations, and the institutions of European space collaboration. Given the intergovernmental characteristics of the negotiations at the European level (see Table 2.1 of chapter 2), the decision at the European level would likely be taken as the 'lowest-common-denominator', which would satisfy the policy logics of all Member States' governments, particularly the big countries whose contribution is more important to the programs. The Spanish delegate to ESA in 1984, Luis de Azcarraga, claimed that the smaller states "can be in the long run more objective, less conditioned by particular interests, more convinced about the necessity of a real cooperation" (Azcarraga 1984, p.19). Their policy logics are relatively stable, mainly focused on the logic of technology, because their industries are rather immature and fragmented so that they need to strengthen the technological competence in the first place. Therefore, the changes in strategies and programs at European level were, in most cases, defined by the big countries. Nevertheless, there have always been conflicts and competitions of policy logics between bigger and smaller countries, and among the big countries. In other words, it is always difficult to reconcile different national policy logics, which are strongly influenced by the institutional arrangements in each Member State.

Importance of National Institutions

The national institutions, which were explained in chapter 6, are important in this account. The national institutions — the rules, procedures and conventions which structure the relationships between actors, and the shared norms and paradigms which underpin and support those rules, procedures and conventions — define the access and influence of logic coalitions to the principal decision makers, and hence, national policy logics are rather stable under usual circumstances. For example, the French policy making institutions are dominated by its space agency, CNES, whose central policy logics were dominated by the logics of autonomy (which brings more funding for CNES) and technology (which brings more interesting programs to CNES). Britain experienced a significant change of policy logics in the mid-1960s under the Wilson government, but the overall institutions were based on the logic of finance and commerce, partly due to the fragmented organization. The German policy logics were mainly based on the logic of technology and science because of the presence of the DLR in the policy-making process. Nevertheless, the British and German space agencies have not been given enough importance to influence national policy logics compared to the French space agency, and therefore were vulnerable to the changes of principal decision-makers.

European Institutions Matter

While national logics were rather divided into different policy logics, it was the flexibility of institutions which kept the European space collaboration within particular frameworks. The separation of ESRO and ELDO ensured the participation of smaller Member States whose policy logics were mainly centered on that of science, while the big Member States were able to protect their logics of national autonomy and technology within the ELDO framework. The principle of *juste retour*, which was introduced in the later years of ESRO, was an institutional arrangement to satisfy the logic of technology and commerce for each Member State. The logics were used not only for protecting embryonic industry by smaller Member States, but also for ensuring that big Member States maintain their control over funding and industrial contracts.

During the ESRO/ELDO years, the policy logics of European governments were mostly oriented toward their 'national' logics, but gradually 'European' oriented logics began to emerge in the ESA years. The Ariane and Space Station programs were two programs that were driven by more 'European' policy logic, namely the logic of European autonomy. However, this does not mean that nationally oriented logics have disappeared. On the contrary, the institutions under ESA were designed to be flexible enough to accommodate different national policy logics. Not only the principle of *juste retour*, but also the rule of optional participation was introduced in the ESA Convention. These institutions enabled the Member States to choose whether and how much they would contribute to ESA programs according to their national policy logics; and if an individual program did not serve their logics, they could choose to leave the program without leaving the ESA organization as a whole. This study displayed extensive evidence that the governments of Member States took full advantage of these institutions.

Institutional Change

Even under such flexible institutions, the difference in policy logics was sometimes not easy to reconcile, particularly when there was a significant shift in policy logic in some Member States. As discussed in chapter 2, institutions are both consciously and unconsciously reproduced, but there is always a moment when actors subjectively and actively intervene in the historical process and re-shape the historical path, which opens up a new future. That 'moment', which Nielsen *et al.* (1995) referred to as the 'path-shaping process', occurred twice in the history of European space collaboration. The first moment took place between the late 1960s and early 1970s, when the British government expressed its willingness to leave Europa development and the German government decided to participate in the post-Apollo programs. The policy logics of the French, British and German governments were split in different directions, which became almost impossible to reconcile within the old institutions, and a more flexible institutional framework under a new organization, ESA, was adopted.

The second moment has been actually taking place since the late 1990s. As discussed in chapter 5, the policy logics of big Member States were shifting towards the logics of finance and commerce under the new circumstances, while smaller Member States were still holding on to their policy logics of national autonomy and technology. The negotiations at the ESA Ministerial Councils in the late 1990s, and the proposal of the 'Union of Centers' showed the difficulty of reconciling the differences in policy logics, even within the flexible ESA framework, because it was not only the rules and procedures, but also the norm of "working together" (Zabusky 1995), which became the subject of change.

The institutions of European space collaboration were, on the one hand, shaping and structuring the policy logics of the actors, but on the other hand, the changes in the balance of policy logics among them required the institutions to adjust to those changes. This study has demonstrated that institutions were not always independent variables, as the historical institutionalists claim, but they are subject to change when the differences in policy logics were not articulated.

The Dynamics of European Space Collaboration

The analysis of the historical dynamics of European space collaboration therefore requires an understanding of the change (and continuity) in national policy logics and national and European institutional settings, and the interaction of these factors. We shall now look back on our findings and put them into this revised analytical framework to see the historical dynamism of European space collaboration.

The Beginning (T₁)

The policy logics of European governments in the late 1950s have two distinguishing characteristics. On the one hand, the idea of European collaboration was inspired by the science logic coalition, led by Amaldi, Auger and Massey, who had successful experiences in CERN, to promote the logic of science at the European level. A strong coherence in the policy logic of science among European governments, including the smaller ones, made it easier to establish new institutions for collaboration based on ESRO. On the other hand, there was no coherence in the policy logics for launcher development: the British logic of finance, the French logic of the military and commerce, and the German and Italian logic of technology. The launcher development organization, ELDO, was therefore created on a fragile balance of policy logics, and the institutional framework of ELDO was designed to be only minimally compelling for Member States. Eventually this weak institutional framework experienced consecutive failures, and bad management. The Member States turned their backs on its unsuccessful and poor institutional performance.

Mid-1960s (T₂)

The emergence of application satellites and the commercial success of Intelsat indicated that space activities had entered a new phase. The governments of both bigger and smaller countries recognized that their first priority was to develop the technological capability in order to catch up with American application satellites and have autonomous access to space by Europeans. The rising logics of technology and commerce brought up the question of industrial return in both ESRO and ELDO. The problem was partly resolved by the eventual introduction of the principle of *juste retour*, at least for ESRO programs, though the shift in policy logic by the Wilson government to the logic of finance clashed with the French logic of autonomy in developing European launchers. The fragile balance of policy logics and the inadequacy of institutions brought on a series of crises in the process of European space collaboration. The creation of the European Space Conference (ESC) provided little help in reconciling the differences in policy logics, particularly with regard to the development of the launcher.

End of ESRO/ELDO Years (T₃)

The American invitation to Europeans to participate in the post-Apollo program had a significant influence on the policy logics of some Member States, particularly Germany and Italy. Their willingness to participate in the Spacelab, driven by the logic of technology and science, was unable to coexist with the French logic of autonomy in launcher development. Together with the British unwillingness to participate in the development of the Europa program, the ELDO framework reached deadlock. In order to break the deadlock, the French government took the initiative to create a new European launcher, Ariane, under a new institutional framework, and the German and British governments accepted this proposal through the 'package deal' with Spacelab and Marots. At the same time, ESRO also faced the difficult problem of application programs. Some Member States, particularly the big ones, were willing to develop application satellites under the ESRO framework, whereas the smaller Member States whose policy logics rested mainly on the logic of science were not happy to jeopardize the scientific programs of ESRO. Thus, the system of '*à la carte*' participation was introduced at the initiative of Hermann Bondi. This new system gave more flexibility to the institutions of European space collaboration, and eventually played a central role in the ESA framework.

Early ESA Years (T₄)

Although the differences in policy logics, particularly among the big countries, ruptured the ESRO/ELDO frameworks, the new institutions under the ESA framework were developed as a reflection of the French policy logic of autonomy. This was greatly facilitated because the German government discovered the importance of maintaining decision-making power and autonomous capability through its bitter experience in the Spacelab program. The logic of European autonomy became the central pillar of ESA programs. But on the other hand, the Member States, particularly the big ones, developed their strategies based on their domestic industrial, financial, and political concerns. The conflicts over the H-Sat/Olympus and TDF/TV-Sat programs told us that operating through ESA institutions was not the obvious choice for the big countries, particularly when the programs had big implications in terms of commercial technologies. The concept of 'Europeanization' of national programs and the rule of optional participation were widely interpreted as meaning that ESA would serve national policy logics and strategies.

Rome and The Hague Ministerial Councils (T₅)

Again, European space collaboration was strongly influenced by the actions of the US government. The American invitation to participate in the International Space

Station programs was, however, treated differently from the Spacelab case, because the policy logics of European governments were more or less united around the logic of autonomy. The 'spirit of Rome' was very high to generate support for three ambitious programs — Ariane 5, Hermes, and Columbus MTFF. Although the re-emergent British logic of commerce posed a question against the logic of autonomy in the Ministerial Council at The Hague in 1987, most European governments stood ready to move on with the decision in Rome.

End of the Cold War and German Reunification (T_6)

The changes in the international structure after the end of the Cold War induced a series of changes in the sphere of European space collaboration and the policy logics of European governments. The German government in particular faced difficulty continuing its policy logics, mainly because of serious budgetary constraints due to reunification. The Franco-German axis was unable to harmonize the French logic of autonomy and the German logic of finance. The strengthening of the logic of finance pushed other logics, the logic of science in particular, away from the European space programs. Sessions of the Ministerial Council, as had been the case in the ESC, became increasingly important for settling the differences in policy logics.

Commercialization of the Space Market (T_7)

While the logic of finance became increasingly powerful in most European governments, the emergence of the commercial space market added the logic of commerce to the governments of big countries. With this logic, they proposed reforming the principle of *juste retour*, which was considered an obstacle to improving the international competitiveness of the European space industry. However, this logic did not spread to the smaller countries, whose industries were more or less detached from competition at the international level, and they jealously protected the rules to maintain their logic of (national) autonomy and technology. The national governments and space agencies of the big countries were frustrated by the resistance of the small countries, as seen in the movement of the ASI-CNES-DLR proposal for the 'Union of Centers'. In this case ESA's institutional structure proved flexible enough to absorb such conflicts. The combination of the logics of finance and commerce also led to the creation of two other institutions; a joint taskforce between ESA and the EU for a 'European Strategy for Space'; and the concept of 'Public-Private Partnership'.

Analysis

This brief review of the findings of this study gives us a perspective on the historical dynamics of European space collaboration from a point of view of policy logics and institutions. Table 8.1 summarizes the changes in policy logics and institutions. Several interesting features can be discerned from this table. First, national and European policy logics are clearly correlated. If there is a harmony of policy logics among all governments, or at least among the leaders, the European policy logics are easily defined. On the other hand, the European policy logics became fragile when there was no coherence among national policy logics, particularly when the leaders were in conflict over their logics. Secondly, the logic of finance appeared on every occasion that the European logic was fragile. The table shows that the force of the logic of finance, in most cases, influenced the discord in European space collaboration, and that it required 'political' fora such as the ESC or ESA Ministerial Councils for settling disputes. Thirdly, a pattern emerged in which new and innovative rules and procedures were created when the logic of commerce became the influential logic among governments. The principle of *juste retour* and the rule of optional participation were somewhat uncharacteristic of conventional international organizations, but they provided more flexibility to the institutions of European space collaboration.

Table 8.1 also gives us interesting pictures of the change and continuity of national policy logics. There is a constant presence of the logic of technology in French policy. This is largely due to the strength of the CNES, particularly the Toulouse Space Center (CST). Although the logic of technology was not always the first priority in the French policy, there were always some elements that the CST promoted in the French-sponsored programs. In practice, the French logic of technology often united with the logic of autonomy, which attracted the political support of the principal decision makers. The combination of these two logics gave distinguishing characteristics to the French space strategy.

The logic of technology also dominated the German policy logics until the end of T_5. This dominance can be explained by the constant engagement of the institutional section of the DLR, even though the agency section often changed. Nevertheless, the logic of technology declined in the 1990s, due to the emergence of the logic of finance. This suggests that German institutions for space policy-making had changed significantly during this period.

The most distinguishable policy logics throughout this history in the British government were the logics of finance and commerce. Apart from the beginning (T_1), the logic of commerce was the main driving force behind the British space programs. On the other hand, the logic of finance influenced the decision of the British government positively to shift in favor of the European option in launcher development, although the reinforcement of the logic of finance from the mid-1960s (T_2) brought difficult moments in the process of collaboration, particularly in the ELDO framework. The British policy logics lost the leadership and influence under the strong French policy logics in the early ESA period; however the acceleration of commercialization in the space market and a congruence of other governments' policy logics re-emphasized the importance of the British logics. As it happened, the concept of PPP and the development of the ESA-EU joint strategy were initiated by the British government.

The governments of the smaller countries,[1] whose policy logics were more or less similar to each other, had the logics of science and technology at their heart. Their logics seemed to be similar to those of France and Germany, but their technological programs heavily depended on the ESA framework. In many cases, their policy logics were satisfied by participating in ESA programs in order to gain particular technological competence. Their logic of technology was safely protected by the rule of optional participation and the principle of *juste retour*. Thus, the governments of smaller countries found the proposal to reform the principle of *juste*

Table 8.1   Historical Changes of Major Policy Logics and Institutions

	T1		T2		T3		T4	T5	T6	T7
External Impacts	Space race, Success of CERN, IGY		Success of Intelsat		Post-Apollo invitation, Failure of Europa		Spacelab problem	Invitation to ISS	End of Cold War	Further Commercialization
Org.	ESRO	ELDO	ESRO	ELDO	ESRO	ELDO	ESA	ESA	ESA	ESA
Leadership	Scientists	GB+F	GB vs. F	GB vs. F	F vs. GB	F vs. D	F+D	F+D	F vs. D	GB(?) or EU(?)
France	S, T	M, A, C	T, C, S	A, T, C	C, T, S	A, T/C	A, C, T	A, T	A, C, T	C, F, A
Germany	S, T	T	T/S	T	C, T/S	F*	T, A, C	T, A, S	F	C, F
Britain	S	F	T, S, F	F	C, T, S	F	C, T	C, F	C, F	C, F
Others	S/T	T	S/T	T, A	T/S, C	T, A	T, A/C	T, A	T, A, F	T, F, C
Europe	S	Fragile	T/S, C	Fragile	C/T, S	Fragile	A, C, T	A, T	Fragile	C, F vs. T
Institutional change	Creation of ESRO/ ELDO, protection of national logics		*Juste retour* (ESRO), 'go it alone' Creation of ESC		*À la carte* participation, package deal, Creation of ESA		European-ization of national programs	Re-emergence of Ministerial Council	Increasing importance of Ministerial Council	Reform of *juste retour,* Union of Centres, 'ESS'

S= Logic of Science, T= Logic of Technology, A= Logic of Autonomy, C= Logic of Commerce, M= Logic of Military, F= Logic of Finance, Tn is shown in the subsections. GB= Great Britain, F= France, D= Germany.
*   German policy logic for ELDO in T3 was based on the logic of finance because the German government wanted to switch their funding to Spacelab, which was driven by the logic of technology and science.

retour in the late 1990s very threatening, and they fought to defend the old institutions.

Concluding Remarks: Lessons for European Integration

The analytical framework of historical dynamics need not be limited in its application to the study of European space collaboration. It can be expanded, for example, to the study of other areas of European integration, particularly in the domain of defense cooperation. Since ESA and the EU are developing an institutional relationship, it would be worth considering whether there are any lessons to be learned from the experiences of European space collaboration for the process of European integration.

Flexible Institutions: Optional Participation

One of the big differences between the ESA and EU frameworks is their institutional arrangement. The ESA framework allows governments to participate in programs optionally, and guarantees an industrial return according to the scale of their contribution (the principle of *juste retour*), whereas in the EU — more precisely the European Community, the first pillar of the EU — the framework is largely based on a preservation of the *acquis communautaire* (accumulated existing legislation and practices) that all Member States shall accept the *acquis* to form a coherent organization and a single market. The role of the *acquis* was significantly important in the history of European integration (see, for example, Shackleton 1993, Wiener 2000) in the way that it anchored the process of European integration and made it more robust. Moreover, the EU has resisted *juste retour* as its budgetary principle and established its unique budgetary system with its own resources.

However, the concepts of preserving the *acquis* and catching up with the pace of integration were challenged by the ideas, on the one hand, of 'two-speed Europe', '*abgestüfte integration*' or 'graduated integration' (Langeheine 1985) and, on the other hand, 'two-tier integration', 'variable geometry', '*Europe à la carte*' (see the summary of these ideas in Wallace 1985). The former proposed relaxing time limits for the slower Member States to implement common objectives, in areas where no satisfactory agreement could be found. The latter accepted that Member States could pick and choose in which policy areas they would like to participate, and thus make coalitions with other Member States, which have similar policy logics, while maintaining some 'core' common objectives (Stubb 1997). These ideas emerged in the late-1970s and the early-1980s, when the EC accepted three (and another one) new Member States whose objectives, strategies, and policy logics were quite different from those of the original six. Though these ideas were quite realistic from a policy logic analysis point of view, the existing institutions, namely the *acquis communautaire*, prevailed in the EC process.

However, further 'deepening' and 'widening' of integration in the 1990s reiterated these ideas to manage diverse policy logics in several policy areas. The British and Danish opt-out from Economic and Monetary Union provided a precedent for operating a kind of '*Europe à la carte*', and the inclusion of the WEU and Schengen agreement added 'variable geometry' to the EU framework. Eventually, the Member States engaged in a debate over 'flexible integration' (Stubb 2000).

What this study on European space collaboration can contribute to this debate is the robust experience of flexible institutional arrangements for collaboration. The rule of optional participation has certainly protected the troubled European frameworks for space collaboration, because it was able to accommodate different policy logics on a single platform. Of course, the EU is not an organization created for a single policy area like ESA, and therefore it would be misleading to imply that the successful method for ESA — optional participation or *'Europe à la carte'* — could produce the same result in the EU. Nevertheless, it would be possible to consider that Member States could optionally participate in some programs, particularly in the second and third pillar issues. Perhaps, the rule of optional participation would work better in common defense policy and issues in the field of justice and home affairs, since there is a limited coherence among the policy logics of EU Member States in these fields. The idea of optional participation may not be suitable and desirable for the EU institution as a whole, but there would certainly be some policy areas where it might produce a better outcome, as the Commission admitted in the European Strategy for Space document (COM(2001)718 final).

And Finally...

European space collaboration is now facing new challenges. Losing the balance in policy logics of the bigger and smaller countries, on the one hand, poses the risk that the ESA might split into two parts, or that big Member States will 'go it alone'. But on the other hand, increasing commercialization in the space market and strengthening of the relationship between ESA and the EU would require a further 'deepening' of collaboration. Either way, the importance of space programs will increase for the foreseeable future, and Europe has little choice but to stay in the game. Space activities are no longer a political toy for politicians or technical experiments for engineers. Space has become a part of social and economic life, and it should enhance the choices and chances for each individual on Earth. The history of European space collaboration reminds us that even though European governments could not strike a balance in their policy logics, they innovated new institutional arrangements to accommodate those logics under a European umbrella. After all, the European governments knew that they would not accomplish the level of technological expertise and competence in space if there was no collaboration, and it will create more opportunity for them to improve their standard of life, commercial potential, and influence in the international scene.

Note

1   Perhaps Italy may not be categorized as a smaller country in terms of its contribution, but since its policy logics were quite similar to those of other smaller countries, it was included in this category.

Bibliography

Aberbach, Joel D., Robert D. Putnam and Bert A. Rockman, (eds.) (1981), *Bureaucrats and Politicians in Western Democracies*. Cambridge, MA: Harvard University Press.

Académie des Sciences (1988), *La recherche et la politique spatiale dans les prochaines décennies*. Paris: 21 March.

Adams, John (1994), 'Economy as Instituted Process: Change, Transformation, and Progress', *Journal of Economic Issues*. vol.28 no.2: pp.331–355.

Adler, Emanuel and Peter M. Haas (1992), 'Conclusion: Epistemic Communities, World Order, and the Creation of Reflective Research Program', *International Organization*. vol.46 no.1: pp.365–390.

Allison, Graham T. (1971), *Essence of Decision: Explaining the Cuban Missile Crisis*. Boston: Little Brown.

Amaldi, Edoardo (1984), 'Why We Need a European Organisation for Space Research', in European Space Agency (ed.) *Europe, Two Decades in Space*. Noordwijk, The Netherlands: ESA: pp.9–11.

Andrews, Bruce (1984), 'The Domestic Content of International Desire', *International Organization*. vol.38 no.2: pp.321–327.

Anson, Peter (1989), 'Skynet Succeeds', *Space*. vol.5 no.2: pp.36–40.

Ashley, Richard K. (1986), 'The Poverty of Neorealism', in Robert O. Keohane (ed.) *Neorealism and Its Critics*. New York: Columbia University Press, pp.255–300.

ASI (Agenzia Spaziale Italiana) (1997), *Piano Spaziale Nazionale 1998–2002: Strategie e Linee Programmatiche*. Roma: ASI.

Atkinson, Harry H. (1993), 'Conclusions of Meeting', in the Proceeding of *The Implementation of the ESA Convention _ Lessons from the Past: Proceedings of the ESA/EUI International Colloquium* in Florence, 25–26 October 1993. pp.223–229.

Atzei, A., K. Pseiner and D. Raitt (1995), 'Future Perspectives for Europe in Space', *ESA Bulletin*. no.82: pp.27–34.

Auger, Pierre (1984), 'The Prehistory of ESRO: A Personal Memoir', in European Space Agency (ed.) *Europe, Two Decades in Space. Noordwijk*, The Netherlands: ESA: pp.12–15.

Ayres, Clarence E. (1944), *The Theory of Economic Progress*. Chapel Hill: University of North Carolina Press.

Ayres, Clarence E. (1961), *Toward a Reasonable Society: The Values of Industrial Civilization*. Austin: University of Texas Press.

Azcarraga, Luis de (1984), 'Spain and Space', in European Space Agency (ed.), *Europe, Two Decades in Space*. Noordwijk, The Netherlands: ESA: SP-1060.

Barbance, Karin, Karl Bergquist, Simonetta Cheli, Valerie A. Hood and Frederic Nordlund (1996), 'Satellite Navigation Activities: The International Context', *Space Communications.* vol.14, pp.155–161.

Barker, Anthony and B. Guy Peters (1993), 'Science Policy and Government', in Anthony Barker and B. Guy Peters (eds.) *The Politics of Expert Advice: Creating, Using and Manipulating Scientific Knowledge for Public Policy.* Edinburgh: Edinburgh University Press: pp.1–16.

Bartelson, Jens (1995), *A Genealogy of Sovereignty.* Cambridge: Cambridge University Press.

Baucom, Donald R. (1995), 'Developing a Management Structure for the Strategic Defense Initiative', in Roger D. Launius (ed.) *Organizing for the Use of Space: Historical Perspective on a Persistent Issue.* Washington D.C.: AAS History Series: pp.187–215.

Baumgartner, Frank R. and Bryan D. Jones (1991), 'Agenda Dynamics and Policy Subsystems', *Journal of Politics.* vol.53 no.4: pp.1043–1074.

Bell, Daniel (1973), *The Coming of Post-Industrial Society.* New York: Basic Books.

Benveniste, Guy (1972), *The Politics of Expertise.* Berkeley: Glendessary Press.

Benyamine, Paul (1995), 'Politique Industrielle et Politique d'Indépendance', in Emmanuel Chadeau (ed.) *L'Ambition Téchnologique: Naissance d'Ariane.* Paris: Editions Rive Droite: pp.247–254.

Bhaskar, Roy (1979), *The Possibility of Naturalism: A Philosophical Critique of the Contemporary Human Sciences.* Brighton: Harvester.

Bignier, Michel (1995), 'Les Choix Industriels et Le Rôle des Entreprises', in Emmanuel Chadeau (ed.) *L'Ambition Téchnologique: Naissance d'Ariane.* Paris: Editions Rive Droite: pp.155–159.

Bildt, Carl, Jean Peyrelevade and Lothar Späth (2000), *Towards a Space agency for the European Union.* Report to the ESA Director General, mimeo.

Bizony, Piers (1996), *Island in the Sky: Building the International Space Station.* London: Aurum Press.

BMBF (Bundesministeriums fûr Bildung, Wissenschaft, Forschung und Technologie) (1997), *Space: Prospects for Research and Applications (Federal Government Strategy Document).* Bonn: BMBF.

BMBF (2001), *German Space Programme.* Bonn: BMBF.

BMWi (Bundesministerium für Wirtschaft) (1996), 'Report by the Coordinator for German Aerospace Affairs in 1996', *BMWi Dokumentation,* no.393.

BNSC (British National Space Centre) (1996), UK Space Policy: *Forward Plan.* London: BNSC.

BNSC (1998), *Draft UK Space Plan 1998: Draft paper prepared for UK Space Policy Seminar, Leeds Friday 3 April 1998.* London: BNSC.

BNSC (1999), *United Kingdom Space Strategy 1999–2002: New Frontiers.* London: BNSC.

Bolland, Jean-Pierre (1995), 'Small National Firms and Large Industrial Consortia', in the Proceedings of *Twenty Years of the ESA Convention* in Munich, 4–6 September 1995: ESA-SP-387, pp.109–113.

Bondi, Hermann (1993), 'Crisis and Achievement: ESRO 1967–1971', in Arturo Russo (ed.) *Science Beyond the Atmosphere: The History of Space Research in Europe.* Noordwijk, The Netherlands: ESA: HSR-Special: pp.139–145.

Bonnet, Roger M. (1993), 'Space Science in ESRO and ESA: An Overview', in Arturo Russo (ed.) *Science Beyond the Atmosphere: The History of Space Research in Europe.* Noordwijk, The Netherlands: ESA: HSR-Special: pp.1–28.

Bonnet, Roger M. and Vittorio Manno (1994), *International Cooperation in Space: The Example of the European Space Agency.* Cambridge, MA: Harvard University Press.

Bourdieu, Pierre (1977), *Outline of a Theory of Practice.* Cambridge: Cambridge University Press (translated by Richard Nice).

Bourély, M. (1992), 'The Institutional Framework for ESA's New Programmes', *ESA Bulletin.* no.30: pp.4–7.

Breckinridge, Robert E. (1997), 'Reassessing Regimes: The International Regime Aspects of the European Union', *Journal of Common Market Studies.* vol.35 no.2: pp.173–187.

Brubaker, Rogers (1984), *The Limits of Rationality: An Essay on the Social and Moral Thought of Max Weber.* Boston: George Allen & Unwin.

Buchanan, James M. and Gordon Tullock (1962), *The Calculus of Consent: Logical Foundations of Constitutional Democracy.* Ann Arbor: University of Michigan Press.

Bull, Hedley (1977), *The Anarchical Society: A Study of Order in World Politics.* New York: Columbia University Press.

Bulmer, Simon J. (1998), 'New Institutionalism and the Governance of the Single European Market', *Journal of European Public Policy.* vol.5 no.3: pp.365–86.

Burns, James MacGregor (1978), *Leadership.* New York: Harper & Row.

Bush, Paul D. (1987), 'The Theory of Institutional Change', *Journal of Economic Issues.* vol.21 no.3: pp.1075–1116.

Bush, Paul D. (1994), 'The Pragmatic Instrumentalist Perspective on the Theory of Institutional Change', *Journal of Economic Issues.* vol.28 no.2: pp.647–657.

Carlier, Armand (2001), 'Prospect of European Space Industry', a keynote speech in SATEL *Conseil Symposium.* Paris, September 4, 2001.

Carlier, Claude and Marcel Gilli (1994), *The First Thirty Years at CNES: The French Space Agency 1962–1992.* Paris: La Documentation Française.

Carlsnaes, Walter (1992), 'The Agency-Structure Problem in Foreign Policy Analysis', *International Studies Quarterly.* vol.36 no.3: pp.245–270.

Causse, Jean-Pierre (1995), 'Les Lanceurs Européens avant Ariane', in Emmanuel Chadeau (ed.) *L'Ambition Technologique: Naissance d'Ariane.* Paris: Rive Droite: pp.15–34.

CEC (Commission of European Communities) (1988), *The Community and Space: a Coherent Approach.* Luxembourg: Office for Official Publication of the European Communities (Com(88)417 final).

CEC (1991), *The European Community – Crossroads in Space: Report by an Advisory Panel on the European Community and Space.* Luxembourg: Office for Official Publication of the European Communities.

CEC (1992), *The European Community and Space: Challenges, Opportunities and New Actions.* Luxembourg: Office for Official Publication of the European Communities (Com(92)360 final).

CEC (1996), *The European Union and Space: Fostering Applications, Markets and Industrial Competitiveness*. Luxembourg: Office for Official Publication of the European Union (Com(96)617 final).

CEC (1999), *Galileo – Involving Europe in a new generation of satellite navigation services*. Luxembourg: Office for Official Publication of the European Union (Com(99) 54 final).

CEC (2000), *On Galileo*. Luxembourg: Office for Official Publication of the European Union (Com(2000)750 final).

CEC (2001), *Global Monitoring for Environment and Security (GMES): Outline GMES EC Action Plan (Initial Period: 2001–2003)*. Luxembourg: Office for Official Publication of the European Union (Com(2001)609 final).

CEC (2001), *Towards a European Space Policy*. Luxembourg: Office for Official Publication of the European Union (Com(2001)718 final).

Chadeau, Emmanuel, (ed.) (1995), *L'Ambition Téchnologique: Naissance d'Ariane*. Paris: Editions Rive Droite.

Chanard, Stephane (1994), 'French Satellites in Uniform', Space. vol.10 no.5: pp.8–12.

Charles, David and Jeremy Howells (1992), *Technology Transfer in Europe: Public and Private Networks*. London: Belhaven Press.

Cheli, Simonetta and Kai-Uwe Schrogl (1999), 'Reshaping European Space Activities', *Space Policy*. vol.15 no.2: pp.61–66.

Chorley (Lord) (1988), 'Economics of Space and the Role of Government', *Space Policy*. vol.4 no.3: pp.180–186.

Christiansen, Thomas and Knud Erik Jørgensen (1999), 'The Amsterdam Process: A Structurationist Perspective on EU Treaty Reform', *European Integration online Papers*. vol.3 no.1: pp.1–19, http://eiop.or.at/eiop/texte1999–001a.htm.

Clerc, Philippe (1997), 'France', in Simone Courteix (ed.) *Le Cadre Institutionnel des Activités Spatiales des États*, Paris: Editions A. Pedone, pp.62–92.

Clerc, Philippe (1998), 'Partnership between CNES and Industry: A New Market Oriented Approach', in G. Haskell and M. Rycroft (eds.) *New Space Markets: Symposium Proceedings, International Symposium, 26–28 May 1997, Strasbourg, France*. Dordrecht: Kluwer Academic Publishers.

Clinton, W. David (1994), *The Two Faces of National Interest*. Baton Rouge and London: Louisiana State University Press.

CNES (Centre Nationale d'Etudes Spatiales) (1988), *Impact de l'Acte Unique Européen sur les Activités Spatiales: Rapport Préliminaire du Groupe de Travail*. Paris, CNES.

CNES (1996), *Plan Stratégique*. Paris: CNES.

CNES (1999), *Plan Stratégique 1999*. Paris: CNES.

Cohen, Elie (1992), Le Corbertisme <<High Tech>>: *Economie des Telecom et du Grand Projet*. Paris: Hachette.

Cole, Alistair (1994), *François Mitterrand: A Study in Political Leadership*. London and New York: Routledge.

Collett, John Peter (1995), 'Space in a European Context: The Making of a National Space Research Policy', in John Peter Collett (ed.) *Making Sense of Space: The History of Norwegian Space Activities*. Oslo: Scandinavian University Press: pp.71–115.

Collette, J.-L. (1987), '"Spacecommerce" – Montreux', *ESA Bulletin*. no.49, pp.37–38.

Collette, René (1992), 'Space Communications in Europe: How did we make it happen?', *History and Technology*. vol.9 pp.83–93.

Collins, Guy (1990), *Europe in Space*. London: Macmillan.

Colucci, Frank (1987), 'Selling SPOT', *Space*. vol.3 no.5: pp.12–16.

Coudy, Henri-Jean, Bruno Deletre, Laurent Moquin, Frédéric Oudea, Henri Osmont d'Amilly and Christian Paul (1988), *L'Espace et la Securité de la France*. Paris: Fondation pour les Etudes de Defense Nationale.

Council of Europe, Consultative Assembly (1960) *Report on European Co-operation on Space Research and Space Technology*. 9th September. Doc. 1175.

Cox, Robert W. (1986), 'Social Forces, State and World Orders: Beyond International Relations Theory', in Robert O. Keohane (eds.) *Neorealism and Its Critics*. New York: Columbia University Press: pp.204–254.

Creola, Peter (1984), 'Ariane: The Road to Independence', in European Space Agency (ed.) *Europe, Two Decades in Space*. Noordwijk, The Netherlands: ESA: pp.31–36.

Creola, Peter (1991), 'ESA Ministerial Meeting: Consensus or Confrontation?', *Space Policy*. vol.7 no.4: pp.289–294.

Creola, Peter (1999), 'Switzerland and Space: How a Small Country Succeeds', *Space Policy*, vol.15 no.1, pp.41–44.

Cunningham, Catherine M. and R. H. Nicholson (1991), 'Central Government Organisation and Policy Making for UK Science and Technology since 1982', in Robin Nicholson, Catherine Cunningham, and Philip Gummett (eds.) *Science and Technology in the United Kingdom*, Harlow: Longman, pp.27–43.

Curien, Hubert (1985), 'A Bold View from France', *Space*. vol.1 no.1: p.10.

Curien, Hubert (1987), 'The Revival of Europe', in Andrew J. Pierre (ed.) *A High Technology Gap?: Europe, America and Japan*. New York: Council of Foreign Relations: pp.44–66.

Curien, Hubert (1988), 'Interview', *La Recherche*, October.

D'Allest, Frédéric (1988), 'The Ariane Family', *Interdisciplinary Science Review*. vol.13 no.2: pp.166–170.

D'Allest, Frédéric (1995), 'Why is the Most Widely Used Launcher in the World European?', in the Proceedings, of *Twenty Years of the ESA Convention* in Munich, 4–6 September 1995: ESA-SP-387, pp.47–50.

Dale, D., F. A. Jagtman and T. Deak (1994), 'Review of Industry/ESA Business Practices within the Scientific Programme: The Industrial Workshops', *ESA Bulletin*. no.78: pp.7–14.

Dauncey, Hugh (1994), *The Making of French Space Policy 1979–1992*. Ph.D Thesis, Bath University.

David, Paul (1985), 'Clio and the Economics of QWERTY', *American Economic Review*. vol.75 pp.332–37.

Davis, Jacquelyn K. (1987), 'SDI and the European Defense Debate', in Steven W. Guerrier and Wayne C. Thompson (eds.), *Perspectives on Strategic Defense*. Boulder, CO: Westview Press.

Day, Dwayne A. (1998), 'A Strategy for Reconnaissance: Dwight D. Eisenhower and Freedom of Space', in Dwayne A. Day, John M. Logsdon and Brian Latell (eds.), *Eye in the Sky: The Story of the Corona Spy Satellites.* Washington: Smithsonian Institution Press: pp.119–142.

De Maria, Michelangelo (1993a), *Europe in Space: Edoardo Amaldi and the Inception of ESRO.* Noordwijk, The Netherlands: ESA: HSR-5.

De Maria, Michelangelo (1993b), 'Italy in Space: The Take-off of the Italian Space Programme and the Birth of ESRIN', in Arturo Russo (ed.) *Science Beyond the Atmosphere: The History of Space Research in Europe.* Noordwijk, The Netherlands: ESA: HSR-Special: pp.113–124.

De Maria, Michelangelo (1993c), *The History of ELDO Part 1: 1961–1964.* Noordwijk, The Netherlands: ESA: HSR-10.

De Maria, Michelangelo and John Krige (1992), 'Early European Attempts in Launcher Technology: Original Sins in ELDO's Sad Parable', *History and Technology.* vol.9 no.1–4: pp.109–137.

DiIulio, J. (1994), 'Principle Agents: The Cultural Bases of Behavior in a Federal Government Bureaucracy', *Journal of Public Administration Research and Theory.* vol. 4: pp.277–318.

DLR (Deutsche Forschungsanstalt für Luft- und Raumfahrt) (1997), *DLR Comprehensive Information.* no.3e/97.

Dondi, G. (1980), 'The Agency's Industrial Policy: Its Principles and Their Implementation Since 1975', *ESA Bulletin.* no.12: pp.76–83.

Duran, Michel (1993), 'La Distribution Géographique: Les Règles, Leur Evolution, Conséquences', in the Proceeding of *The Implementation of the ESA Convention _ Lessons from the Past: Proceedings of the ESA/EUI International Colloquium* in Florence, 25–26 October 1993. pp.73–76.

Eberle, James and Helen Wallace (1987), *British Space Policy and International Collaboration.* London, New York and Andover: Routledge & Kegan Paul for The Royal Institute of International Affairs.

Edgerton, David (1996), 'The "White Heat" Revisited: The British Government and Technology in the 1960s', *Twentieth Century British History.* vol.7 no.1: pp.53–82.

Edgren, John (1996), 'Modeling Institutional Change: Some Critical Thoughts', *Journal of Economic Issues.* vol.30 no.4: pp.1017–1029.

Edmonds, Martin, Matthew Uttley and George Hayhurst (1990), 'UK and US Dependence on Foreign Technology in Defence Research and Development', *Science and Public Policy.* vol.17 no.3: pp.157–169.

EP (European Parliament) (1995), *Proceedings of European Space Forum.* 6–7 November 1995, Brussels.

EP (2002), *REPORT on the proposal for a Council regulation on the establishment of the GALILEO Joint Undertaking.* (Committee on Industry, External Trade, Research and Energy) A5–0005/2002.

ESA (European Space Agency) (1978), *Recommendations on the Development of Space Science in the 1980s.* Noordwijk, The Netherlands: ESA: SP-1015.

ESA (ed.) (1984a), *Twenty Years of European Cooperation in Space: An ESA Report.* Paris: ESA.

ESA (1984b), *European Space Science: Horizon 2000,* Paris, France: ESA SP-1070.

ESA (1993), Europe at the Crossroads: *The Future of Its Satellite Communications Industry.* Noordwijk, The Netherlands: ESA: SP-1166.

ESA (1995), *Rendezvous with the New Millennium: The Report of ESA's Long-Term Space Policy Committee.* Noordwijk, the Netherlands: ESA: SP-1187.

Euroconsult (1994), *Space Business in Europe.* Paris: Euroconsult.

Eurospace (1995), 'Space: A Challenge for Europe', *Space Policy.* vol.11 no.4, pp.227–232.

Evans, Peter B., Harold K. Jacobson, and Robert D. Putnam (eds.) (1993), *Double-edged Diplomacy: International Bargaining and Domestic Politics.* Berkeley, Los Angeles and London: University of California Press.

Favier, Pierre and Michel Martin-Roland (1990), *La Décennie Mitterrand: Tome1, Les Ruptures* (1981–1984). Paris: Seuil.

Finke, Wolfgang (1975), 'Foreword', *ESA Annual Report 1975.* Noordwijk, The Netherlands: ESA.

Finnemore, Martha and Kathryn Sikkink (1998), 'International Norm Dynamics and Political Change', *International Organization.* vol.52 no.4: pp.887–917.

Fischer, Frank (1990), *Technocracy and the Politics of Expertise.* London: Sage.

Fischer, Peter (1994), *The Origins of the Federal Republic of Germany's Space Policy 1959–1965.* Noordwijk, The Netherlands: ESA, HSR-12.

Fleury, Jean (1987), 'Armées, Espace et Europe', *Défense Nationale.* March 1987: pp.19–20.

Forschungsinstitut der Deutschen Gesselschaft für Auswärtige Politik, Institut Français des Relations Internationales, Istituto Affari Internazionali, Nederlands Instituut voor Internationale Betrekkingen 'Clingendael', and Royal Institute of International Affairs (1988), *Europe's Future in Space: A Joint Policy Report.* London, New York and Andover: Routledge & Kegan Paul for The Royal Institute of International Affairs.

Friend, Julius W. (1991), *The Linchpin: French-German Relations, 1950–1990.* New York: Praeger/The Center for Strategic and International Studies.

Fuchs, Gerhard (1994), 'Policy-Making in a System of Multi-Level Governance: The Commission of the European Community and the Restructuring of the Telecommunications Sector', *Journal of European Public Policy.* vol.1 no.2: pp.177–194.

Galbraith, John Kenneth (1967), *The New Industrial State.* Boston: Houghton Mifflin.

Garrett, Geoffrey (1992), 'International Cooperation and Institutional Choice: The European Community's Internal Market', *International Organization.* vol.46 no.2: pp.533–558.

Garrett, Geoffrey and Barry R. Weingast (1993), 'Ideas, Interests, and Institutions: Constructing the European Community's Internal Market', in Judith Goldstein and Robert O. Keohane (eds.) *Ideas and Foreign Policy: Beliefs, Institutions, and Political Change.* Ithaca, NY: Cornell University Press: pp.173–206.

Geens, Gaston (1984), 'The Birth of the European Space Agency', in European Space Agency (ed.) *Europe, Two Decades in Space.* Noordwijk, The Netherlands: ESA: pp.46–50.

Gibson, Roy (1988), 'Britain's Space Future', *Spaceflight.* vol.30: pp.76–77.

Gibson, Roy (1995), 'The Advent of European Application Satellites', in the Proceedings of *Twenty Years of the ESA Convention* in Munich, 4–6 September 1995: ESA-SP-387, pp. 39–41.

Giddens, Anthony (1976), *New Rules of Sociological Method: A Positive Critique of Interpretative Sociologies*. London: Hutchinson.

Giddens, Anthony (1979), *Central Problems in Social Theory: Action, Structure and Contradiction in Social Analysis*. London: Macmillan.

Giddens, Anthony (1984), *The Constitution of Society*. Cambridge: Polity Press.

Giget, Marc, Rachel Villain and Sylvie Bellin (1996), *Les retombées et effets d'entrainement des technologies spatiales: Mythes et réalités*. Paris: Ministère délégué à la Poste, aux Télécommunications et à l'Espace.

Gill, Stephen (1990), *American Hegemony and the Trilateral Commission*. Cambridge: Cambridge University Press.

Gilpin, Robert G. (1987), *The Political Economy of International Relations*. Princeton: Princeton University Press.

Goldstein, Judith and Robert O. Keohane (eds.) (1993), *Ideas and Foreign Policy: Beliefs, Institutions, and Political Change*. Ithaca, NY: Cornell University Press.

Golich, Vicki L. (1992), 'From Competition to Collaboration: The Challenge of Commercial-class Aircraft Manufacturing', *International Organization*. vol.46 no.4: pp.899–934.

Gordon, Philip H. (1993), *A Certain Idea of France: French Security Policy and the Gaullist Legacy*. Princeton: Princeton University Press.

Gourevitch, Peter (1978), 'The Second Image Reversed: The International Sources of Domestic Politics', *International Organization*. vol.32 no.4: pp.881–911.

Grande, Edgar (1996), 'The State and Interest Groups in a Framework of Multi-Level Decision-Making: The Case of the European Union', *Journal of European Public Policy*. vol.3 no.3: pp.318–338.

Greenberg, Joel S. and Henry R. Hertzfeld (1992), *Space Economics*. Washington D.C.: American Institute of Aeronautics and Astronautics.

Gregson, N. (1987), 'Structuration Theory: Some Thoughts on the Possibilities for Empirical Research', *Society and Space: Environment and Planning D*. vol.5 no.1: pp.73–91.

Grieco, Joseph (1990), *Cooperation among nations: Europe, America, and non-tariff barriers to trade*. Ithaca: Cornell University Press.

Grillo, Wolfgang (1993), 'Germany's Future Role in ESA', *Space Policy*. vol.9 no.2, pp.85–88.

Grouard, Serge (1989), *Stratéies Européennes et Espace Militaire*. Paris: Fondation pour les Etudes de Défense Nationale.

Haas, Peter M. (1992), 'Introduction: Epistemic Communities and International Policy Coordination', *International Organization*. vol.46 no.1: pp.1–35.

Hall, Peter (1986), *Governing the Economy: The Politics of State Intervention in Britain and France*. Oxford: Oxford University Press.

Hall, Peter A. and Rosemary C.R. Taylor (1996), 'Political Science and the Three New Institutionalisms', *Political Studies*. vol.44 no.4: pp.936–957.

Harrison, M.H. (1987), 'Decisions Draw Near', *Space*. vol.3 no.4: pp.48–52.

Hartl, P. and M. Wlaka (1996), 'The European Contribution to a Global Civil Navigation Satellite System', *Space Policy*. vol.12 no.3: pp.167–175.

Hartley, Keith (1983), *NATO Arms Co-operation: A Study in Economics and Politics*. London: George Allen & Unwin.

Hayward, Jack (1986), *The State and the Market Economy: Industrial Patriotism and Economic Intervention in France*. Brighton: Wheatsheaf Books.

Hayward, Jack (ed.) (1995), *Industrial Enterprise and European Integration: From National to International Champions in Western Europe*. Oxford: Oxford University Press.

Hayward, Keith (1986), *International Collaboration in Civil Aerospace*. New York: St. Martin's Press.

Hayward, Keith (1988), 'Airbus: Twenty years of European collaboration', *International Affairs*. vol.64 no.1: pp.11–26.

Hayward, Keith (1989), *The British Aircraft Industry*. Manchester: Manchester University Press.

Hayward, Keith (1993), 'International Collaboration in Space: The Case of the International Space Station, Freedom', *Science and Public Policy*. vol.20 no.5: pp.333–341.

Hayward, Keith (1994a), *The World Aerospace Industry: Collaboration and Competition*. London: Duckworth and RUSI.

Hayward, Keith (1994b), 'European Union policy and the European aerospace industry', *Journal of European Public Policy*, vol.1 no.3, pp.347–365.

Hayward, Keith (1996), *British Military Space Programmes*. London: RUSI Whitehall Paper Series.

Heclo, Hugh (1974), *Modern Social Politics in Britain and Sweden: From Relief to Income Maintenance*. New Haven: Yale University Press.

Heisbourg, François (1998), 'French and German Approaches to Organizing Europe's Future Security and Defense: A French Perspective', in David P. Calleo and Eric R. Staal (ed.) *Europe's Franco-German Engine*. Washington D.C.: Brookings Institution Press: pp.47–70.

Henk, Gregory G. (1998), 'Privatization and the Public/Private Partnership', *Journal of Management in Engineering*, vol.14 no.4, pp.28–29.

Heppenheimer, T.A. (1997), *Countdown: A History of Space Flight*. New York: John Wiley & Son.

Heseltine, Michael (1987), 'Britain and the Strategic Defense Initiative', in Steven W. Guerrier and Wayne C. Thompson (eds.), *Perspectives on Strategic Defense,* Boulder, CO: Westview Press.

Hickman, Peter L.V. (1995), 'The Commercialisation of Space: The Case of Communications Satellites', in the Proceedings of *Twenty Years of the ESA Convention* in Munich, 4–6 September 1995: ESA-SP-387, pp.143–147.

High Level Group (1996), *Development and Competitiveness of Space Industries in Europe: Report of the Industry's High Level Group to the European Commission,* mimeo.

Hix, Simon (1994), 'The Study of the European Community: The Challenge to European Politics', *West European Politics*. vol.17 no.1, pp.1–29.

Hobe Stephan and Mathias Spude (1991), 'Impact of Unification of German Space Activities', *Space Policy*. vol.7 no.4, pp.323–327.

Hochmuth, M.S. (1974), 'Aerospace', in Raymond Vernon (ed.), *Big Business and the State: Changing Relations in Western Europe*, Cambridge, MA: Harvard University Press.

Hoffmann, Hans E.W. (1995), 'The Spacelab Programme', in the Proceeding of *Twenty Years of the ESA Convention* in Munich, 4–6 September 1995: ESA-SP-387, pp. 43–46.

Högenauer, E. (1988), 'Sänger: European Reusability', *Space*, vol.4 no.3: pp.4–6.

Hollis, Martin and Steve Smith (1991), 'Beware of Gurus: Structure and Action in International Relations', *Review of International Studies*. vol.17 no.4: pp.393–410.

Hood, Christopher (1994), *Explaining Economic Policy Reversals*. Buckingham: Open University Press.

Horner, David (1993), 'The Road to Scarborough: Wilson, Labour and the Scientific Revolution', in Richard Coopey, Steven Fielding, and Nick Tiratsoo (eds.), *The Wilson Governments, 1964–1970*. London: Pinter Publishers: pp.48–71.

House of Commons, Trade and Industry Committee (2000), *UK Space Policy*. London: HMSO, HC 335.

House of Lords, Select Committee on Science and Technology (1987), *United Kingdom Space Policy*, 17 December, HL paper 41.

House of Lords, Select Committee on Science and Technology (1988), *United Kingdom Space Policy: Government Response to the Second Report of the Selected Committee (Session 1987–88)*, 11 October, HL paper 105.

House of Representatives (the United States) (1990), *Report of the Advisory Committee on the Future of the U.S. Space Program (Augustine Report)*. Washington, D.C.: U.S. Government Printing Office.

Hultqvist, Bengt (1993), 'The Start of Space Research in Sweden during the COPERS and Early ESRO Years, with Personal Recollections', in Arturo Russo (ed.) *Science Beyond the Atmosphere: The History of Space Research in Europe*. Noordwijk, The Netherlands: ESA: HSR-Special: pp.89–105.

Imbert, P. and G. Grilli (1994), 'La Politique Industrielle de l'ESA: Le Concept Evolutif du "Juste Retour"', *ESA Bulletin*. no.78: pp.16–19.

Intelsat (1999), *Intelsat Annual Report*. Washington D.C.: Intelsat.

Jasani, Buphendra and Toshio Sakata (eds.) (1987), *Satellites for Arms Control and Crisis Monitoring*. Oxford: SIPRI/Oxford University Press.

Jenkins-Smith, Hank C. and Paul A. Sabatier (1993a), 'The Study of Public Policy Processes', in Paul A. Sabatier and Hank C. Jenkins-Smith (eds.) *Policy Change and Learning: An Advocacy Coalition Approach*. Boulder, CO: Westview Press: pp.1–9.

Jenkins-Smith, Hank C. and Paul A. Sabatier (1993b), 'The Dynamics of Policy-Oriented Learning', in Paul A. Sabatier and Hank C. Jenkins-Smith (eds.) *Policy Change and Learning: An Advocacy Coalition Approach*. Boulder, CO: Westview: pp.41–56.

Johnson-Freese, Joan, and Roger Handberg (1997), *Space, the Dormant Frontier: Changing the Paradigm for the 21st Century*. Westport, CT: Praeger Publishers.

Jones, Christopher (1996), 'Aerospace', in Hussein Kassim and Anand Menon (eds.) *The European Union and National Industrial Policy*. London and New York: Routledge: pp.88–105.

Jourdain, Laurence and Isabelle Sourbès-Verger (1995), *L'Europe Spatiale – Filiation et Spécificité: Adaptation aux Contraintes Actuelles*. Paris: Ministère des Technologies de l'Information et de la Poste.

Kahn, Phillipe (ed.) (1992), *L'exploitation Commerciale de l'Espace: Droit Positif, Droit Prospectif*. Dijon; Université de Bourgogne et CNRS.

Kapstein, Ethan Barnaby (1992), 'International Collaboration in Armaments Production: A Second-Best Solution', *Political Science Quarterly*. vol.106 no.4: pp.657–675.

Katzenstein, Peter (1978), *Between Power and Plenty*. Madison: University of Wisconsin.

Keck, O. (1976), 'West German Science Policy since the Early 1960s: Trends and Objectives', *Research Policy*. vol.5 no.2: pp.116–157.

Keohane, Robert O. (1984), *After Hegemony: Cooperation and Discord in the World Political Economy*. Princeton: Princeton University Press.

Keohane, Robert O. (1989), *International Institutions and State Power: Essays in International Relation Theory*. Boulder, San Francisco, London: Westview Press.

Keohane, Robert O. and Joseph S. Nye (1977), *Power and Interdependence*. Boston: Little Brown.

Kiewiet, D. Roderick and Mathew D. McCubbins (1991), *The Logic of Delegation : Congressional Parties and the Appropriations Process*. Chicago: University of Chicago Press.

Klepper, Gernot (1991), 'The Aerospace Industry', in David G. Mayes (ed.) *The European Challenge: Industry's Response to the 1992 Programme*. New York: Harvester: pp.184–207.

Kolodziej, Edward A. (1987), *Making and Marketing Arms*, Princeton NJ; Princeton University Press.

Kraft, Michael E. and Norman J. Vig (eds.) (1988), *Technology and Politics*. Durham: Duke University Press.

Krasner, Stephen D. (1978), *Defending the National Interest: Raw Materials Investments and U.S. Foreign Policy*. Princeton: Princeton University Press.

Krasner, Stephen D. (ed.) (1983), *International Regimes*. Ithaca: Cornell University Press.

Krasner, Stephen D. (1984), 'Approaches to the State: Alternative Conceptions and Historical Dynamics', *Comparative Politics*. vol.16 no.2: pp.223–246.

Krasner, Stephen D. (1991), 'Global Communications and National Power: Life on the Pareto Frontier', *World Politics*. vol.43: pp.336–66.

Kratochwil, Friedrich V. (1989), *Rules, Norms, and Decisions: On the Conditions of Practical and Legal Reasoning in International Relations and Domestic Affairs*. Cambridge: Cambridge University Press.

Krige, John (1992a), *The Prehistory of ESRO, 1959/60: From the First Initiatives to the Formation of the COPERS*. Noordwijk, The Netherlands: ESA, HSR-1.

Krige, John (1992b), 'Britain and European Space Policy in the 1960s and Early 1970s', *Science and Technology Policy*. vol.5 no.2: pp.13–18.

Krige, John (1992c), 'The Rise and Fall of ESRO's First Major Scientific Project, The Large Astronomical Satellite (LAS)', *History and Technology*. vol.9 no.1–4: pp.1–26.

Krige, John (1993a), *The Early Activities of the COPERS and the Drafting of the ESRO Convention*. Noordwijk, The Netherlands: ESA: HSR-4.

Krige, John (1993b), 'How Space Scientists and Governments Saw ESRO in the Early 1960s', in Arturo Russo (ed.) *Science Beyond the Atmosphere: The History of Space Research in Europe.* Noordwijk, The Netherlands: ESA: HSR-Special: pp.29–40.

Krige, John (1993c), *The Launch of ELDO.* Noordwijk, The Netherlands: ESA: HSR-7.

Krige, John (1993d), *Europe into Space: The Auger Years (1959–1967).* Noordwijk, The Netherlands: ESA: HSR-8.

Krige, John (1993e), 'An Historical Looks at the ESA Convention', in the Proceeding of *The Implementation of the ESA Convention _ Lessons from the Past: Proceedings of the ESA/EUI International Colloquium* in Florence, 25–26 October 1993. pp. 13–19.

Krige, John (1994), 'The European Space System', in John Krige and Arturo Russo (eds.) *Reflections on Europe in Space.* Noordwijk, The Netherlands: ESA: HSR-11: pp.1–11.

Krige, John (1999), 'The Commercial Challenge to Arianespace: The TCI Affair', *Space Policy.* vol.15 no.2: pp.87–94.

Krige, John and Arturo Russo (1994), *Europe in Space: 1960–1973.* Noordwjik, The Netherlands: ESA SP-1172.

Krugman, Paul (1995), 'Dutch Tulips and Emerging Markets', *Foreign Affairs.* vol.74 no.4: pp.28–44.

Kubbig, Bernd W. (1990), 'The SDI Agreement between Bonn and Washington: Review of the First Four Years', *Space Policy.* vol.6 no.3: pp.231–247.

La Serre, Françoise de, and Phillippe Moreau Defarges (1983), 'France: A Penchant for Leadership', in Christopher Hill (ed.) *National Foreign Policies and European Political Cooperation.* London: George Allen & Unwin, pp.56–70.

La Serre, Françoise de, and Helen Wallace (1990), 'The European Dimension: Conflict and Congruence', in Françoise de la Serre, Jacques Leruez, and Helen Wallace (eds.) *French and British Foreign Policies in Transition.* New York: Berg Publishers, pp.96–128.

La Vaillée, Paternotte (1984), 'Belgium and Space', in European Space Agency (ed.) *Europe, Two Decades in Space.* Noordwijk, The Netherlands: ESA: pp.96–98.

Lafferranderie, Gabriel (1988), 'Les Procédures et Régles de Vote dans la Convention de l'Agence et Leur Pratique', *ESA Bulletin.* no.54: pp.72–77.

Lafferranderie, Gabriel (1996), 'Le Conseil Réuni au Niveau Ministériel: Son Histoire, Son Evolution', *ESA Bulletin.* no.85: pp.80–86.

Lakoff, Sanford and Herbert F. York (1989), *A Shield in Space?: Technology, Politics and the Strategic Defense Initiative.* Berkeley: University of California Press.

Lambright, W. Henry (1976), *Governing Science and Technology.* New York: Oxford University Press.

Landmark, Bjørn (1984), 'ESA and Norway', in European Space Agency (ed.) *Europe, Two Decades in Space.* Noordwijk, The Netherlands: ESA: pp.77–80.

Langeheine, Bernd and Ulrich Weinstock (1985), 'Graduated Integration: A Modest Path Towards Progress', *Journal of Common Market Studies.* vol.23 no.2, pp.185–197.

Launius, Roger D. (1994), NASA: *A History of the U.S. Civil Space Program.* Malabar, FL: Krieger Publishing.

Layder, Derek (1981), *Structure, Interaction, and Social Theory*. London: Routledge & Kegan Paul.

Lebeau, André (1976), 'The Changing Role of Europe in Space', *ESA Bulletin*. no.6: pp.3–5.

Lebeau, André (1979), 'Planning within the Agency: Its Difficulties and Limitations', *ESA Bulletin*. no.18: pp.8–10.

Lebeau, André (1990), *Les Structures Institutionnelles et les Modes de Fonctionnement de l'Europe Spatiale*. Paris: Ministre des Postes, des Télécommunications et de l'Espace.

Lévy, Maurice (1984), 'Some Recollections of the Period 1970–75', in European Space Agency (ed.) *Europe, Two Decades in Space*. Noordwijk, The Netherlands: ESA: pp.81–87.

Lévy, Maurice (1993), 'The ESRO Scientific Programme during the Transition Period, 1971–1975', in Arturo Russo (ed.) *Science Beyond the Atmosphere: The History of Space Research in Europe*. Noordwijk, The Netherlands: ESA: HSR-Special: pp.143–145.

Logsdon, John (1991), *Together in Orbit: The Origins of International Participation in Space Station Freedom*. NASA Contract NASW-4237.

Loosch, Reinhard (1993), 'Decision-Making and Voting', in the Proceeding of *The Implementation of the ESA Convention _ Lessons from the Past: Proceedings of the ESA/EUI International Colloquium* in Florence, 25–26 October 1993. pp.59–68.

Lord Reay (1991), 'UK space policy', *Space Policy*. vol.7 no.4: pp.307–315.

Lüst, Reimer (1984), 'The Preparation for the European Collaboration in Space Science', in European Space Agency (ed.) *Europe, Two Decades in Space*. Noordwijk, The Netherlands: ESA: pp.88–90.

Lüst, Reimer (1987), 'Europe's Role in Space', *PSIS Occasional Papers*. no.3: pp.1–23.

Lüst, Reimer (1991), 'Where is Europe's Place in Space?', *Space Policy*. vol.7 no.4: pp.295–299.

Lüst, Reimer (1993), 'Introduction', in the Proceedings of *The Implementation of the ESA Convention – Lessons from the Past: Proceedings of the ESA/EUI International Colloquium* in Florence, 25–26 October 1993. pp.9–11.

Luton, Jean-Marie (1992a), 'Consequences of the Changing Political Landscape for Future Space Projects', *ESA Bulletin*. no.70: pp.10–12.

Luton, Jean-Marie (1992b), 'The Granada Ministerial Conference: The Issues and the Outcome', *ESA Bulletin*. no.72: pp.8–11.

Madders, Kevin (1997), *A New Force at a New Frontier*. Cambridge: Cambridge University Press.

Madders, K.J. and W.M.Thiebaut (1992), 'Two Europes in One Space: The Evolution of Relations between the European Space Agency and the European Community in Space Affairs', *Journal of Space Law*. vol.20 no.2: pp.117–132.

Manahan, Michael C. (1984), 'Ireland's Involvement in Space-Related Activity: A Personal Account', in European Space Agency (ed.) *Europe, Two Decades in Space*. Noordwijk, The Netherlands: ESA: pp.91–93.

March, James G. and Johan P. Olsen (1989), *Rediscovering Institutions: The Organizational Basis of Politics*. New York: Free Press.

Mark, Hans (1987), *The Space Station: A Personal Journey.* Durham: Duke University Press.

Marsh, Peter (1991), 'Britain in Space, 1945–90', in Robin Nicholson, Catherine M. Cunningham, and Philip Gummett (eds.), *Science and Technology in the United Kingdom.* Harlow: Longman: pp.192–210.

Massey, Harrie and M.O. Robins (1986), *History of British Space Science.* Cambridge: Cambridge University Press.

Masters, Roger D. and Arthur R. Kantrowitz (1988), 'Scientific Adversary Procedures: The SDI Experiments at Dartmouth', in Michael E. Kraft and Norman J. Vig (eds.) *Technology and Politics.* Durham: Duke University Press: pp.278–305.

McCurdy, Howard E. (1990), *The Space Station Decision: Incremental Politics and Technological Choice.* Baltimore and London: The Johns Hopkins University Press.

McDougall, Walter A. (1985a), *The Heavens and the Earth: A Political History of the Space Age.* Baltimore: Johns Hopkins University Press.

McDougall, Walter A. (1985b), 'Space-Age Europe: Gaullism, Euro-Gaullism and the American Dilemma', *Technology and Culture.* vol.26 no.2: pp.179–203.

McLean, Alasdair (1992a), 'European Military Space Programmes', *Military Technology.* pp.10–19.

McLean, Alasdair (1992b), *Western European Military Space Policy.* Aldershot: Dartmouth.

Milner, Helen V. (1997), *Interests, Institutions and Information: Domestic Politics and International Relations.* Princeton: Princeton University Press.

Ministère du Développement Industriel et Scientifique (1970), *Rapport Aigrain sur la Politique Spatiale.* Mars 1970.

Mitterrand, François (1986), *Réflexions sur la politique extérieure de la France: Introduction à vingt-cinq discours (1981–1985).* Paris: Fayard.

Montague, Geoffrey (1995), 'Europe on Firm Ground', *Space.* vol.11 no.6: pp.17–18.

Montluc, Bertrand de (1991), 'Perspective of government official', in the Proceedings of *The Globalization of Technology: Implications for the Future in Space* at Space Policy Institute, The George Washington University, Washington D.C., 26 November 1991. pp.84–92.

Montluc, Bertrand de (1992), 'L'Environnement International des Prochaines Décisions Européennes sur l'Espace', *Politique Etrangère.* vol.57 no.1: pp.159–164.

Montluc, Bertrand de (1993), 'Les Politiques Spatiales en France et en Allemagne', *La Recherche.* vol 24, pp.1298–1304.

Montluc, Bertrand de (1997), 'The Changing Face of the European Space Sector: The Policies of Germany, Italy and the United Kingdom', *Space Policy.* vol.13 no.1, pp.9–14.

Moravcsik, Andrew (1990), 'The European Armaments Industry at the Crossroads', *Survival,* vol.32 no.1: pp.65–85.

Moravcsik, Andrew (1991a), 'Negotiating the Single European Act: National interest and conventional statecraft in the European Community', *International Organization.* vol.45 no.1: pp.19–56.

Moravcsik, Andrew (1991b), 'Arms and Autarky in Modern European History', *Daedalus*. vol.120 no.4: pp.23–45.

Moravcsik, Andrew (1993a), 'Integrating International and Domestic Theories of International Bargaining', in Peter B. Evans, Harold K. Jacobson, and Robert D. Putnam (eds.) *Double-Edged Diplomacy: International Bargaining and Domestic Politics*. Berkeley, Los Angeles and London: University of California Press: pp.1–42.

Moravcsik, Andrew (1993b), 'Armaments among Allies: European Weapons Collaboration, 1975–1985', in Peter B. Evans, Harold K. Jacobson, and Robert D. Putnam (eds.) *Double-Edged Diplomacy: International Bargaining and Domestic Politics*. Berkeley, Los Angeles and London: University of California Press: pp.128–167.

Moravcsik, Andrew (1993c), 'Preference and Power in the European Community: A Liberal Intergovernmentalist Approach', *Journal of Common Market Studies*. vol.31 no.4: pp.473–524.

Moravcsik, Andrew (1998), *The Choice for Europe: Social Purpose and State Power from Messina to Maastricht*. Ithaca, N.Y.: Cornell University Press.

Moreau Defarges, Phillippe (1992), 'Les différents modèles d'état concurrentiel', in René Lenoir and Jacques Lesourne (eds.), *Où va l'état: La souveraineté économique et politique en question*. Paris: Le monde éditions: pp.140–155.

Morgenthau, Hans J. and Kenneth W. Thompson (1985), *Politics among Nations: The Struggle for Power and Peace, Sixth edition*. New York: McGraw-Hill.

Müller, Joachim (1989), 'Policy Options for Government Funding of Advanced Technology: The Case of International Collaboration in the European Telecommunication Satellite Programme', *Research Policy*. vol.18 no.1: pp.33–50.

Nau, Henry R. (1974), *National Politics and International Technology: Nuclear Reactor Development in Western Europe*. Baltimore: Johns Hopkins University Press.

Nielsen, Klaus, Bob Jessop, and Jerzy Hausner (1995), 'Institutional Change in Post-Socialism', in Jerzy Hausner, Bob Jessop and Klaus Nielsen (eds.) *Strategic Choice and Path-Dependency in Post-Socialism: Institutional Dynamics in the Transformation Process*. London: Edward Elgar: pp.3–44.

North, Douglass C. (1990), *Institutions, Institutional Change and Economic Performance*. Cambridge: Cambridge University Press.

O'Connell, Kevin M., John C. Baker, and Ray A. Williamson (eds.) (2001), *Commercial Observation Satellites: At the Leading Edge of Global Transparency*. Washington DC: RAND/ASPRS.

OECD (Organisation for Economic Co-operation and Development) (1985), *The Space Industry: Trade Related Issues*. Paris, OECD.

Office Parlementaire d'Evaluation des Choix Scientifiques et Technologiques (1991), *Rapport sur les Orientations de la Politique Spatiale Française et Européenne*. (Loridant Report), Paris: Assemblée Nationale: no.501.

Olson, Mancur (1965), *The Logic of Collective Action: Public Goods and the Theory of Groups*. Cambridge, MA: Harvard University Press.

Onuf, Nicholas G. (1991), 'Sovereignty: Outline of a Conceptual History', *Alternatives*. no.16: pp.425–446.

Oye, Kenneth A. (ed.) (1993), *Cooperation Under Anarchy*. Princeton: Princeton University Press.

Paillon, Michel (1993), 'L'Effort Spatial Européen et la Necessité d'une Action Communautaire', in the Proceedings of *The Implementation of the ESA Convention – Lessons from the Past: Proceedings of the ESA/EUI International Colloquium* in Florence, 25–26 October 1993. pp.209–212.

Palacios, J. (1978), 'Quelques Aspects de la Politique Industrielle de l'ESA', *ESA Bulletin*. no.12: pp.24–29.

Paolini, Jérôme (1987), 'Politique spatiale militaire française et coopération européenne', *Politique Etrangère*. vol.52 no.1: pp.435–449.

Parker, Ian (1992), 'Spacecraft in the Balance', *Space*. vol.8 no.2: pp.35–37.

Pattie, Geoffrey (1985), 'Britain's Role in Space', *Defense and Foreign Affairs*. pp.16–38.

Peebles, Curtis (1997), *The Corona Project: America's First Spy Satellites*. Annapolis, MD: Naval Institute Press.

Pelton, Joseph N. (1992), 'Organizing Large Space Activities: Why the Private Sector Model Usually Wins', *Space Policy*. vol.8 no.3, pp.233–244.

Peters, B. Guy (1994), 'Agenda-setting in the European Community', *Journal of European Public Policy*. vol.1 no.1: pp.9–26.

Peters, B. Guy and Anthony Barker, (eds.) (1992), *Advising West European Governments: Inquiries, Expertise and Public Policy*. Edinburgh: Edinburgh University Press.

Peterson, John (1993), *High Technology and the Competition State: An Analysis of the Eureka Initiative*. London and New York: Routledge.

Peterson, John (1995), 'Decision-making in the European Union: Towards a framework for analysis', *Journal of European Public Policy*. vol.2 no.1: pp.69–93.

Peterson, John (1996), 'Research and Development Policy', in Hussein Kassim and Anand Menon (eds.), *The European Union and National Industrial Policy*. London and New York: Routledge: pp.226–246.

Peterson, John and Margaret Sharp (1998), *Technology Policy in the European Union*. London: Macmillan.

Pfaltzgraff, Robert L. and James L. Deghand (1968), 'European Technological Collaboration: The Experience of the European Launcher Development Organization (ELDO)', *Journal of Common Market Studies*. vol.7 no.1: pp.22–34.

Philippart, Eric and Geoffrey Edwards (1999), 'The Provisions on Closer Cooperation in the Treaty on European Union: Politics of a Multi-faceted System', *Journal of Common Market Studies*. vol.37 no.1, pp.87–108.

Pierson, Paul (1996), 'The Path to European Integration: A Historical Institutionalist Analysis', *Comparative Political Studies*. vol.29 no.2: pp.123–163.

Polanyi, Michael (1968), 'The Republic of Science: Its Political and Economic Theory', in Edward Shils (eds.), *Criteria for Scientific Development: Public Policy and National Goals: A Selection of Articles from Minerva*. Cambridge, MA: MIT Press: pp.1–20.

Powell, Walter W. and Paul J. DiMaggio (eds.) (1991), *The New Institutionalism in Organisational Analysis*. Chicago: University of Chicago Press.

PricewaterhouseCoopers (2001), *Inception Study to Support the Development of a Business Plan for the GALILEO Programme.* A report to the European Commission, mimeo.

Pucci, Andrea (1993), 'Problems in Europe's Budget: Andrea Pucci, MD and CEO of Alenia Spazio, Expresses His View', *Space.* vol.9 no.5: p.17.

Putnam, Robert D. (1988), 'Diplomacy and Domestic Politics: The Logic of Two-Level Games', *International Organization.* vol.42 no.3: pp.427–460.

Quilès, Paul (1991), 'Europe's Future in Space: The Challenges Ahead', *ESA Bulletin.* no.66: pp.13–14.

Radaelli, Claudio M. (1995), 'The Role of Knowledge in the Policy Process', *Journal of European Public Policy.* vol.2 no.2: pp.159–183.

Reagan, Ronald (1983), 'Address on the Strategic Defense Initiative', Nationwide radio and television address on March 23, 1983, reproduced in Steven W. Guerrier and Wayne C. Thompson (eds.), *Perspectives on Strategic Defense.* Boulder, CO.: Westview Press, 1987.

Rees, G. Wyn (1998), *The Western European Union at the Crossroads: Between Trans-Atlantic Solidarity and European Integration.* Boulder, CO: Westview.

Reibaldi, Giuseppe G. (1996), 'Future Italian Space Policy', *Space Policy.* vol.12 no.1. pp.9–11.

Reiss, Edward (1992), *The Strategic Defense Initiative.* Cambridge: Cambridge University Press.

Ruggie, John G. (1993), 'Territoriality and Beyond: Problematizing Modernity in International Relations', *International Organization.* vol.47 no.1: pp.139–174.

Russo, Arturo (1992a), *ESRO's First Scientific Satellite Programme: 1961–1966.* Noordwijk, The Netherlands: ESA: HSR-2.

Russo, Arturo (1992b), *Choosing ESRO's First Scientific Satellites.* Noordwijk, The Netherlands: ESA: HSR-3.

Russo, Arturo (1993a), *The Early Development of the Telecommunications Satellite Programme in ESRO (1965–1971).* Noordwijk, The Netherlands: ESA: HSR-9.

Russo, Arturo (1993b), 'Cooperation and Competition: The European Space Science Community and ESRO', in Arturo Russo (ed.) Science Beyond the Atmosphere: *The History of Space Research in Europe.* Noordwijk, The Netherlands: ESA: HSR-Special: pp.81–88.

Russo, Arturo (ed.) (1993c), *Science beyond the Atmosphere: The History of Space Research in Europe.* Noordwijk, The Netherlands: ESA: HSR-Special.

Russo, Arturo (1994), ESRO's *Telecommunications Programme and the OTS Project.* Noordwijk, The Netherlands: ESA: HSR-13.

Russo, Arturo (1997a), *Big Technology, Little Science: The European Use of Spacelab.* Noordwijk, The Netherlands: ESA: HSR-19.

Russo, Arturo (1997b), *The Definition of ESA's Scientific Programme for the 1980s.* Noordwijk, The Netherlands: ESA: HSR-20.

Russo, Arturo (1998), 'The Advocacy Coalition Framework: Revisions and Relevance for Europe', *Journal of European Public Policy.* vol.5 no.1: pp.98–130.

Sabatier, Paul A. (1993), 'Policy Change over a Decade or More', in Paul A. Sabatier and Hank C. Jenkins-Smith (eds.) Policy Change and Learning: An Advocacy Coalition. Boulder, CO: Westview: pp.13–39.

Sabatier, Paul A. and Hank C. Jenkins-Smith, (eds.) (1993), *Policy Change and Learning: An Advocacy Coalition Approach*. Boulder: Westview.

Sandholtz, Wayne (1992), *High-tech Europe: The Politics of International Cooperation*. Berkeley, Los Angeles, Oxford: University of California Press.

Scharpf, Fritz W. (1988), 'The Joint Decision Trap: Lessons from German Federalism and European Integration', *Public Administration*. vol.66: pp.239–278.

Scharpf, Fritz W. (1994), 'Community and Autonomy: Multi-level Policy-making in the European Union', *Journal of European Public Policy*. vol.1 no.2: pp.219–42.

Scharpf, Fritz W. (1997), *Games Real Actors Play: Actor-Centered Institutionalism in Policy Research*. Boulder, CO: Westview.

Schwarz, Michiel (1979), 'European Policies on Space Science and Technology 1960–1978', *Research Policy*. vol.8 no.3: pp.204–243.

Sebesta, Lorenza (1994a), *United States-European Cooperation in Space during the Sixties*. Noordwjik, The Netherlands: ESA HSR-14.

Sebesta, Lorenza (1994b), 'The Politics of Technological Cooperation in Space: US-European Negotiations on the Post-Apollo Programme', *History and Technology*. vol.11 no.3: pp.317–341.

Sebesta, Lorenza (1995), *United States-European Space Cooperation in the Post-Apollo Programme*. Noordwijk, The Netherlands: ESA: HSR-15.

Sebesta, Lorenza (1996), *The Availability of American Launchers and Europe's Decision 'To Go It Alone'*. Noordwijk, The Netherlands: ESA: HSR-18.

Sebesta, Lorenza (1997), *Spacelab in Context*. Noordwijk, The Netherlands: ESA: HSR-21.

Servan-Schreiber, Jean-Jacques (1967), *Le Défi Americain*. Paris: Denoel.

Shachar, J. and E. Zuscovitch (1991), 'Spin-offs and Technology Policy in High-Tech Networks: The Case of the European Space Program', in H. Inose, M. Kawasaki and F. Kodama (eds.), Science and Technology Policy Research: *What Should Be Done? What Can Be Done?* Tokyo: Mita Press, pp.165–180.

Shackleton, Michael (1993), 'The Delors II Budget Package', in Nigel Nugent (ed.) *The European Community 1992: Annual Review of Activities*. Oxford: Blackwell.

Shaffer, Stephen M. and Lisa R. Shaffer (1980), *The Politics of International Cooperation: A Comparison of U.S. Experience in Space and in Security*. Denver: University of Denver. Monograph series in world affairs, vol.17.

Sheehan, Michael and Alasdair McLean (1990), 'Lost Leadership: Britain's Thirty Year Failure in Space', *Contemporary Review*. vol.257 no.1499: pp.281–284.

Skocpol, Theda (1979), *States and Social Revolutions: A Comparative Analysis of France, Russia, and China*. Cambridge: Cambridge University Press.

Skolnikoff, Eugene B. (1993), *The Elusive Transformation: Science, Technology, and the Evolution of International Politics*. Princeton: Princeton University Press.

Smith, Dexter Jerome (1995), 'European Leader: France's Space Industry Is Still Gaullist', *Space*. vol.11 no.3: pp.4–8.

Sourbès-Verger, Isabelle and Xavier Pasco (2001), 'The French Pioneering Approach on Global Transparency', in Kevin M. O'Connell, John C. Baker and Ray A. Williamson (eds.), *Commercial Observation Satellites: At the Leading Edge of Global Transparency*. Washington DC: RAND/ASPRS.

SpaceVest, KPMG Peat Marwick, Space Publications, Center for Wireless Telecommunications (eds.) (1997), *State of the Space Industry.* Monograph.

Spude, Mathias (1997), 'Allemagne', in Simone Courteix (eds.) *Le Cadre Institutionnel des Activités Spatiales des Etats: Etude Comparative.* Paris: Edition A. Pedone, 1997, pp.43–62.

Steinmo, Sven, Kathleen Thelen and Frank Longstreth (eds.) (1992), *Structuring Politics: Historical Institutionalism in Comparative Analysis.* Cambridge: Cambridge University Press.

Stiernstedt, J. (1984), 'ESRO and ESA from the National Point of View', in European Space Agency (ed.) *Europe, Two Decades in Space.* Noordwijk, The Netherlands: ESA: pp.99–102.

Stubb, Alexander C-G. (1997), 'The 1996 Intergovernmental Conference and the Management of Flexible Integration', *Journal of European Public Policy.* vol.4 no.1, pp.37–55.

Stubb, Alexander C-G. (2000), 'Negotiating Flexible Integration in the Amsterdam Treaty', in Karlheinz Neunreither and Antje Wiener (eds.) *European Integration after Amsterdam: Institutional Dynamics and Prospects for Democracy.* Oxford: Oxford University Press, pp.153–174.

Suzuki, Kazuto (2000), 'Government Intervention in the Commercialisation of Launch Services: Japan and Europe', in M. Rycroft (ed), *The Space Transportation Market: Evolution or Revolution.* Kluwer Academic Publishers, pp.257–265.

Thelen, Kathleen and Sven Steinmo (1992), 'Historical Institutionalism in Comparative Politics', in Sven Steinmo, Kathleen Thelen and Frank Longstreth (eds.) *Structuring Politics: Historical Institutionalism in Comparative Analysis.* Cambridge: Cambridge University Press: pp.1–32.

Thoma, W. (1983), 'The Sophia Antipolis Workshop on the Relationship between ESA and Industry', *ESA Bulletin.* no.34: pp.13–15.

Thompson, John B. (1989), 'The Theory of Structuration', in David Held and John B. Thompson (eds.) *Social Theory of Modern Societies: Anthony Giddens and His Critics.* Cambridge: Cambridge University Press: pp.56–76.

Thornton, David Weldon (1995), *Airbus Industries: The Politics of an International Industrial Collaboration.* London: Macmillan.

Thrift, Nigel J. (1983), 'On the Determination of Social Action in Space and Time', *Society and Space.* vol.1 no.1: pp.23–57.

Tilly, Charles (ed.) (1975), *The Formation of National States in Western Europe.* Princeton: Princeton University Press.

Tomsa, Branko (1987), *Les Dimensions Economiques des Programmes Spatiaux Civils.* PSIS Occasional Papers, London: Programme for Strategic and International Security Studies.

Tsebelis, George (1994), 'The Power of the European Parliament as a Conditional Agenda Setter', *American Political Science Review.* vol.88 no.1: pp.128–142.

Ugur, Mehmet (1997), 'State-Society Interaction and European Integration: A Political Economy Approach to the Dynamics and Policy-Making of the European Union', *Review of International Studies.* vol.23 no.4: pp.469–500.

Usunier, Pierre (1984), 'Competition and Cooperation in Space: 20 Years' Apprenticeship', in European Space Agency (ed.) *Europe, Two Decades in Space*. Noordwijk, The Netherlands: ESA: pp.120–124.

Valentine, Burl (1972), 'Obstacles to Space Cooperation: Europe and the Post-Apollo Experience', *Research Policy*. vol.1 no.2: pp.104–121.

Van Fenema, H. Peter (1999), *The International Trade in Launch Services: The Effect of U.S. Laws, Policies and Practices on Its Development*. Leiden, The Netherlands: University of Leiden (Self-Publication).

Van Reeth, George P. (1995) 'The Evolution of Industrial Policy', in the Proceedings of *Twenty Years of the ESA Convention* in Munich, 4–6 September 1995: ESA-SP-387: pp.101–104.

Van Traa-Engelman, Hanneke L. (1996), 'Commercialization of Space Activities: Legal Requirements Constituting a Basic Incentive for Private Enterprise Involvement', *Space Policy*. vol.12 no.2: pp.119–128.

Vernon, Raymond, (ed.) (1974), *Big Business and the State: Changing Relations in Western Europe*. Cambridge, MA: Harvard University Press.

Vig, Norman J. (1968), *Science and Technology in British Politics*. Oxford: Pergamon Press.

Walker, William and Philip Gummett (1993), *Nationalism, Internationalism and the European Defence Market*. Paris: Institute for Security Studies and Western European Union.

Walker, William and Susan Willett (1993), 'Restructuring the European Defense Industrial Base', *Defence Economics*. vol.4: pp.141–160.

Wallace, Helen (with Adam Ridley) (1985), Europe: *The Challenge of Diversity*. London: Routledge & Kegan Paul for the RIIA.

Wallace, Helen (2000), 'Flexibility: A Tool of Integration or a Restraint on Disintegration?', in Karlheinz Neunreither and Antje Wiener (eds.) *European Integration after Amsterdam: Institutional Dynamics and Prospects for Democracy*. Oxford: Oxford University Press: pp.175–191.

Waltz, Kenneth N. (1965), *Man, the State, and War: A Theoretical Analysis*. New York: Columbia University Press.

Waltz, Kenneth N. (1979), *Theory of International Politics*. Reading, Mass.: Addison-Wesley.

Weber, Max (1978), *Economy and Society*. Berkeley: University of California Press. (translated by Guenther Roth and Claus Wittich).

Wendt, Alexander E. (1987), 'The Agent-Structure Problem in International Relations Theory', *International Organization*. vol.41 no.3: pp.335–370.

Wendt, Alexander E. (1992), 'Anarchy is What States Make of It: The Social Construction of Power Politics', International Organization. vol.46 no.2: pp.391–423.

Wendt, Alexander E. (1999), *Social Theory of International Politics*. Cambridge Cambridge University Press.

Wendt, Alexander and R. Duvall (1989), 'Institutions and International Order', in Ernst-Otto Czempiel and J.N. Rosenau (eds.) *Global Changes and Theoretical Challenges: Approaches to World Politics for the 1990s*. Lexington, MA: Lexington Books: pp.51–73.

WEU (Western European Union) (1984), *The Military Use of Space: Report by the Committee on Scientific, Technical and Aerospace Questions*. Document 976.

Whyte, Neil (1989), *Europe and Space*. London: PNL Press for The European Documentation Centre: The European Dossier Series 13.

Whyte, Neil and Philip Gummett (1997), 'Far Beyond the Bounds of Science: The Making of the United Kingdom's First Space Policy', *Minerva*. vol.35 no.2: pp.139–169.

Wiener, Antje (2000), 'The Embedded *Acquis Communautaire*: Transmission Belt and Prism of New Governance', in Karlheinz Neunreither and Antje Wiener (eds.) *European Integration after Amsterdam: Institutional Dynamics and Prospects for Democracy*. Oxford: Oxford University Press: pp.318–341.

Wild, Wolfgang (1991), 'Cornerstones of German Space Strategy', *Space Policy*. vol.7 no.1: pp.5–8.

Williams Roger (1993), 'The House of Lords Select Committee on Science and Technology within British Science Policy and the Nature of Science Policy Advice', in B. Guy Peters and A. Barker (eds.) *Advising West European Governments: Inquiries, Expertise and Public Policy*. Edinburgh: Edinburgh University Press: pp.137–150.

Williamson, Mark (1992), 'The UK Parliamentary Space Committee: The Emergence of a Space Lobby?', *Space Policy*. vol.8 no.2.

Williamson, Mark (1997), 'Merge or Die', *Space & Communications*. vol.13 no. 5: pp.5–8.

Williamson, Oliver (1985), *The Economic Institution of Capitalism*. New York: Free Press.

Young, Oran R. (1989), *International Cooperation: Building Regimes for Natural Resources and the Environment*. Ithaca, NY: Cornell University Press.

Zabusky, Stacia E. (1995), *Launching Europe: An Ethnography of European Cooperation in Space Science*. Princeton NJ: Princeton University Press.

Zegveld, Walter and Christien Enzing (1987), *SDI and Industrial Technology Policy: Threat or Opportunity?* London: Frances Pinter.

Index